# PROGRESSIVE WRITING SKILLS

## W.S. Fowler

Addison Wesley Longman Limited
Edinburgh Gate, Harlow
Essex CM 20 2JE, England
and Associated Companies throughout the world.

© W.S.Fowler 1989

First published by Thomas Nelson and Sons Ltd 1989
This impression Longman Group Ltd. 1996
Third impression 1997

ISBN 0-17-555747-0

All rights reserved. This publication is protected in the United Kingdom by the Copyright Act 1988 and in other countries by comparable legislation. No part of it may be reproduced or recorded by any means without the permission of the publisher. This prohibition extends (with certain very limited exceptions) to photocopying and similar processes, and written permission to make a copy or copies must therefore be obtained from the publisher in advance. It is advisable to consult the publisher if there is any doubt regarding the legality of any proposed copying.

Produced through Longman Malaysia, PP

**ACKNOWLEDGEMENTS**
Texts
The publishers are grateful to the following for permission to reproduce copyright material: The Illustrated London News Picture Library for the extracts from *Catching Halley's Comet* by Patrick Moore p54 and *The Race to Cross the Channel* by James Bishop p56.

Photographs
The publishers wish to thank the following for permission to reproduce copyright photographs: J. Allan Cash Limited pp38, 48, 51, 83; The Wasa Museum, Stockholm, Sweden p51; Camera Press p62; Popperphoto p64; Kobal Collection pp73, 74, 75, 81; Thomas Nelson and Sons, Penni Bickle p79; Wandsworth Public Libraries p79; Weidenfeld (Publishers) Limited p80.

Every effort has been made to trace owners of the copyright, but if any omissions can be rectified the publishers will be pleased to make the necessary arrangements.

# Contents

| | | Page |
|---|---|---|
| **Introduction** | | v |
| Unit 1 | Personal letters: invitation, acceptance, refusal | 1 |
| Unit 2 | Narrative: telling a story in chronological order | 4 |
| Unit 3 | Description: people | 6 |
| Unit 4 | Formal letters: requesting and giving information | 10 |
| Unit 5 | Discussion: comparison | 12 |
| Unit 6 | Guided writing: instructions | 14 |
| Unit 7 | Personal letters: directions | 16 |
| Unit 8 | Narrative: sequence of tenses | 18 |
| Unit 9 | Description: objects | 22 |
| Unit 10 | Formal letters: applications for jobs | 24 |
| Unit 11 | Discussion: for and against (1) | 27 |
| Unit 12 | Guided writing: making choices | 30 |
| Unit 13 | Personal letters: narrative | 32 |
| Unit 14 | Narrative: direct and indirect speech | 34 |
| Unit 15 | Description: places | 38 |
| Unit 16 | Formal letters: complaint, apology and explanation | 40 |
| Unit 17 | Discussion: for and against (2) | 43 |
| Unit 18 | Guided writing: using a diary | 46 |
| Unit 19 | Descriptive narrative: human scenes | 48 |
| Unit 20 | Making and reporting speeches: informal | 50 |
| Unit 21 | Discussion: for or against | 52 |
| Unit 22 | Summary: fact | 54 |
| Unit 23 | Formal writing: reports | 57 |
| Unit 24 | Guided writing: using graphs | 60 |
| Unit 25 | Descriptive narrative: biography | 62 |
| Unit 26 | Making and reporting speeches: formal | 66 |
| Unit 27 | Summary: opinion | 68 |
| Unit 28 | Discussion: solutions to problems | 70 |
| Unit 29 | Formal writing: commenting on a book or film | 73 |
| Unit 30 | Guided writing: classified advertisements | 76 |
| Unit 31 | Descriptive narrative: changes in people and places | 78 |
| Unit 32 | Making and reporting speeches: newspaper reports | 82 |
| Unit 33 | Discussion: choosing an approach | 84 |
| Unit 34 | Summary: dialogue | 87 |
| Unit 35 | Formal writing: letters to the editor | 90 |
| Unit 36 | Guided writing: solving problems | 92 |
| **Reference Section** | | 94 |
| **Index** | | 119 |

# Introduction

*Progressive Writing Skills* is intended to provide students at intermediate level with models, techniques and practice enabling them to carry out any writing task they may be asked to perform. Although it covers all the tasks customarily required by an examination like Cambridge First Certificate, it is by no means limited to them. In my view, the book will be used most effectively if it is begun in a pre-First Certificate level course, but some of the tasks included, such as writing summaries for different purposes, go beyond the requirements of the First Certificate curriculum.

The book can be taught in one of two ways. It is genuinely 'progressive' in the sense that the tasks steadily increase in difficulty and the level of structural competence required, when different kinds of writing task are re-cycled (see Contents), rises correspondingly. This means that the units can be taught in the order presented. On the other hand, students who need to concentrate on certain kinds of task, such as official letters, can begin with the relevant units and complete the sequence before attempting other types of writing. In this case, I would emphasise that the order within the sequence should be retained, so that students begin with Unit 4 and then go on to Unit 10 and Unit 16.

**Approach**
In my opinion, students cannot write successfully in a foreign language without models, and these models must be accessible to them in the sense that they can be imitated. I have therefore provided models for all the writing tasks in the book that exemplify techniques but are within the structural and vocabulary range an intermediate student already possesses or can easily learn or revise.

These models lend themselves to analysis in terms of organisation as well as usage. Students often fail to appreciate that the organisation of ideas in a discussion composition, for example, is more important than the ideas themselves and as important as the control of language. Throughout the book, therefore, models and exercises are used to draw students' attention to such things as the importance of paragraphing and the use of connectors and modifiers. In the same way, the techniques that make a story interesting, and these are similar in all languages, depend on knowing where as well as how to employ different structures. Therefore, these narrative techniques must be analysed and practised, as well as the sequence of tenses and the use of direct and indirect speech.

**Input**
Every kind of writing task requires a certain technique, and in all cases there is also an input in terms of structural competence, vocabulary and register (socially appropriate language) which varies according to the task. My objective has therefore been, not only to analyse and exemplify the skills themselves through models and exercises, but also to predict the input.

It is not within the scope of a book like this to provide grammatical exercises for every structure that may be needed or to predict and pre-teach every item of vocabulary. The techniques and input (what the student must learn to perform the task successfully) are clearly very different when the interpretation of the task depends largely on the student's imagination, as in narrative, from those in official letters written with a well-defined purpose.

At the same time, at least in terms of structural competence and register, the input can be calculated with reasonable accuracy, and in consequence, I have included a detailed Reference Section at the back of the book.

**Reference Section**
This section explains the use of all the structures that appear in models, unit by unit, and in some cases suggests items of vocabulary appropriate for different tasks. Since tasks are re-cycled throughout the book, I have also suggested which structures are most likely to need revision for a given task, as well as those occurring in a unit for the first time. Persistent structural difficulties can be overcome by using the cumulative index to the Reference Section that appears at the end.

**Summary of Content and Objectives**
Writing well in a foreign language demands suitable preparation. In this book, preparation consists of the following elements:

1. models exemplifying the specific techniques required by different writing tasks; these models and the accompanying exercises enable students to analyse their content, organisation and technique, as well as to recognise the sequences of structures that customarily appear in them;
2. further exercises aimed at drawing students' attention to the different components of a piece of writing and enabling them to practise techniques and sequences before attempting to put what they have learnt into practice in open-ended tasks;
3. a choice of comparable writing tasks at the end of each unit – I would normally expect students to choose only one of these – requiring the use of the skills they have been taught and the successful employment of appropriate structures, vocabulary and register;
4. a reference section, accompanied by a cumulative index, explaining the use of structures, connectors and modifiers, and, where necessary, vocabulary and register. Each unit of the Reference Section from 7 to 36 lists items that have previously appeared but are likely to be needed and so may need to be revised before students attempt the new tasks.

The results obtained in pretesting this material encourage me to believe that intermediate students with this kind of preparation can be successfully trained to deal with any writing task appropriate to their level of English.

*WILL FOWLER, Barcelona, June 1988*

# 1 Personal Letters:
## invitation, acceptance and refusal

## Invitation

Jane Calder is seventeen. She has a pen-friend in Greece called Katerina, and has just received a letter from her. Read her reply. Study the layout of the letter, and the content of each paragraph.

Decide where Jane does the following, writing the paragraph number (1, 2 or 3) against each point; if Jane does not include the point in her letter, write 0. Jane:

(a) invites Katerina to her house
(b) asks her to reply soon
(c) tells her she will have her own bedroom
(d) refers to the content of her letter
(e) says she will go to Cambridge
(f) thanks her for her letter
(g) suggests how long Katerina could stay
(h) suggests the dates when Katerina must come
(i) mentions Katerina's family
(j) mentions her own family

Now put the points in order of appearance in each paragraph and decide if the main purpose of the paragraph is: to find out if Katerina can come to stay; to invite her to stay; to assure her that she will be welcome

Which phrases introduce the main topic? Which phrases are conventional endings to a letter?

---

93 Riverside Avenue
Bedford
CP2 1AP

April 17th 1989

Dear Katerina,

Thanks so much for your letter, which arrived yesterday. I'm very happy to hear that you're coming to England this summer. You say that your English course in Cambridge lasts a month, but you'll be on holiday so I hope you'll be able to come and see us.

We have a spare room, so there's no problem about putting you up, and you're welcome to stay for as long as you like. We're not going away this summer, so there's no problem about arranging dates.

Please write soon and tell me if you can come. My best wishes to your parents and your brother and sister. My parents send their kindest regards.

Love,
Jane.

---

## Practice

Study Jenny Marshall's letter to her friend Anne. Complete the letter by putting the sentences and phrases in the appropriate places.

..........1
..........2 ..........3
..........4

..........5,
..........6 to you for such a long time. I've been so busy at the university. But now something has come up that would give us the chance to meet. The university drama department are organising a trip to Stratford on ..........7 to see Twelfth Night. I know you and Bob live nearby, but if you haven't seen this production yet, ..........8? If so, I can get two extra tickets.

We're planning to come up by coach on Friday, but my new boy-friend, Trevor, lives in Warwick, and his parents have invited me for the weekend. It would be lovely to see you on Saturday if you were free. ..........9

..........10 by next Friday. Could you let me know before then if you would like to come? In any case, I hope we can meet at the weekend.

..........11 Love to Bob.
..........12

---

I have to book the tickets
Friday, May 5th    4th April, 1989
Love    Dear Anne    46 Cranford St.,
would you like to join us    London
I'm sorry I haven't written
Looking forward to hearing from you
NW3 5PQ    I'd like you to meet Trevor

1

# 1 Personal letters

##  Acceptance and Refusal

Study Richard's acceptance of this invitation, and then study the letter from Marian Winslow to Margaret Stafford, explaining why she and her husband cannot accept a similar invitation. Then answer the questions that follow.

---

James and Eileen Stafford
have pleasure in inviting
Richard and Sandra Connor
to the marriage of their daughter
Margaret
to
Frank Atkinson
at St. Anne's Church, Abberley, Sussex
on Saturday, 23rd June at 12.00 p.m.
and to the reception at The Fox and Hounds, Abberley

19 Horsham Road
Abberley, Sussex
HR3 1AB                                             RSVP

---

53 Murray Avenue
Birmingham B14 8KH

May 22nd 1989

Dear Mr and Mrs Stafford,
    Thank you very much for your kind invitation to your daughter Margaret's wedding. Sandra and I are delighted to accept.
    It was very thoughtful of you to enquire in your accompanying note whether we were coming down on the previous evening and to offer to find us somewhere to stay in the village. As we have a small baby, we do not want to be away for too long, so we plan to drive down in the morning. Frank tells us that the reception is likely to go on for some time, but for the same reason we will only stay to drink the health of the bride and groom, and then we'll have to make an early start for home. Thanks, anyway, for thinking of us.
    We look forward to meeting you on Saturday, 23rd June.

               Yours sincerely,
               Richard Connor

---

27 Hillside Close,
Bournemouth,
Dorset BA12 3BO

May 24th 1989

Dear Maggie,
    It was very kind of your parents to invite John and me to your wedding. Unfortunately, we won't be able to come, and I have written to them, expressing our regret, but I felt that I had to write to you personally to say how sorry we are that we can't make it.
    The trouble is that the last two weeks in June are the only ones when John and I can both get away from work together, so we booked our holiday to the Greek Islands as soon as we realised this, and there's no way we can change it.
    It's such a pity, because I was looking forward very much to seeing you married. Naturally, we'll be thinking of you on the day. Have a marvellous time! We wish you all the best for the future, we're sure that you'll be happy. Frank is such a wonderful man!
    John sends his love. Our kindest regards to Frank.

               Love
               Marian.

---

1. Compare the beginnings and ends of the two letters. In what ways are they different, and why?
2. Whose friend is Richard, and whose friend is Marian? How do we know this from the content of the letters?
3. Compare the three main paragraphs in each case. In what way is their purpose alike? Account for the differences.

# 1 Personal letters

## Practice

Martin Hardy is celebrating his twenty-first birthday party on Saturday, November 12th, and he has invited two of his friends, Julian and Stephen. Complete their letters, inventing addresses and dates, and writing the paragraphs that are missing.

In Julian's letter (first paragraph) he should thank Martin for his invitation and accept; in the last, he should say he is looking forward to the party, and end appropriately.

Stephen (second paragraph) should explain why his job prevents him from accepting; in the last, he should say he is sorry to miss it and end appropriately, with regards to friends who will be there.

Julian

........................

........................,
................ first paragraph ........................
It's very kind of you to offer to put me up for the night, and I'd like to take advantage of your offer. I'll be coming on my scooter, and I don't much like the idea of celebrating your birthday in style and then going out into the cold night air for a thirty-mile ride home. Thanks very much.
................ third paragraph ........................
........................

Stephen

........................

........................
Thanks very much for your invitation to your twenty-first birthday party. I'm sorry to say that I won't be able to make it. It really is annoying, because I was looking forward to seeing you again, and meeting all our old friends from school. But on this occasion work comes first, I'm afraid.

As you know, I'm working as a trainee computer programmer for IXL, and they're sending me on a course...
................ third paragraph ........................
........................

## Further Practice

1 Write a letter to a pen-friend in Britain, inviting him/her to spend a fortnight in your country.
2 Write Katerina's answer to Jane (p. 1), accepting her invitation and suggesting dates for your arrival and departure.
3 You and some friends are planning to go to a folk/music/dance festival about 100 km from where you live. Write to a friend who lives in another town and invite him/her to go with you.
4 Some of your classmates at your former school are planning a reunion in honour of your favourite teacher, who is retiring. Write to a friend from your schooldays and invite him/her to the dinner.
5 You have received the invitation in question 4. Write (a) accepting the invitation and asking if you can help in any way (b) explaining why you will not be able to attend the reunion.

# 2 Narrative:
## telling a story in chronological order

### Telling a story

Before reading the story, look at the notes on the use of tenses and narrative in the Reference Section (p.95). When you have read the story, answer the questions that follow.

### Blackout in Barcelona

The blackout in Barcelona happened on a typical autumn night in October 1987, about ten o'clock. I was writing a letter, my wife was reading a book, and my son was watching a film on TV. Suddenly, all the lights in the house went out.

'Just when the film was getting interesting,' my son said in disgust.

I went out onto the landing to see if the blackout was affecting the whole block of flats. Everything was in darkness. Then I went back into the living-room. Our flat is on the top floor and we have a good view of half of the city. The only lights I could see were in two villages on the outskirts and a few near the port, beside the sea.

'It looks as if the whole city is affected,' I told my wife.

She went into the kitchen to look for some candles, and my son turned on an old radio that worked with batteries to see if he could find out what was going on. I went out onto the terrace at the back of the house and looked down. A few cars were moving slowly up the hill; the drivers were taking more care than usual because the traffic lights were not working. Some people at the bus-stop were arguing in loud voices, wondering if the bus would arrive on time and if they would be able to get home.

The local radio stations were giving conflicting reports, but the main news was that the power failure was affecting the whole of Catalonia. Towns like Gerona and Tarragona, a hundred kilometres away, were also blacked out.

'Maybe the Martians have landed, Dad,' my son said hopefully.

The experts were trying to discover the cause of the blackout, but we did not find out the real reason, a failure in the main generator outside the city, until the next day. Gradually, however, as I stood looking out of the window, I saw lights beginning to come on again; the light was spreading across the city and slowly coming towards us. Suddenly, the lights went on in the next street, and almost immediately afterwards, power was restored in our own flat. I looked at my watch. It was half-past eleven.

My son turned on the TV. 'It's past your bedtime,' my wife said.

'Not really,' he said. 'That hour and a half doesn't count. Besides, I want to see the end of the film.'

---

1 In a narrative it is important to establish from the beginning where and when the action took place. How does the narrator do this?
2 Put the narrator's actions that night in the correct order, writing a number next to each letter.
   (a) he listened to the radio
   (b) he told his wife what he could see through the window
   (c) he went out onto the terrace
   (d) he watched the lights coming on in the city
   (e) he wrote a letter
   (f) he watched the traffic in the street
   (g) he looked at his watch
   (h) he heard some people arguing
   (i) he found out the reason for the power failure
   (j) he went out onto the landing
3 What *were* the narrator, his wife and his son *doing* when the lights went out?
4 What *did* they *do* when the lights went out?
5 There are four important stages in the narrative. What are they, and how does the narrator draw attention to them?
6 The sentence beginning: 'Our flat is on the top floor . . .' (l.10) is written in the present tense. Why is this information important, and why is this tense used, instead of a past tense?
7 Look at the tenses used with reference to the people at the bus-stop and then put what they said to each other into direct speech.

4

# 2 Narrative

## Practice

David Curtis is a taxi-driver. Here, he tells the story of two incidents that occurred one day in the course of his work. The story is told chronologically, but the paragraphs are out of order and the sentences within each paragraph are also out of order *except* for the first one (in **bold** type).

Decide first on the order of the paragraphs, and then put the sentences in the correct order.

Direct speech is used at four points in the story. Find the most appropriate places in the paragraphs indicated for the direct speech to be inserted.

A **About a hundred yards from the hospital, I saw a big black car at the side of the road.** (a) When he saw me, he waved me down, and I saw a girl sitting in the back of the car. (b) The driver was standing beside it, dressed in a chauffeur's uniform, and a young man was arguing with him.

B **Nothing special happened during the morning but about half-past two I was driving along Clarence Road, when a young man suddenly ran out of his house, waving his arms madly.** (a) I only hoped she wouldn't have it in the back of the car. (b) I stopped, and he asked me to wait. (c) Then he went back into the house, and came back a moment later with his wife leaning on his arm. (d) I could see that straightaway. (e) Anyway, they got in, and five minutes later I dropped them off at St. John's.

C **There was one more coincidence, in fact.** (a) It was a boy, and they were going to call him David. (b) When I went round to Clarence Road for my fare, the first Mr Barlow said his wife and the baby were getting on well. (c) And that's my name!

D **One day is very like another in my job, but there are some that stand out in your memory – last Wednesday, for instance.** (a) I picked up a lot of passengers on short journeys. (b) When I got up, it was raining, and that's always a good sign for a taxi-driver because it's easy to get fares.

E **It was an emergency, but of a different kind.** (a) The man said it was a pity his brother couldn't come to the wedding because his wife was expecting a baby, and hoped she was all right. (b) The young couple were on their way to the airport. (c) It turned out that it was, so I told them about my other fare, dropped them at the airport, and wished them luck as well. (d) They were going on their honeymoon, and were afraid they would miss their flight.

F **The young man was so worried about his wife that he got out without paying me.** (a) But he gave me his name and address, and I said I'd call round one evening to collect the fare. (b) I wished them luck, and they went into the hospital. (c) When I reminded him he put his hand in his pocket and looked desperate.

(A) 'I hope it's not another emergency' I thought. 'Not another baby.'

(B) 'Drive to St. John's Hospital as fast as you can,' the young man said. 'My wife's going to have a baby.'

(E) 'Excuse me,' I said, 'but your name isn't Barlow, is it?'

(F) 'Oh, my God,' he said. 'I was in such a hurry that I came out without any money.'

## Further Practice

1 Write a story about a fire in your own or a neighbour's house.
2 Write a story about a mother getting dinner ready, when her son/daughter arrives home with two or three hungry friends.
3 Write a story about a day in your own life or that of a friend or relative in which some unusual things happened.
4 Write a story like the taxi-driver's on this page including some incidents involving either (a) a nurse (b) a teacher (c) a policeman/woman (d) a group of children on holiday.

# 3 Description: people

## ✎ Describing someone

Read the description of the writer's aunt, and then answer the questions that follow.

### Aunt Barbara

My aunt Barbara is my father's sister. She is about 35, but she looks much younger. She is a very attractive woman, with fair, curly hair, large, green eyes, and a beautiful fresh complexion. She is quite tall, but looks even taller because she dresses very well and always wears high-heeled shoes. She has a lovely, slim figure and I would like to look like her when I am her age.

Aunt Barbara is married, and lives quite near us with her husband, my uncle Stephen, and their son Martin, who is ten. She works as a teacher at the local comprehensive school. She is very energetic and never stops moving. At the weekend she plays tennis with my uncle, but she also goes to keep-fit classes three times a week and is very fond of dancing. She sometimes sits down quietly to read a book, but she can't stand watching television. She prefers to go out for a long walk if the weather is fine.

I think of her as warm and friendly, with a lively personality, because she has always been kind to me. But some of her students at the comprehensive school say she is strict and can be quick-tempered if they don't pay attention. I think that she gets impatient with people who are bored or inattentive, because she is so active herself. I never feel bored in her company, and so I have always got on very well with her.

Find references in the text to the following characteristics, and group them according to the paragraph in which they appear. Then give each paragraph a general heading:
age, defects, dislikes, dress, eyes, family, figure, hair, height, interests, likes, personality, qualities, temperament, writer's opinion of her aunt, work.

~~~~~~~~~~~~~~~~~~~~~~~~~~~~~~~~~~~~~~~~~~~~~

## Physical characteristics check-list

Use this chart to describe someone you know. Note that in some cases words are normally used only for men or for women. Note that we do not usually use less attractive words for people we know and like: 'He's not very good-looking' (He's rather ugly).

|  | Men | Women |
|---|---|---|
| **Age** | old ... elderly ... middle-aged ... young ... is (looks) about (30) ||
| **Appearance** | good-looking ... handsome ... ugly | beautiful ... pretty ... plain |
| **Height** | tall ... of average (medium) height ... short ||
| **Figure** | well-built ... broad-shouldered | ... has a good figure |
| **Shape** | plump ... slim (favourable) ... fat ... thin (unfavourable) ||
| **Face** | round ... long ... square ... oval ... wrinkled ... freckled ||
| **Features** | beard ... moustache ... bald head | |
| **Hair** | black ... dark ... fair ... red | long ... short ... straight ... curly ... wavy |
| **Eyes** | blue ... brown ... green ... grey ... hazel ||

# 3 Description

## Practice

Complete the text below, choosing the most appropriate phrase in the right-hand column to fill the gaps.

When I was young, my favourite film star was Gary Cooper. He was about 50 when I first saw him, but he was still very ___(1)___ and ___(2)___ In cowboy films, he wore a check shirt and ___(3)___, but I have seen him in others where his ___(4)___ figure made him look elegant in a ___(5)___ He got into films because he ___(6)___ horses well. He was ___(7)___ on a farm in Montana, and at that time had no idea that he would become a famous ___(8)___ At first, people said he didn't ___(9)___ at all, but then they realised that he did everything naturally, without effort. I don't know ___(10)___, but biographies suggest that he was the same in real life as he was on the screen. He was ___(11)___ but determined. A journalist once ___(12)___ him if he always said, 'Yup' instead of 'Yes', as he did in westerns, and Cooper simply replied 'Yup'. His greatest quality as an actor, however, was that he looked so honest that he always played the part of the ___(13)___ He seemed good without being ___(14)___, which is one of the ___(15)___ things an actor can do.

(1) tall/short  (2) handsome/pretty
(3) jeans/trousers
(4) slim/thin  (5) dress/suit
(6) drove/rode
(7) brought up/educated
(8) actor/artist
(9) act/play

(10) how he really was/what he was really like

(11) noisy/quiet  (12) asked/said

(13) hero/villain
(14) dull/unfeeling
(15) easiest/hardest

1 Compare the description of Gary Cooper with the description of Aunt Barbara. How many of the words from the physical characteristics check list are mentioned? Are they mentioned in the same paragraphs? Which are left out and which are expanded? Can you think of a reason for this?
2 Give each paragraph a general heading. Compare them with the headings for the description of Aunt Barbara.
3 How does the story about the journalist help you to understand the whole paragraph better?

## Personality Check-list

Match the favourable adjectives on the left with the corresponding unfavourable adjectives on the right. Write the number to match the appropriate letter. Then use this check-list in your own descriptions of people.

1 amusing, entertaining
2 intelligent, clever
3 calm
4 cheerful
5 generous
6 hard-working
7 pleasant, charming
8 polite
9 sensitive
10 sincere
11 smart
12 tolerant

a dim, stupid
b disagreeable
c dull, boring
d hypocritical
e lazy, idle
f mean
g miserable, depressing
h narrow-minded
i quick-tempered
j rude
k unfeeling
l untidy

# 3 Description

## 3 Describing daily routine

Dr Ronald Fletcher is a busy general practitioner (GP) in a London suburb. Look at his diary for a typical day, and then read his full account of what usually happens.

**FEBRUARY 24 WEDNESDAY**

- 9.00 Surgery
- 10.30? Rounds
- 1.30? Lunch
- 2.30 Complete rounds
- 4.00 Forms for Min. of Health
  Read article in Lancet
- 6.00 Surgery
- 8.00 Ring Dr Bradley about weekend arrangements
- 8.15 Early dinner
- 9.00 Night duty

I have to get up every day about seven because work really begins about an hour before surgery when the 'phone calls start to come in. My wife helps me with that because she usually answers the 'phone and that gives me time to have breakfast and read the paper. We open the waiting-room about 8.30, and there are often a dozen people there when I start surgery at nine.

People at surgery generally have coughs and colds and just need a prescription for the chemist or a doctor's certificate to stay away from work, but occasionally an examination suggests there may be something seriously wrong with them. In such cases, I have to arrange appointments for them at the hospital to check my diagnosis. On an average day, I can finish surgery by 10.30 or so, and start my rounds. My wife makes a list of the visits I have to make from the 'phone calls during the morning and often helps me by working out the best route from one patient's house to another.

I usually try to get back to lunch by 1.30, though I sometimes have to continue my visits in the afternoon. On a good day, I have a couple of hours before surgery begins again at six when I can catch up with the paper work, completing forms for the health authorities, and sometimes read an article in one of the medical journals to keep up with the latest developments.

Evening surgery usually lasts till about eight, but often goes on much longer. I belong to a group of five doctors in the area who share night duty between us. That means that we are on call once a week between Monday and Friday and every fifth weekend. As a result, my wife and I normally have dinner about nine, I have time to talk to the children, and we sometimes watch TV before going to bed around eleven. When I am on call, however, we have dinner as soon as surgery is over, so that I can go out immediately if I am needed. Occasionally, there are emergencies, of course. If one of my own patients is very seriously ill or dies, I like my colleagues to let me know and always visit them or the family myself, even when I am officially off duty.

# 3 Description

1 How is the day indicated in Dr Fletcher's diary different from the normal day he describes in his account of his work?
Underline the following adverbs in the text:
always, usually, generally, normally, often, sometimes, occasionally.
When no adverb is used: Paragraph 1, sentence 1; paragraph 1, sentence 3; paragraph 2, sentence 4 ('makes a list of the visits'), which one is implied?
Underline the expressions:
every day, on an average day, on a good day.
Which adverb of frequency comes closest to their meaning?
2 Which periods of the day are described in each paragraph of Dr Fletcher's account? Compare this to the taxi-driver's story of an exceptional day on p. 5. Did David Curtis give the same importance to each period of the day? If not, why not?
3 Imagine that everything happened on the day indicated in Dr Fletcher's diary as he expected. Write a short narrative based on the text and the diary, giving an account of the day. Link it together with time expressions (then, afterwards, etc.).
Begin like this: 'I got up about seven, as usual. My wife helped me with the calls, answering the 'phone while I was having breakfast. We opened the waiting room at 8.30, and there were a dozen people there when I started surgery at nine.
I finished surgery at . . . and . . .'
4 Make plans similar to Dr Fletcher's diary for a normal day in (a) your own life (b) the life of a member of your family (c) one of the following:
a bank clerk; a businessman/businesswoman who lives outside the city where he/she works; a university student.
Take into account the preparation for the day, and what the person does after work, as well as the working day in itself.

## Further Practice

1 Describe a member of your family or a friend.
2 Describe someone you dislike, and explain why.
3 Describe a film actor/actress or pop star that you admire.
4 Describe a character in a book, film or television serial.
5 Write an account of a normal day in your own life, or in that of any of the people indicated in question 4 above.

# 4 Formal Letters:
## requesting and giving information

### ✎ Requesting information

Juan Martinez read this advertisement in the *ELT Monthly*, and decided to write for further information. First, he made a note of questions he wanted to ask. Study Reference Section (p.98) and then look at his notes and the letter he wrote. Find the expression in the letter for each note. Pay attention to the address, the way he began and ended the letter, and the form for asking for information.

## CAMFORD POLYTECHNIC

Summer Courses for Advanced Students of English

The Polytechnic is organising a number of courses of one month's duration for advanced students of English this summer in language studies with options in literature, business English and English for tourism. Enquiries to:
The Director of Courses,
Camford Polytechnic,
Camford CM2 8JT

---

Calle Mallorca 34,
05061 Valencia

The Director of Courses,
Camford Polytechnic,
Camford CM2 8JT

March 20th 1989

Dear Sir,
 I am writing to you with reference to your advertisement in the ELT Monthly for one-month courses in English at the Polytechnic this summer.
 I would be grateful if you would send me further information on these courses, indicating the dates on which they will start, the timetable and the fees. I am particularly interested in Business English and would like to know how much time is spent on this option every day.
 Could you also give me details of accommodation? Are students lodged at the Polytechnic or with families outside? I would also like to know whether groups of students with the same first language are lodged together or whether it is possible to meet others from different language backgrounds.
 I look forward to hearing from you.
  Yours faithfully
  Juan Martinez
  JUAN MARTINEZ

---

When do courses start? How many hours of English a day? How many hours business English? Cost? Accommodation — in Polytechnic or with family? Groups with other Spanish speakers or mixed?

---

Find words or phrases in Juan's letter that mean:
(a) in connection with (b) Please (c) My main interest is (d) want to (e) Please . . ., too.
What is the purpose of each paragraph? To ask for information, to ask for additional information, or to introduce the topic?

# 4 Formal letters

## Practice

Complete Anne Morley's letter to Jim Courtney, choosing from the alternatives given in the right-hand column.

18 Grenville Avenue,
Norwich NR4 3CK

Mr Jim Courtney,
193 Winsford Road,
London SW19 4WH

April 17th, 1989

Dear ___(1)___,
   I ___(2)___ you ___(3)___ your ___(4)___ for adventure holidays for young people in the *Observer*. I ___(5)___ grateful ___(6)___ send me ___(7)___ information about them.
   I am particularly interested ___(8)___ your holidays in Asia. ___(9)___ you give me details of dates of departure and costs? I ___(10)___ some advice about arrangements I ___(11)___ to ___(12)___ before joining the group, ___(13)___ visas required for different countries and certificates of inoculation against diseases.
   I look forward to ___(14)___ from you.
     Yours ___(15)___
     Anne Morley

(1) (a) Mr Courtney (b) Sir
(2) (a) am writing to (b) write
(3) (a) for (b) in connection with
(4) (a) advertisement (b) announcement
(5) (a) am (b) would be
(6) (a) if you would (b) that you
(7) (a) another (b) further
(8) (a) in (b) on
(9) (a) Could (b) Please
(10) (a) also wish (b) would also like
(11) (a) needed (b) would need
(12) (a) do (b) make
(13) (a) as (b) such as
(14) (a) hear (b) hearing
(15) (a) faithfully (b) sincerely

**ADVENTURE HOLIDAYS**
Join a mixed group of young people on the adventure of your life! Drive a jeep across Asia or the Sahara Desert. Further information from Jim Courtney, 193 Winsford Road, London SW19 4WH.

## Further Practice

In writing any of these letters, remember to introduce the subject clearly; think of what information you need, and any particular questions to ask. Devote one paragraph to each.

1. You are going to visit England and would like to go to a Shakespeare play in Stratford. Write to the Royal Shakespeare theatre. (Dates of visit, plays, price of tickets – advance booking, payment in advance).
2. You want to take an examination in English. Write to the British Council in your country, asking for information. (Dates, cost, papers in examination – registration in advance, entrance forms, payment by post).
3. You are taking part in a project at school studying different towns in England. Write to a British Council library for information. (Books in library, obtainable from other libraries – borrowing conditions, payment, post).
4. You are interested in spending two weeks' holiday in the country or by the sea somewhere in Britain. Write to the town hall, asking for information. (Tourist leaflets, hotels, accommodation – opportunities for personal interests, sport, etc.).
5. You want to buy some computer programs you cannot obtain in your country. Write to a firm in England for information. (Programs available, cost – means of payment, delivery time).

# 5 Discussion: comparison

## ✎ Comparing information

Before reading the text, study Reference Section (p.99), Comparative forms.

### Hotels in Rome

| Hotel | Room facilities | Restaurant | Bar | Lounge | Cost per night |
|---|---|---|---|---|---|
| Michelangelo | Tel, TV, mini-bar, bath, shower | yes | yes | yes | 150.000 lire |
| Giotto | | | | | 80.000 lire |
| Tiziano | | | | | 95.000 lire |

Arthur Buckley is going to visit Rome, and has written to a friend, Mark Constable, asking for advice on hotels.

Read Mark's reply, and use the information given to complete the chart. Then give each of the four paragraphs a short heading.

Which hotel does Mark recommend, and why?

---

I've stayed in three hotels in Rome this year. The Michelangelo is beautiful but very expensive. I had a very comfortable room, with telephone, colour TV, separate bathroom and shower, mini-bar.. There is a magnificent restaurant on the roof and a pleasant lounge. It's certainly the best hotel if you can afford it.

The Giotto costs less than half the price. It does not have a restaurant but the worst thing about it is that the lounge is so crowded and noisy, and there is no bar. The room I had was very small, and there was a TV but no shower in the bathroom. It's much cheaper than the Michelangelo but not nearly as comfortable. I don't recommend it.

On the whole I think the Tiziano is the most reasonable. It costs a little more than the Giotto, but I had a pleasant room, with the same facilities as the Michelangelo, except for the mini-bar. The lounge was smaller and quieter than in the other hotels, but better for doing business with customers.

To sum up, the Michelangelo is the most impressive, but I prefer the Tiziano. In the first place, it's much cheaper; secondly, the food is better value for money; thirdly, it's more friendly. The staff were more helpful, moved faster, and seemed to do everything more cheerfully.

# 5 Discussion

## Practice 1

An English friend of yours wants to stay at a small seaside resort on a Mediterranean island. You know the place well, and can give him/her information on its three hotels.

Use the map and information provided to write a letter giving him/her advice. Begin and end the letter appropriately, but follow the format of Mark's letter for the middle four paragraphs. Invent names for the hotels and your opinion of them and say where they are situated.

|       |                  | Room facilities |    |      |        |             | Hotel facilities |     |        |       |               |                                      |                      |
|-------|------------------|-----------|----|------|--------|-------------|------------|-----|--------|-------|---------------|------|--------------------|
| Hotel | Number of rooms  | Telephone | TV | bath | shower | view of sea | Restaurant | Bar | Lounge | Disco | Swimming pool | Tennis court | Cost, two weeks in £ meals included | Location |
| A     | 180              | ✓         | ✓  | ✓    | ✓      | ✓           | ✓          | ✓   | —      | —     | ✓             | —    | 450 | facing beach |
| B     | 50               | —         | —  | ✓    | —      | —           | ✓          | ✓   | —      | ✓     | —             | —    | 200 | side street, beach 300 m |
| C     | 120              | ✓         | —  | ✓    | ✓      | ✓           | ✓          | ✓   | —      | ✓     | ✓             | ✓    | 350 | cliffs, beach 1 km |

## Practice 2

In the student's composition printed below, the paragraphs have been put in the wrong order (but not the sentences) and some words and phrases have been left out. First, decide on the correct order of the paragraphs. Then complete the composition by inserting the words and phrases given at the end in the correct spaces.

A ...........¹ my father bought a larger car, a Renault 14. It was bigger and faster, and easier to get into, because it had four doors; ...........², it was more comfortable. I never liked it as much as the first Renault, ...........³, probably because we had two accidents with it ...........⁴, ...........⁵ they were not due to any defect in the car.

B ...........⁶ I like the Sierra best, ...........⁷ when we are on the motorway, but it is only fair to say that it cost more than ...........⁸ so it should have more advantages.

C I can remember three cars in our family. ...........⁹, when I was about five, we had a Renault 5. It was bright red, with a hatchback, so it took all our luggage in the boot. It was ...........¹⁰, because it was easier to park than the two we have had since, but it had two defects. One was that it started to rock if my father drove faster than 60 miles per hour; ...........¹¹ was that it was difficult to start on winter mornings.

D My father's new car is a Ford Sierra. There is no doubt that it is the best car we have had. ...........¹², it is the biggest and has much more space in the boot than the Renaults; ...........¹³, it is the most powerful, so it is ...........¹⁴; ...........¹⁵, it is the most elegant, painted grey with a thin red stripe.

A few years later    above all

although    apart from that

especially    however

In the first place    On the whole

secondly    the other

the other    soon after we bought it

the best for long journeys    the others

the most convenient in the city

Several years ago

## ✎ Further Practice

Make sure that you know how to use comparative forms before attempting any of these topics, and check in the Reference Section if you are in doubt. In each case you can compare either two or three things. In choosing a topic, consider how much of the necessary vocabulary you know, as well as which is the most interesting topic.

1. Compare two or three houses you or members of your family have lived in.
2. Compare two or three places where you have spent holidays.
3. Compare two or three cars your family have owned.
4. Compare two or three schools you have attended.

13

# 6 Guided Writing: instructions

## ✍ Giving Instructions

Sheila Watson is baby-sitting this evening for Mr and Mrs Crane, who are going to have dinner at a friend's house. Before leaving at 6.30, Mrs Crane gives her some instructions, and Sheila takes notes so that she will not forget anything. Read what Mrs Crane says, and then complete Sheila's notes.

*Notes:*
1. When the Cranes have gone out,...
2. If children get bored,...
3. 8.00
4. 8.30
5. 8.45

Callers:
Telephone calls:
Emergency:

---

The children have had their tea, and they won't need anything more until about eight o'clock. I always give Simon a cup of chocolate and some biscuits before he goes to bed at 8.30. Kate has hot milk. The biscuit tin is in the kitchen on the second shelf, but don't let them eat too many. Three each.

They're watching their favourite programme on TV at the moment, and then they'll play, but if they get bored read them a story. Simon will give you a book to read but let Kate choose a story, too.

Make sure they're in bed by 8.30. Leave the door open, and leave the light on in the hall. Then go back after about a quarter of an hour and turn it off when you see they're asleep.

If anyone rings, please write the name and telephone number on the pad on my husband's desk by the 'phone. We don't expect anyone to call at the house, so don't let anyone in; there have been a lot of burglaries in the district recently. Lock the front door from the inside when we've gone. We'll be back about 11 o'clock, but in case of emergency, if anything really serious happens, you can get us at the Taylors'. That's 147 2864.

~~~~~~~~~~~~~~~~~~~~~~~~~~~~~~

## Practice 1

Julie Walker's neighbour, an old lady called Mrs Marshall, is ill, so Julie has offered to do her shopping for her and any other errands she needs. Read what Mrs Marshall says, and then make out the list Julie makes to remind herself of what she has to do. Use the map to decide on the best route for Julie to follow to and from the house so that she does not waste time, and put the errands in the right order according to the route you choose.

---

You can get all the shopping at the supermarket, Julie, except for the bread. I don't like that sliced bread, so would you mind going to Bassett's the baker's? It's a bit out of your way, but I hope you won't mind. On the way, would you call at the library, please, and take these two books back? Don't worry about choosing two more. Just bring the library tickets back. The most important thing is my pension, though. Could you call in at the post office and collect it for me? Mrs Webster knows you, but I've written a note to her authorising you to pick it up for me. I think that's all – oh, there's one other thing. Could you buy the *TV Times* for me at the newsagent's? Thank you so much.

---

*Map:* baker's — library — post office — supermarket — newsagent's — Mrs Marshall

# 6 Guided writing

## Practice 2

Bernard Morris is the Managing Director of a printing firm. It is Friday afternoon, and he has to go abroad on business immediately. He plans to be back in the office on Thursday morning. The Deputy Managing Director, Gordon Scott, is on holiday, but he will be back on Monday. Bernard asks his secretary, Judy Cole, to write a memo to Mr Scott telling him what needs to be done while Bernard is away.

Read what Bernard says to Judy. Then write her memo, using the same format. Number each topic according to the date and time when the action must be taken, not according to importance. Remember that in the context of the memo, Mr Scott will become 'you' and Judy will become 'Judy' or 'my secretary'.

```
MEMORANDUM

From: Bernard Morris     To: Gordon Scott

                         November 8th, 1989

1  _____
2  _____
3  _____
4  _____
5  _____

If anything important happens while I'm away,
please contact me at my hotel.  A list of
hotels and telephone numbers is attached.

             Judy Cole
             P.P. Bernard Morris
                  Managing Director

(Dictated by Mr. Morris and signed in his
absence)
```

Of course the most important thing is the visit from Graham Miles of Wellington Publishers. He's coming about eleven on Monday morning, and he knows I can't be there myself, and Mr Scott is going to look after him. Tell Gordon to take him round the works, introduce him to all the technical staff and give him a good lunch at 'The Half Moon'. You can book a table for him, but Gordon must tell you if he wants to invite anyone else.

Then there's a meeting with the staff representatives about the Christmas party. That's on Wednesday afternoon at 3.30. I leave the details to them, but Gordon must make sure they don't go over the budget of £300.

Talking of parties, we've arranged a goodbye party for John Walton to mark his retirement, haven't we? That's on Tuesday evening at 'The Half Moon'. I'm sorry I won't be there, but ask Gordon to apologise for me and make the presentation.

The other thing that's really urgent is that we must finish the *Basic Geography* books next week and get them to the binders on Friday. That's the first priority on Monday morning, because we're behind schedule. Ask Gordon to speed up the work on that. He can pay the men overtime, if necessary.

If anything really important happens while I'm away, you have the list of the hotels where I'm staying and the telephone numbers, so you can attach it to the memo.

## Further Practice

1. You are going away on holiday for a fortnight and have asked a friend or neighbour to feed your cat. Make a list, showing the times when the cat must be fed, and say where the food is.
2. You are going away for the weekend, but your brother/sister is coming to the house with a friend. Make a list reminding him/her of where things are, and ask him/her to do two things for you while you are away.
3. You are going abroad on business for five days, staying in three cities in a foreign country. Decide on a schedule, and then write a memo for your secretary, asking her to book flights and hotels. Help her by indicating hotels where you have stayed before and alternatives if they are booked up.
4. You are planning a party for twenty people. Make a list of the food and drink you will need, and write it out for a friend, showing where he/she can buy the different things. Imagine there is no supermarket near you.
5. You are the English teacher at your school, with five different classes during the day. You have to go to a conference, and another teacher is going to substitute for you one day. Make a list of the times and levels of the classes, the books used, and what you would like the teacher to do in each class.

# 7 Personal Letters: directions

## ✏ Finding the way

Mark and Penny Wallace have just moved into a new house and want to invite all their friends to a 'housewarming' party. Read their letter to Angela Vickers, and in particular compare the second paragraph to the map Mark and Penny have attached to help Angela find her way. Then complete the tasks that follow.

Use the map to write different second paragraphs, giving directions to (a) Steve, who is coming by bus from the west (b) Mary, who is coming by train to Walbury from the south (c) Maurice, who is coming by underground to Walbury Park from the north.

28 Walbury Park Road,
London SW31 6WB

May 18th, 1989

Dear Angela,
  At last we've got everything more or less straightened out in our new house and to celebrate this we're having a party on Friday, June 2nd. We very much hope you can come, and look forward to seeing you any time from seven onwards. The phone hasn't been installed yet, so I'm writing to you instead. If you can't make it, please drop me a line or ring me at the office (634 2891).
  I imagine you'll be coming by car, so I've drawn you a map to help you find the house. You can take the main road into London from Chillington until you come to the crossroads at Walbury station. About a hundred yards further on, you'll come to Woodside Road. There's a pub on the corner called 'The Woodcutter'. Turn left along Woodside Road, and take the second on the right, Vine Road. Vine Road joins Walbury Park Road, and our house is the third on the left, facing the park.
  We look forward to seeing you.

    Love,
    Penny

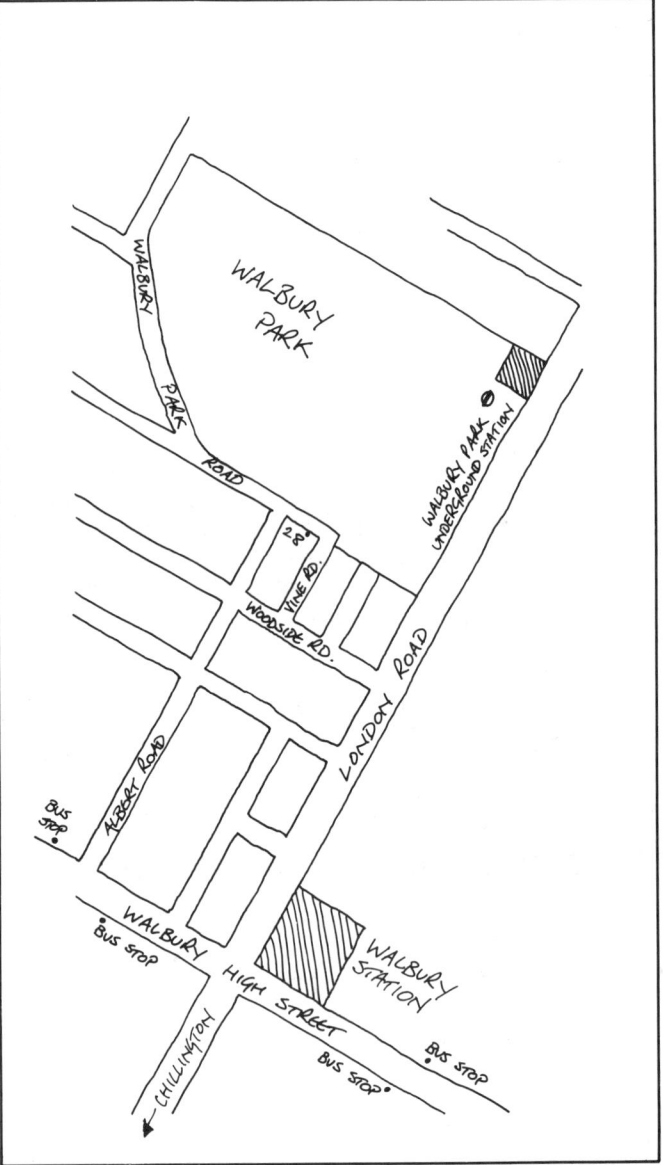

# 7 Personal letters

## Practice

John Long is expecting a visit from an Italian friend, Giovanni, but Giovanni has just written to him to say he has had to change his flight. He will arrive at Gatwick airport on Friday afternoon next week, instead of Saturday morning, and John cannot now meet him at the airport as he planned.

Complete the extract from John's reply with the correct word or phrase from this list: *at, for, from, in, on, opposite, out of, over, to, under*.

---

... I'm very sorry that I won't be able to meet you ..........¹ the airport, because I will be ..........² work ..........³ Friday afternoon. I'm therefore going to give you some instructions so that you can make your own way ..........⁴ my flat. I'll certainly leave the office ..........⁵ time to get home to welcome you.

You can get either a train or a coach ..........⁶ Gatwick to Victoria. The train is better, because you will already be ..........⁷ the station when you arrive. If you take the coach, you will have to come ..........⁸ the Coach Station, turn left and walk along Buckingham Palace Road ..........⁹ about a hundred yards. The railway station is ..........¹⁰ the other side of the road.

..........¹¹ Victoria, get a single ticket ..........¹³ ..........¹² Penge East, which is ..........¹⁴ the Orpington line. It's the fifth station, ..........¹⁵ Penge East fact. When you come ..........¹⁶ the station, you will see a footbridge ..........¹⁷ the bridge, and turn railway line. Cross ..........¹⁸ the end of the road, turn left and right. ..........¹⁹ walk along Crampton Road. Turn right ..........²⁰ the corner of Penge High Street, and this time go ..........²⁰ a railway bridge. Lawrie Park Road is then the first turning ..........²¹ the right, and I live ..........²² number 279, ..........²³ a tennis ..........²⁴ my club. I can see people playing ..........²⁵ the bedroom window. My flat is upstairs, ..........²⁵ the second floor.

---

1 How do you think John began and ended his letter? Write a beginning to the first paragraph and a short last paragraph.
2 Draw a map that John could have enclosed to direct Giovanni from Penge East station to his house.

## ✎ Further Practice

1 Write a letter to a friend who lives in another part of your town or city inviting him/her to a party at your house and giving directions. Assume that he/she is coming by public transport.
2 Write instructions for a group of tourists coming to your town or city to help them spend an interesting morning sightseeing. Imagine that they are staying at a hotel in the centre, and want to walk from one place to another.
3 Imagine you are Angela and cannot go to the 'housewarming' party. Write to Mark and Penny, making an apology. (For guidance, look at Marian's letter on p.2.)

# 8 Narrative: tense changes

## ✍ Telling a story

Before reading the story, study the notes on the use of tenses in narrative and of time expressions (Reference Section 8). Then answer the questions that follow.

### The Level Crossing Keeper

It was one of those cold, wet, miserable February afternoons when no one wants to go out. It *had started* raining about midday and the rain *was* still *falling* steadily. Now it *was beginning* to get dark, and mist *was forming* on the other side of the railway line. Jack looked at the clock over the little desk in his hut. Then he put on his coat and cap and went out to shut the crossing. He *was expecting* a goods train to come through in three minutes' time, at 4.37, and he imagined it *would be* on time because no one *had rung* to say it *was running* late.

It was a lonely spot, with very little traffic either on the road or the railway. When Jack retired the following year, they *would* probably *replace* him with an automatic crossing, but meanwhile he still had his job to do. He brought the lever down to lower the barrier, and then went back into the doorway of his hut to shelter from the rain while the train went through. The mist *was growing* thicker.

As the train passed, Jack counted the wagons from habit. There were eighty-seven. When the last *had gone* by, he raised the lever and the gates swung back. As he did so, he saw a big black car waiting on the far side of the crossing. He could just make out the figure of a man, sitting upright in the driving seat. He waved, but there was no answer, so he turned on his heel and went back into his hut. He *would have* time for a warm cup of tea before the next train appeared about ten past five.

He put the kettle on the stove, lit a cigarette and waited for the water to boil. Five minutes later, he *was enjoying* his tea when he happened to look out of the window. To his surprise, the car *was* still *standing* at the crossing. Perhaps it *had broken down*. He decided he *would go out* to see if the driver needed help, but first he *would finish* his tea.

The car still *had not moved* when Jack went out again, buttoning up his coat, because the rain *was dripping* down his neck. As he approached the car, peering through the mist, he was surprised that there was no sign of the driver. It was not until he came level with the front window that he saw that the man *had fallen* on his side onto the passenger's seat.

'Perhaps he's had a heart attack,' Jack said aloud to himself.

But then, as he opened the door, he saw the small round hole in the windscreen and another, similar hole in the man's forehead.

---

1 Read through the first two paragraphs again to obtain the maximum information you can about the time and place where the events occurred, and about the weather. Point to all the details that provide you with this information.

2 What time, exactly, does the story begin and approximately how long does the action last? Give reasons for your answer.

3 Make a list of all the actions in the Past Simple tense in chronological order, beginning with: 'Jack looked at the clock . . .' (l.5), and put an approximate time against them. Then complete the table below for the verbs in other tenses and compare it to your list. What is the pattern that emerges?

4 Continue the story. Decide what Jack did immediately, and what happened the same evening. You need not solve the crime, but you should decide how and when the man was killed, and how these facts were established.

| Past Continuous | | Past Perfect | | Conditional | |
|---|---|---|---|---|---|
| was falling | 4.34 | had started | midday | would be | 4.37 |
| was beginning | ... | had rung | ... | would replace | ... |
| was forming | ... | had gone by | ... | would have | ... |
| was expecting | ... | had broken down | ... | would go out | ... |
| was running | ... | had not moved | ... | would finish | ... |
| was growing | ... | had fallen | ... | | |
| was enjoying | ... | | | | |
| was standing | ... | | | | |
| was dripping | ... | | | | |

# 8 Narrative

## Practice

Read the whole story below before (a) choosing the correct time expression from the list below; (b) putting the verbs into one of the following tenses, Past Continuous, Past Perfect or Conditional. Then answer the questions that follow. Note: the time in Spain is six hours ahead of Miami and eight ahead of Mexico City.

### An unexpected stop

I (sit) in the airport restaurant in Miami having lunch. At the hotel they (tell) me that my flight (leave) at 4.30 ..................¹ but ........................² I did not trust their announcements. I was in a country I (not expect) to visit on my way to a city where people (come) to meet me ........................³. Apart from that, the clock said 1.15 and my watch said 7.15 but I understood everything people (say) at the tables around me and because of all the films I (see) everything was strangely familiar. I found myself in the United States ........................⁴ ........................⁵, by accident.

The trouble (start) ........................⁶ when I (wait) for the Mexico City plane in Madrid airport. The plane (come) from Paris on its return journey to Mexico but someone just (discover) that it (not take off) yet.

According to schedule, the plane was due in Mexico City about eight o'clock ........................⁷, local time, (which would be four ........................⁸ by my watch). ........................⁹ Luis (take) me to a hotel and I (have) a day's rest ........................¹⁰ meeting an important customer for dinner ........................¹¹. ........................¹² the extra waiting period I sent a telegram to Luis, warning him that I (be) late, and sat down to wait for further information. ........................¹³, we took off.

Nothing much happened on the flight across the Atlantic but ........................¹⁴ we (get out) of the plane at Miami for a 10-minute stop to refuel, all the lights went out. We waited in a lounge hour after hour until late ........................¹⁵. ........................¹⁶, they told us to fill in a temporary immigration form and sent us to a hotel.

At the hotel a clerk (try) to issue room numbers to a lot of very tired Spanish-speaking travellers who did not understand him. I could see that we (stand) in the queue ........................¹⁷ unless someone did something, so I translated all the numbers ahead of me and ........................¹⁸ got to the front.

'Do you mean you can speak their language?' the man said to me in astonishment, looking at my British passport.

I nodded. Since then, I have discovered that 40% of the population of Miami speak it but he was evidently not one of them. ........................¹⁹ I got up, ........................²⁰ a few hours' sleep, I tried to ring Luis but the telephone operator told me they didn't know the code for Mexico. I had a shower and breakfast, and set off for the airport.

Now, over lunch, I (worry) about Luis. (stay up) he waiting for me ........................²¹? (be) he at the airport to meet me? (meet) we the customer for dinner, as we (plan)? (keep) I awake if we did?

---

About four hours later    after all night    As soon as    at night
by this time    at the moment when
before    During    for the first time
finally    in my life    in the morning
in the afternoon    in the evening
in a few minutes    Then
the previous evening    the next evening
the night before    the day before

1. Compare the time scale here with that of the story on the opposite page. How is it different? How does the second writer avoid telling the whole story in the Past Perfect tense?
2. Continue the story for two more paragraphs, assuming the flight took off at 4.30. What happened when the writer arrived in Mexico City?

# 8 Narrative

## ✍ The beginning and the end

At the beginning of a story, the writer should set the scene so that we understand the events and their importance. The story should end with a logical climax. The first and last paragraphs of this story are missing.

Read the main body of the story and then answer the questions that follow.
Use your answers to decide which of the beginnings and endings on the opposite page you prefer, and why.

### The Cross-Country Race

As Tom stood waiting for the race to start, he glanced at his main rivals, Julian Mayne and Gary Cummings from the big city. They both looked confident and relaxed, while Tom was nervously shifting from one foot to the other. But the race mattered more to him. He did not look at his father or Jenny, his girl-friend, in the crowd. It was important to them, too.

His first task was to get away from the mass of runners. Then he would be able to run freely at his own pace. The moment the race started, he moved alongside Mayne and they were soon part of a group of about twenty who led the rest up the steep slope away from St. Mary's church into the fields at the top of the hill.

For the next two miles the course ran downhill across muddy fields before turning sharply at the foot of another hill. When they reached the top, they would see the spire of St. Mary's standing out clearly in the distance two miles further on. He kept close to Mayne and Cummings but as they came over the hill, looked back and saw that the rest were a long way behind. The race would be decided between the three of them.

Mayne and Cummings sprinted away from him down the hill and Tom had to hold himself back to keep to his plan. His only hope was to trust in his knowledge of the course. St. Mary's stood on flat ground and someone who did not know the course well would imagine that the last mile, through the village streets, was even, too. But Tom had trained over every yard of it. The slope they had climbed at the beginning of the race was really the end of a long hill.

As he left the fields and turned back onto the road, Tom saw Mayne disappearing round a bend a hundred yards ahead of him. Cummings was further ahead, out of sight. Now he would have to trust in the plan his father had worked out during the winter. He still felt strong as he forced himself to run faster, uphill.

Beginning  Where was the race taking place? What time of year was it, do you imagine? What other information do we need to understand the atmosphere? Why do you think the race mattered more to Tom? What part had his father played in preparing him for the race?

Ending  Do you want Tom to win, and if so, how? What evidence is there for deciding how the race is likely to continue? Who is more tired? Who is Tom likely to pass first? If he passes both runners, where would you like this to happen?

# 8 Narrative

Beginning 1  The first cross-country race in Tom's village had taken place many years before. His father had won it and had received a medal. Now a lot of runners from the city entered for the race, and the village runners did not have much chance. But Tom had been training all winter, and his father had given him some advice. He did not think he would win because the city runners were more experienced.

Beginning 2  The cross-country race took place in Tom's village every year in March. It was a great event for the villagers, but for a long time now runners from the city had taken the prizes. The last local victory had been twenty years before but the medal that hung on the wall at home always reminded Tom that the winner had been his father. Tom had been training hard all winter over the course and his father had planned his tactics. Now, on a bright sunny morning after three days of rain, he was impatient to put his plan into action.

Ending 1  He soon caught Mayne, and now he could see Cummings in front of him. The village was full of people. They were shouting his name and telling him that he could win. He ran faster, and Cummings came nearer. When he saw the church a hundred yards ahead, he was not sure if he could catch him, but he did. As they reached the line, his father and Jenny ran out of the crowd to congratulate him. His father said that he was very proud of him.

Ending 2  Mayne was very tired, and Tom soon overtook him, but Cummings was still a long way ahead. Everyone from the village was shouting his name, but Tom kept to his plan, reserving his energy for his final effort. As the church came in sight, he sprinted at last. Cummings heard him breathing at his shoulder, and looked back, but at that moment Tom passed him and crossed the line a yard ahead.

His father and Jenny came out of the crowd to greet him.
'You were wonderful, Tom,' Jenny said.
'Just good planning,' his father said, but from his smile Tom knew he was proud and happy.

## 3 Further Practice

In attempting the topics below, decide when you begin the story where it is taking place, what time of year it is, what the weather is like, and how much information the reader needs about the background to the story to understand what happens.

End the story with a comment that summarises its meaning, either of your own or spoken by one of the characters.

1. A robbery. *Either* the main character comes home and suspects something wrong as he/she approaches the house *or* some thieves have what they think is a perfect plan to rob a bank or country house.
2. A ghost story or a story about a person who thinks he/she sees a flying saucer (UFO).
3. Blackmail. A story about a person who has a guilty secret. Someone who has discovered it tries to get money from him/her in return for keeping the secret.
4. Your own story of one of the themes of the stories in this unit: a murder story, the account of a journey or a story about a race.

# 9 Description: objects

## ✎ Describing a room

Look at the drawing of William's room, and name each of the numbered features, using the list below:

bed   book shelves   drawers
mat   posters   table lamp   wardrobe
window   writing desk

My room at home has to serve two purposes; it is a bedroom but also a study. It is not very large, but I like it because it has a large window opposite the door, and my desk is on the right near the window, so I do not need to use the table lamp during the day.

I have a writing desk that folds down so I can do my homework comfortably. I keep my pens and pencils in the top part of the desk, and it has three drawers, where I keep all my notebooks. There is a table lamp on top of the desk, and some bookshelves above it, fixed to the wall, for all my school books. I have decorated the room by sticking some posters on the wall above my bed.

On the other side of the room, opposite my bed, is the wardrobe. It has two sections, and is very convenient because it is built into the wall, and so it does not take up much space. I keep my jackets and trousers in one section, and the other section consists of little drawers for shirts and socks and underwear. At the bottom there is a big drawer, where I keep sweaters.

## Practice

Now look at the drawing of William's elder sister's room, and name each of the additional numbered features, using the list below. Then write a description of the room. Begin like this:

  My sister Anna's room is different from mine...

bedside lamp   bedside table   carpet
chest of drawers   dressing table   mirror

## ✎ Further Practice

Write a description of your own room at home or your brother or sister's room or a friend's room.

22

## 9 Description

### ✏️ Describing an object

First, read the text; then use it, together with the list below the drawing, to number all the features on the drawing; finally, answer the questions on the text.

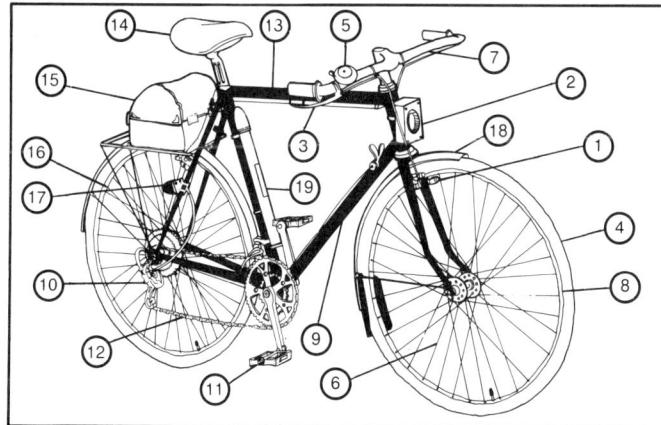

back wheel   bell   brake   brake block
chain   crossbar   dynamo   frame
front wheel   handlebars   lamp   mudguard
pedal   pump   saddle   saddle bag
spokes   three-speed gear   tyre

### My first bicycle

I got my first real bicycle as a birthday present when I was twelve. It was made of shining steel and the frame was painted black. It had a three-speed gear on the cross-bar, a dynamo driven by the back wheel that produced electricity for the lamp, a socket on the frame for the pump, a saddle-bag attached to the saddle for my school books, and a bell on the handle-bars.

I knew how to ride a bicycle, because I had had a child's bicycle before that, but I was very excited because in future I would be able to ride to school, instead of going on the bus. In the first few weeks after my birthday, I rode my new bicycle every day, and gradually discovered all its advantages, compared to the one I had had until then. When I came to a steep hill, I could change gear with my three-speed and pedal up it, instead of getting off and pushing the bike. I was not afraid of getting home after dark because the lamp provided a good light, and the faster I rode the brighter it was.

I also discovered the risks and the disadvantages. I liked to free-wheel down the hills without pedalling, but I soon learnt that it was risky to put the front brake on first. That was a sure way to go over the handlebars, head first. I also learnt that bicycles need constant maintenance. I had to pump up the tyres and oil the gears and there were times when I had to mend punctures and replace the brake blocks. The thing I hated most was when the chain came off, and I had to take hold of the black, oily links and put it on again. But it was a good bicycle, and it lasted me until I was grown up.

1. Give each paragraph a heading. What is its purpose? Does it describe the bicycle or the writer's experience with it, or both?
2. Why does the writer describe this as his first 'real' bicycle?
3. What was the purpose of the five special features the writer describes in the first paragraph?
4. In what ways was this bicycle an improvement on the previous one?
5. What sort of things could go wrong with the bicycle, and what did the writer have to do to solve these problems?

### ✏️ Further Practice

1. Write about: my first camera; my first record-player; my first watch.

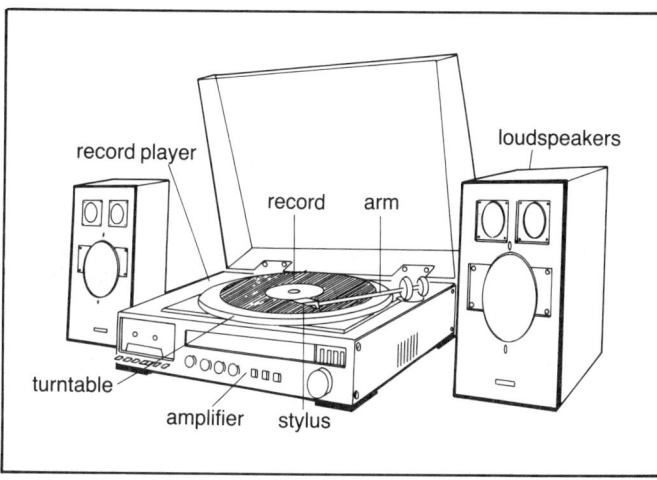

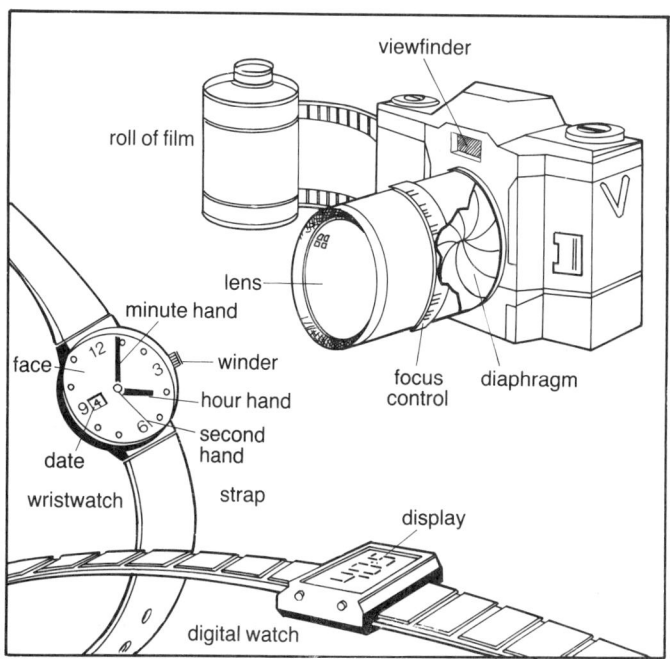

23

# 10 Formal Letters: applications for jobs

## Letters of application

> Small company based in North London seeks enthusiastic secretary with cheerful telephone manner. Experience with word processors an advantage. Write with full c.v. to Harriet Finlay, Grayling Communications Ltd., 98 Hamden St., London NW19 MH6.

Read the two letters of application for this job, comparing them to the information contained in the curriculum vitae each applicant encloses. Then answer the questions.

---

34 Stag Lane,
London SW9 3SB

May 7, 1989

Dear Miss Finlay,
    I have seen your ad for a job as a secretary with your company in the paper, and I am quite interested in it so I enclose my curriculum vitae.

    I have been working as a secretary for the past eighteen months at an insurance company, but now I feel I need a change.

    We have not got a word processor at the office but my boy-friend has one, and I am sure I would soon pick it up.

    I hope you will give me an interview, and look forward to hearing from you.

    Yours sincerely,
    *Christine Jones*
    Christine Jones

---

8 Albion Road
London SW7 1ST

May 7, 1989

Ms Harriet Finlay
Grayling Communications Ltd.,
London NW19 MH6

Dear Ms Finlay,
    I was very interested to see your advertisement in the Daily Telegraph this morning for a secretary. I believe I have the appropriate qualifications and experience for this post, and am therefore enclosing my curriculum vitae.

    While I enjoy the job I am doing at present, I haven't very much opportunity to deal with people from outside the office, as I had in my previous job, and the post you advertise seems very attractive to me for this reason.

    Word processors have not yet been installed at the office where I am working, but I have been attending evening classes for the last three months in order to gain experience with them, and believe I have made progress.

    I very much hope you will take my application into consideration, and look forward to hearing from you.

    Yours sincerely,
    *Angela Coxon*
    Angela Coxon

---

(1) Christine Jones
(2) 34 Stag Lane, London SW9 3SB
(3) 267 1958
(4) 28th February, 1969
(5) single
(6) St. Mary's College, Watford (1980–1985) Major Secretarial College (1985–1986)
(7) GCE 'O' level (5 subjects) Secretarial Diploma
(8) Secretary, Marble Ltd. (1986–7) Secretary, Consolidated Insurance Co. (1987–now)
(9) dancing, swimming, reading
(10) Joshua Plumb, Claims Dept. Consolidated Insurance Co. (my boss)

---

(1) Angela Coxon
(2) 8 Albion Rd., London SW7 1ST
(3) 197 5246
(4) 8th April, 1969
(5) single
(6) Wesbiton Comprehensive School (1980–1985) Branley Secretarial College (1985–6)
(7) GCE 'O' level, Maths., French, English Language, History, Geography (1985) Secretarial diploma (Pitman) (1986)
(8) Secretary, Hall & Coates (travel agents) (1986–Oct. 1987) Secretary, Bore & Bore (solicitors) (since Oct. 1987)
(9) languages, travel, tennis
(10) Ms Rachel Barnett, Principal, Branley Secretarial College, 17 Oxford St., London W1 2PY
Ms Caroline Longley, branch manager, Hall & Coates, 16 Ransome Rd., London SW6 2HR

# 10 Formal letters

1. First, look at the two curricula vitae submitted. Give a brief heading, such as 'name', to each of the ten points mentioned. In what ways are the curricula vitae similar, and in what ways is Angela's more convincing?
2. Now compare the letters, taking into account the form of the advertisement. Why do you think Harriet Finlay interviewed Angela, but did not interview Christine? In particular, study (a) the form of the address (b) the reference to the advertisement (c) interest expressed in the present job and the job the girls are applying for (d) interest in the requirements of the job (e) the form of ending the letter.

---

## Practice 1

### Travel Representative

International tour operators with head office in London require a local representative based in Athens to assist in organising holidays. Duties involve meeting groups, checking hotel and excursion arrangements and guaranteeing smooth organisation. The successful candidate will be familiar with Athens and the surrounding area, and have had previous experience in the field. Apart from speaking fluent English and modern Greek, he/she must show a capacity to work with tact and initiative. Apply in writing, enclosing full c.v. to Stephen Craig, Manager (Greece), Med Tours Limited, Ksiromerou 74, Ambelokipi, Athens

 MED TOURS Ltd

Making a successful application for a job is not only a matter of writing correct English but using the right sort of language. It is important not to be too aggressive and colloquial, but also not to sound impractical and use rhetorical phrases. Complete Nikos's application, choosing the most acceptable language for each of the blanks.

(1) (a) I want the job (b) I am very anxious to serve you (c) I believe I have the qualifications and experience you require
(2) (a) I am therefore (b) That's why I'm (c) It is for this reason that I am
(3) (a) had a long and pleasurable connection (b) done a lot of work (c) had a great deal of experience
(4) (a) my understanding of the problems is considerable (b) I have a good knowledge of the problems involved (c) I know all the tricks
(5) (a) made a lot of good friends in the hotel business (b) developed an excellent relationship with hotel managers (c) extended my acquaintance among the hoteliers
(6) (a) am confident (b) 've got the feeling (c) have the impression
(7) (a) give satisfactory service in resolving difficulties (b) fix things up (c) deal with any problems that might arise
(8) (a) expand my already wide knowledge of the English language (b) keep my English going (c) practise my spoken and written English
(9) (a) would be grateful if you would consider my application (b) reckon that if you give me an interview, you won't be sorry (c) have pleasure in presenting my application for your kind consideration
(10) (a) I await your reply at your earliest convenience (b) I look forward to hearing from you (c) Please reply soon

```
                                    G. Michaelis 115
                                    Pangrati
                                    Athens
Mr Stephen Craig,
Area Manager (Greece), Med Tours Ltd.,
Ksiromerou 74
Ambelokipi
Athens.
                                    February 9th, 1989
```
Dear Mr Craig,
   I was very interested to see your advertisement in today's *Athens Daily News* for a travel representative, as ___(1)___. ___(2)___ enclosing my cirriculum vitae.
   I have ___(3)___ with tourists. I have been working for a travel agency here for the past five years and ___(4)___. During this time, I have ___(5)___ so I ___(6)___ that I would be able to ___(7)___. This experience has also enabled me to ___(8)___.
   I ___(9)___. ___(10)___.
   Yours sincerely,
   Nikos Lanitis

25

# 10 Formal letters

## Practice 2

John Targett is a successful salesman interested in this job. The text of his letter consists of six sentences, divided into four paragraphs, but here they are printed out of order. Re-order them, indicating the beginning of each paragraph, and then give each paragraph a topic heading. Afterwards, answer the questions that follow.

### Sales Representative

Ferguson and Walker, one of the leading suppliers of stationery in the UK, require a salesman/woman with a proven track record as a Sales Rep. for Buckinghamshire and Berkshire. Applications are invited from dynamic men and women in the age range 25-40. The person we are looking for has the opportunity to develop an expanding market in this area. Write, enclosing full C.V. to The Sales Manager, Ferguson and Walker Ltd., Shankly Road, Ely, Cambridgeshire, EL9 5EY.

F&W
Ferguson & Walker

(a) Another advantage is that the area would be more suitable to me than my present area south of the Thames as I have just bought a house in Buckinghamshire.
(b) In all cases, I have been able to increase sales in my area, and I have therefore attached to my c.v. a summary of the percentage increases I have achieved in the four firms I have worked for as evidence of my track record.
(c) I was very interested to read your advertisement in yesterday's *Sunday Times* for a sales representative in Buckinghamshire and Berkshire, and am therefore enclosing my c.v., as requested.
(d) I trust my application will be of interest, and look forward to hearing from you.
(e) At the age of 32, I am looking for the opportunity this post seems likely to offer to make further progress in a firm with good future prospects.
(f) From that you will see that I have considerable experience as a sales rep. with a variety of products, including stationery.

1 What forms should John use to begin and end his letter?
2 What information usually contained in a curriculum vitae would the Sales Manager obtain from John's letter?
3 What additional information is he going to provide, and how should this help him with his application?
4 Compare John's last paragraph to Angela's on p.24. In what way is John more confident, and why is that appropriate in his case?

## Further Practice

Imagine that the following advertisements have appeared in English in a newspaper in your country. Apply for one or more of the posts advertised. You are free to invent a name and address for the company advertising, and you should assume a curriculum vitae for yourself that would make you a suitable candidate. It is not necessary to write a separate c.v., but you should include useful information in your letter.

> Travel agency requires bright, energetic person aged 20-25 to help with enquiries on information desk June-September. Good English essential.

> International company requires top-flight secretary as personal secretary to the Area Manager. This is a responsible position demanding tact and initiative. The person selected will be required to make frequent trips abroad. Previous experience at executive level and fluent English essential.

> Camp-Aid is a dynamic company supplying the needs of tourists on holiday throughout Europe. Applications are invited from residents in all Western European countries for salesmen/women as local Reps. to expand our share of a growing market.

> Couriers wanted to accompany groups on coach tours starting from Britain. Fluency in English and one other European language essential. Previous experience an advantage, but not obligatory.

> The National Arts Council needs students of art history, architecture, history and archaeology from June-September as guides on organised tours of monuments of historical interest. Candidates must be fluent in a least one foreign language. Apply, giving full details of qualifications and previous experience.

# 11 Discussion: for and against

## ✐ Contrasting points of view

Before working on this unit, study Reference Section, p.108 (connectors and modifiers).
Spoken and written discussion reaching a balanced conclusion obey different rules. First, read the dialogue between Jim, Kate and Laura.

JIM: I see the Russians are planning to go to Mars now. It makes me sick to think of all the money spent on space research. How can they throw money away like that when millions of people on Earth are hungry?

KATE: I don't think it's thrown away. You can't stop scientific progress. People naturally want to find out about other planets, and what we find out may be very useful to the human race in the future.

JIM: But it doesn't do us much good now, does it? All that effort and expense to land two people on the Moon, and we found out that no one lives there, and we couldn't, either. We knew that already.

KATE: Yes, but when I saw the film, I thought it was thrilling. It caught people's imagination. And that's why there have been so many technological advances in other areas. I've read that the investment has been repaid nine times. All the computers, even things like digital watches, have developed much faster because of space research.

JIM: Well, they don't feed hungry people or improve social services, either, do they? What do you think, Laura?

LAURA: I think you're both right in a way, though personally I'm more on Kate's side. The main argument in favour is that because it's spectacular, it encourages research everywhere. Some things they have found out help cure people in hospital, for instance, so it does have a practical value now, not just in the future. But of course if you think that raising the standard of living of poor people in the world is the most urgent problem we need to solve, any expense on research that doesn't affect that directly must seem wasteful.

Now read Laura's written version of this discussion. Note (a) the way it is organised in paragraphs (b) the order in which the discussion is presented (c) the use of phrases that connect the argument.

Space research is still a controversial issue. For some people it is an exciting proof of man's adventurous spirit, bringing scientific progress, *while* for others it is a waste of money that should be spent on improving living conditions here on Earth and solving the problems of poverty and hunger.

*This* is the main argument against space research. The vast sums of money spent on it could be better used in other ways. *Apart from that*, it is thought that the successful landing on the Moon, *for example*, *although* it was spectacular, did not advance human knowledge very much, *since* we already knew it was uninhabited.

*On the other hand*, those who defend space research argue that scientific progress is inevitable, and *what is more*, the effort to reach the Moon led to technological advance in other areas. *Consequently*, it is wrong to think that space research only benefits certain people, *because* all kinds of everyday objects have developed faster because of it. It is *therefore* wrong to think that the money is wasted.

*On balance*, I am in favour of space research because of the advantages it has already brought in terms of life on Earth today, *for instance* in developing techniques in hospitals. *Nevertheless*, I sympathise with those who are so concerned about the condition of people in Third World Countries that they would like to spend all the money available to governments on helping them.

# 11 Discussion

## Practice

Complete the article below comparing bicycles and scooters as a means of transport for teenagers by choosing from the list of connectors below. Only one word or phrase is correct.

Thirty years ago, most teenagers had bicycles, but now they are comparatively rare, and even those boys and girls who have them do not use them as often. ___(1)___, motor scooters are much more common. ___(2)___, this may seem a sign of progress but ___(3)___ the change is not necessarily for the better.

It is easy to see why young people prefer scooters. ___(4)___, they are much faster and do not require much physical effort; ___(5)___, you can take a passenger with you on the pillion seat behind; ___(6)___, they give young people a feeling of independence, because they can travel further and impress their friends. ___(7)___, the disadvantages are equally obvious. ___(8)___, scooters are more expensive to buy and to maintain, and ___(9)___ those under 16 are not allowed to have them. ___(10)___, greater freedom brings danger because speed encourages young people to take risks and ___(11)___ scooters are involved in more accidents, and the accidents are ___(12)___ more serious.

Bicycles are safer and easier to control. Years ago, teenagers had more experience with them because they had learnt to ride as young children, and ___(13)___ knew what they were capable of. ___(14)___, many young people overestimate what a scooter can do and pretend it has the power of a motor-cycle. ___(15)___, ___(16)___ bicycles are not very safe, either, in cities these days because there are more cars and drivers are not used to them and do not make allowances for them.

___(17)___, those who are old enough to ride scooters naturally prefer them, but they should realise that they are the most dangerous form of transport on the road. Those who are too young or cannot afford to buy a scooter probably find bicycles slow and uncomfortable ___(18)___, and riding a bicycle requires more experience of traffic than before. ___(19)___, the change has been for the worse, ___(20)___ for the 13- and 14-year-olds, but the only safe solution would be to have special lanes for cyclists.

(1) (a) At the other end (b) On the contrary (c) On the other hand
(2) (a) At first sight (b) In the beginning (c) In the first place
(3) (a) apart from that (b) in fact (c) indeed
(4) (a) At first (b) In the beginning (c) In the first place
(5) (a) also (b) as well (c) secondly
(6) (a) above all (b) mostly (c) over all
(7) (a) Although (b) However (c) in spite
(8) (a) At first sight (b) In principle (c) To begin with
(9) (a) consequently (b) in any case (c) meanwhile
(10) (a) Apart from that (b) As a result (c) On the other hand
(11) (a) as a result (b) for this (c) secondly
(12) (a) as well (b) generally (c) however

(13) (a) consequently (b) for this (c) to begin with
(14) (a) However (b) In contrast (c) On the contrary
(15) (a) But (b) In spite (c) Nevertheless
(16) (a) indeed (b) it is the fact that (c) the fact is that

(17) (a) In the end (b) Lastly (c) To sum up

(18) (a) by comparison (b) in contrast (c) on the other hand
(19) (a) Above all (b) At last (c) On balance
(20) (a) especially (b) generally (c) mostly

The plan for this article is similar to that of the previous one on space research, but a different technique is used in the second and third paragraphs. What is it?

# 11 Discussion

## ✎ A balanced article

Look at the detailed plan below for a balanced article on animals in captivity. The introductory first paragraph has been completed for you. Use the points for and against to develop the second and third paragraphs. If you can think of better arguments include them or replace those given. Finally, use the notes to summarise points for and against in the last paragraph, and include your personal opinion.

Most important cities have a zoo and people, especially children, enjoy visiting it. Teachers often take their classes there because of the educational value a visit may provide. On the other hand, many people feel it is wrong to keep animals in captivity, like prisoners, and think they should all be allowed to live freely in their natural surroundings.

1 Animals in captivity provide valuable educational experience. People would never see, recognise them in natural surroundings.
2 Zoos improved, animals better looked after, species preserved.
3 Situation still artificial. Animals have protected existence, sometimes no freedom.
4 Personal opinion.

**For**
1 Educational value, people learn about animals, zoologists study habits.
2 Preservation of species; rare animals may disappear. Can often breed in captivity. Better food.
3 Zoos improved. More space. Advantages of safari parks. Most animals can run about.

**Against**
1 Cruel, unnatural. Animals kept in cages.
2 Destroys natural abilities, changes behaviour. Animals born in zoos would die in the wild.
3 Even in safari parks, limited space, not all animals given freedom – e.g. birds like eagles.

## ✎ Further Practice

Use the organisation of paragraphs in the examples in this unit for guidance. Make a plan, listing points for and against like the plan above. In choosing questions, choose one or more where you can see points for and against, not a topic where you feel strongly on one side or the other.
1 The advantages and disadvantages of travelling by bus/coach and by train.
2 Travelling by air or by ship to an island 200 km. away.
3 Going to the cinema and going to the theatre or similar live performance, such as a 'pop', 'rock' or classical concert.
4 Co-educational schools (where boys and girls are in the same class) compared to schools where they are separated.
5 Private television channels, paid for by advertising, and state television channels, assuming there is one, paid for by public money.

# 12 Guided Writing: making choices

## 3 Choosing a holiday

**Sicily Club.** The perfect family break. Couriers on hand at all times to take care of the children. Wonderful old village turned into a holiday paradise. Tennis, sailing, windsurfing. Separate discos for adults, teenagers, children. Two weeks' holiday, including flight, £700, children under 12 half price.

**Have you always wanted to sail a yacht?** You can have a week in a villa in the Mediterranean with sailing lessons every day and then join experienced yachtsmen on a week's sailing in the Greek islands. £800 for a fortnight, including flight to Greece and meals on board.

**All the sun and fun you need for next to nothing.** For only £150 you can have a fortnight in Ibiza at the Hotel Rocamar. Swimming pool, beach, bar, night life.

**Looking for adventure?** Go sledging and drive a team of husky dogs across Swedish Lapland. A fascinating way to make the most of eighteen hours of daylight, and meet friends who will share your adventure. £1200, including flight and all expenses.

**Sun, sand and unspoilt beaches.** Get away from the rest of the crowd, and rent a room in a house where your host will show you the beautiful surroundings of his native village on the Yugoslavian coast. £150 for two weeks' escape. Includes air fares, bed and breakfast.

Ingrid Freeman is a student, aged 19. She belongs to a large family. Apart from her parents, she has an elder brother, Ian, who is 26, and three younger brothers and sisters aged 14, 11 and 10. Her parents are going to take the younger children with them on holiday, but Ingrid wants to go somewhere sunny with her friend Judith, where she can meet the local people. Her brother Ian is an adventurous type. He always wants to go somewhere on his own and have new experiences.

Before reading the text, decide which of the holidays would be most attractive for different members of the family, giving reasons. Then complete Ingrid's account, explaining the choice they have made.

Finally, decide which holiday you would like to go on yourself, and write a paragraph, explaining why.

I haven't made up my mind yet about my holiday this summer. My parents are going to ........................[1] with the three young ones because they saw an advertisement for a holiday where the family live together in a village. The advantage for the children is that they have couriers ........................[2]. Apart from that, Mum and Dad like tennis, and enjoy going to a disco in the evening, but there they'll be able to relax in the evenings, because the children ........................[3]. One of the best things about it is the price, because two of the children are under 12 and ........................[4].

I'm planning to go somewhere with my friend Judith, but we don't agree about where to go. We both want to get some sun in the Mediterranean, and she's seen an advertisement for ........................[5] but I don't think I would like that because ........................[6]. I'd rather find a quieter place where you can ........................[7], so I'm trying to persuade her to go with me to ........................[8]. There we can ........................[9].

My brother Ian hasn't made up his mind, either. He likes doing adventurous things, and he really wants to go to ........................[10] because ........................[11]. The only thing is that these holidays are expensive, so he may decide to ........................[12]. He's never ........................[13], and the advantage is that you can ........................[14] before you ........................[15].

# 12 Guided writing

## Choosing a television programme

Mark Farmer, 42, is a businessman who likes to relax in the evenings. He enjoys films, plays, detective series and above all, anything connected with sport. His wife, Maureen, 39, is a teacher; she prefers news programmes and documentaries. Janet, 16, is fond of music, classical and modern, and also likes series but not crime stories; her brother, Jason, 14, likes quiz shows, sports programmes and comedy series.

Decide which programmes each member of the family wants to watch this evening, giving reasons, and write a paragraph for each. Remember that sometimes they may have to choose between two programmes that interest them that are on at the same time.

Begin: Mark would like to watch *Hard Cases* at 9.00 because... Later he would have to choose between...

### Tonight's Viewing

**BBC1**
- 7.00 **WOGAN.** Terry Wogan interviews three bishops on the church's role today.
- 7.35 **GOING FOR GOLD.** European general knowledge quiz.
- 8.00 **KENNY EVERETT SHOW.** Last of the popular comedian's series.
- 8.30 **WATCHDOG** looks at shoppers' problems.
- 9.00 **NEWS, REGIONAL NEWS, WEATHER**
- 9.30 **PANORAMA.** Interview with the Prime Minister of India, Rajiv Gandhi.
- 10.10 **STUDIO MURDERS** (1981). Mystery film. **(11.45 weather, close down)**

**BBC2**
- 7.00 **THE JOY OF LIVING** (1938) Lively musical with Jerome Kern songs.
- 8.30 **BARRY DOUGLAS.** Pianist plays Beethoven's Waldstein Sonata.
- 9.00 **HORIZON.** Documentary on how depression affects people.
- 9.50 **MOONLIGHTING.** American detective series.
- 10.30 **SPLIT SCREEN.** Series that examines controversial issues by presenting two opposing views. Tonight: public and private health care.
- 10.45 **NEWSNIGHT (11.30 weather, close down)**

**ITV Thames**
- 7.00 **WISH YOU WERE HERE** compares holidays abroad.
- 7.30 **CORONATION STREET.** The long-running series from the North.
- 8.00 **AFTER HENRY.** Family series.
- 8.30 **WORLD IN ACTION** looks at where the money from bank robberies goes.
- 9.00 **HARD CASES.** New drama series in six parts, first tonight, about the probation service.
- 10.00 **NEWS AT TEN.**
- 10.35 **SPORTSNIGHT,** featuring golf and highlights of European Cup football.

**Channel 4**
- 7.00 **CHANNEL 4 NEWS,** with commentary and weather forecast.
- 8.00 **BROOKSIDE.** Series.
- 8.30 **RUDE HEALTH.** Comedy play set in a doctor's surgery.
- 9.00 **MERELY MORTAL.** Second of a five-part series examining attitudes towards death.
- 10.00 **HILL STREET BLUES.** The American detective series.
- 11.00 **RADIO BIKINI.** Documentary about atomic-bomb tests in the Pacific.

## Further Practice

1. Either use the television guide on this page or the different television programmes available on the same evening in your own country to write about the preferences of your own family. You should expect to begin on these lines: 'At 7.00 I would like to watch..., but my father, mother etc. would rather see..., because...'
2. Ask three friends in class which foreign country they would most like to visit and why, and then write four paragraphs explaining their preferences and your own.
3. Do the same thing, asking them which famous person they would most like to meet and why.
4. If different members of your family like to spend the weekend in different ways, explain their preferences.

# 13 Personal Letters: narrative

## ✍ Thanks and apologies

Jane Thompson is a teacher at a village school in Sussex. Last weekend she invited three friends from different periods in her life to her house: Alison, who was at school with her and is now a secretary in London; Kate, who was at university with her and also works in London as a librarian; Mary, who lives in the town of Lewes a few miles away, where she is a nurse in the County Hospital. Today she has received letters from them all thanking her for her hospitality. Read all three letters before answering the questions.

---

Flat 3, Stanford Court
94, Stanford Road
London SW9 HH12

March 10th, 1989

Dear Jane,

Just a few lines to say how much I enjoyed last weekend. You are a wonderful host, and it was so nice to get away from the office.

It was a good idea to invite three friends of yours who had never met before. Even though we took a little while to get used to one another, I thought we all got on well together. Kate rang me to ask me if I'd like to go to the cinema with her later this week. We found we had so much in common, including a love of good films, so thanks to you I've found a new friend in London.

Thanks once again, and please let me know when you're next going to be in London. I'd be happy to put you up.

Love,
Alison

---

196 Lingfield Road
Lewes

10th March 1989

Dear Jane,

It seems silly to write to say 'thank you' for the lovely weekend when we live so close and we'll be seeing each other on Saturday, but I thought I should apologise for one or two things that happened. I was too embarrassed to go on about it in front of the others, and I know you said I was exaggerating but I felt such a fool.

To start with, I've been to your house before so I can't imagine how I got lost and kept you all waiting for dinner on Friday night. I suppose I was very tired after working on night-shift all week. After that, I felt I had made a bad impression from the beginning, and when I woke up next morning and realised I had slept till 10 and you'd all had breakfast, I felt even worse. So I was just trying to make up for it by saying something bright and cheerful when I saw Kate reading a book and said: 'How can you bury yourself in a book on a lovely day like this? Are you a librarian or something?' I'd completely forgotten that you had said she was one when you introduced us. Then, in the afternoon, when Alison started criticising the health service because of her mother's operation, I kept telling myself to shut up but I just couldn't help getting involved. I hope she didn't take what I said personally.

So all I can say is that I'm really sorry if I did anything to spoil the atmosphere you'd worked so hard to create. I really did enjoy myself very much. I look forward to seeing you here on Saturday afternoon. Thank God I'm not on night shift this week, so I won't be so tired.

Love,
Mary

# 13 Personal letters

## Practice

When you have read Kate's letter, complete it with the most appropriate expression from the choices given, taking word order into account.

89 Redlands Ave.,
London SE3 BH
10.3.89

Dear Jane,
    I __(1)__ had to write to say how much I enjoyed last weekend. You said beforehand that you were taking a risk inviting three women who didn't know one another, but I thought we got on __(2)__ well. Alison and I made friends from the start, and we're going to the cinema together on Thursday.
    The next time you see Mary, please tell her that I __(3)__ didn't take offence when she made that joke about librarians. __(4)__, I thought it was quite funny, but __(5)__ when I said I was one, she was __(6)__ embarrassed. __(7)__ she was tired after such a hard week at the hospital, and had forgotten what I was, so I didn't take it __(8)__. Quite __(9)__, I admire anyone who is prepared to do that sort of job and still have the energy to go on a long country walk.
    So thank you once again for having us, and please let me know when you're going to be in London again. Looking forward to seeing you soon,
      __(10)__,
    Kate

(1) (a) actually (b) surely (c) really

(2) (a) eventually (b) extremely (c) frankly

(3) (a) actually (b) certainly (c) of course
(4) (a) Actually (b) Naturally (c) Surely
(5) (a) luckily (b) surprisingly (c) unfortunately
(6) (a) naturally (b) of course (c) properly
(7) (a) Of course (b) Seriously (c) To my surprise

(8) (a) on purpose (b) personally (c) properly
(9) (a) certainly (b) frankly (c) surely

(10) (a) frankly (b) honestly (c) sincerely

1 Although the content of the three letters is different they follow a similar plan. What is it? Give each paragraph a heading.
2 Which two of Jane's friends got on best, and what did they discover that they had in common?
3 Why does Mary think she must apologise to Jane? Which four mistakes does she think that she made, and why did she make them? What was the attitude of the other three to these mistakes, in so far as we can see from the letters?

## Further Practice

1 You have spent two weeks as the guest of a family in England. On your return home, write to the person who invited you, thanking him/her for his/her hospitality.
2 During your stay in England, you were invited to another family's house for the weekend. When you return to your host's house, write to thank them for their hospitality, and apologise for two or three things that happened without your meaning them to, such as arriving late, breaking a glass, making a tactless remark etc.
3 Write in English to a friend abroad who entertained you last year. Say once again how much you enjoyed your visit, remind him/her of interesting things that happened, and invite him/her to your country this year.
4 A friend of yours wrote to say that he/she would be in your country for two days, and you arranged to meet at his/her hotel. Write, explaining why you could not keep the date, and apologising.
5 You promised to send an English friend, who is studying your language, a book only obtainable in your country. Write, explaining why you have not been able to send it yet, and apologising.

# 14 Narrative: direct and indirect speech

## ✍ Reporting a conversation

Telling a story by reporting a conversation is not a matter of changing direct into reported speech word for word, though you need to know how to do this. Before beginning work on this unit, look at the notes in the Reference Section, p.110 (Reported speech and introducing verbs). Then answer the questions.

Trevor Lonsdale, a newspaper reporter, and a photographer, Bill Hanley, are in Victoria Street in London, reporting the annual January sales at the Army and Navy stores.

BILL: It's a waste of time coming here. You never get any interesting pictures. Just a lot of people excited because they've bought something they don't really want, and think it's a bargain.

TREVOR: Well, people like reading about the sales. And sometimes famous people come to the shops. You never know. For instance – hey, Bill! – look at that fair-haired girl in the smart coat. I'm sure it's her. I can't see any detectives with her in this crowd, but perhaps she's come by herself. Come on, quick. Take some pictures before she goes into the shop.

BILL: Why? Hey, I think you're right. It *is* her. OK, go and talk to her.

TREVOR: Excuse me – er, your Royal Highness, er – would you mind answering a few questions?

FIONA: What are you talking about? And why is he taking pictures?

TREVOR: Well, you see, we're interested to see you here, mixing with the crowd. It's very democratic, I must say.

FIONA: I suppose this is some sort of joke, but I don't think it's funny. I've only got twenty minutes to do my shopping, and then I must get back...

TREVOR: Of course, to the Palace. Is the Prince looking after the children?

FIONA: I haven't got any children! You must be mad! Look, if you don't go away and leave me alone, I'll call the police!

TREVOR: No, that's not necessary. I won't bother you any more, your Royal Highness.

FIONA: What is this? Why do you keep calling me 'your Royal Highness'?

TREVOR: Well, I thought you were Princess er... But now I look at you closely, perhaps I was wrong. If so, I'm very sorry. Who are you, in fact?

FIONA: My name's Fiona Jackson. I'm 22, and I live in Clapham. I work as a secretary for Westminster City Council, just round the corner. Does that satisfy you?

TREVOR: Of course, but if you don't mind me saying so, you look just like her, and she has her hair done in the same way.

FIONA: Yes, that's what my mother always says, though I can't see it. Well, it was an honest mistake, I suppose.

TREVOR: Well, thank you, anyway. I must let you get on with your shopping.

BILL: A whole reel of film wasted!

TREVOR: No, don't worry, Bill. We can use this. You'll see.

1 Who did Trevor think the girl was?
2 Why was he almost sure that it was her and what made him doubtful? How did he explain it?
3 Why was the girl in a hurry?
4 Where did Trevor think she was going after doing her shopping?
5 What did the girl threaten to do if he didn't go away?
6 What information did Fiona give him?
7 What does Fiona's mother say about her and the Princess?
8 Why did Trevor tell Bill not to worry?

# 14 Narrative

## Practice

Trevor wrote a story about his experience which was printed in the newspaper, but before the newspaper arrived the next morning, he told his wife about it.
You must complete the version on the left with appropriate verbs in the correct tense.
Then compare it with the version on the right, and compare both with the original dialogue.
Note (a) which parts of the conversation are summarised, or not mentioned at all, in each reported version
(b) which parts are reported, and whether reported speech is used or the phrase is shorter because an introducing verb is used instead
(c) which parts are reported without a change in tenses.

Bill was complaining that it ..................¹ a waste of time going to the sales when I suddenly saw this young woman who ..................² just like the Princess. I ..................³ (not) see any detectives with her, but Bill ..................⁴ I was right, so I went up to her and ..................⁵ her if she ..................⁶ mind answering some questions. I ..................⁷ it was very democratic to see her mixing with the crowd. She was annoyed, because she only ..................⁸ twenty minutes to do her shopping, and then she ..................⁹ to get back. I supposed she meant to the Palace. I even asked her if the Prince ..................¹⁰ the children, and then she got really angry and ..................¹¹ to call the police. I still thought it was *her*, but then she asked me why I ..................¹² calling her 'Your Royal Highness'. And then I realised that I ..................¹³ a mistake, so I apologised. I asked her who she really ..................¹⁴, and she told me her name and her age and where she ..................¹⁵ and ..................¹⁶. She was a secretary called Fiona Jackson, but she certainly ..................¹⁷ just like the Princess. She was well-dressed, and she ..................¹⁸ her hair ..................¹⁹ in the same way. She admitted that her mother always ..................²⁰ the same thing. Bill started complaining again about the waste of film but I ..................²¹ him we ..................²² use it, and we have. Look, here it is in the paper!

## SPOT THE PRINCESS!

Our reporter, Trevor Lonsdale, was covering the sales in Oxford Street yesterday when he spotted an attractive young woman who looked just like 'You know who', doing a little lunch-time shopping and mixing with the crowd. She thought it was a joke when he addressed her as 'Your Royal Highness', but got quite annoyed when he asked her if her husband was at home in the Palace looking after the children, and threatened to call the police. That was when Trevor realised his mistake, and apologised.

An understandable mistake, in our opinion, because one of the young ladies pictured here is Fiona Jackson, 22, who lives in Clapham and works as a secretary for the Westminster City Council.

Trevor is not the first to have taken her for the Princess. Fiona's mother thinks they are very much alike, and so do we. Can you tell the difference? Which of these two young ladies is the real Princess? (Answer on back page).

## Further Practice

Imagine you saw someone you thought was a famous person alone in your country, either at a station or airport or on holiday, dressed in ordinary clothes, and you decided to ask him/her if he/she really was that person, and what he/she was doing there. You can choose whether the person was in fact the one you supposed or you made a mistake, but in either case the dialogue must continue for a little while.

1 Write the conversation from the moment when you met the person.
2 Write what you told your family or friends about it afterwards, explaining how and where the conversation took place.
3 Write a brief report for the local newspaper, and give it a headline. In this case, the story will be very different if the person was famous, and you must say if he/she is still in your country.

# 14 Narrative

## ✏ Telling a story

Julia Davies works for an advertising agency. The account below is part of a letter she wrote to her parents in Wales. Read it, and then answer the questions.

I had to go to Nuneaton last Wednesday. Our client there (1) *suggested that I should take the fast afternoon train to Glasgow, which only stops once before Nuneaton, at Watford Junction*. He said (2) *he would meet me at the station and take me to my hotel*. Then we could have dinner together and discuss the project before I visited his factory on Thursday morning.

I was pleased that I had the compartment to myself when we left Euston. I (3) *thought I would be able to spread my papers on the seat and work quietly* but when we got to Watford Junction a big man with a heavy suitcase opened the door, and sat down opposite me.

I supposed he had just come from the USA because his case was covered with labels from places like Miami and he was wearing an enormous hat, but when he spoke I realised that he was English.

(A) 'I bought that hat in Texas,' he said loudly, throwing it on the rack. (4) *I offered to move my papers so he could put his case on the rack*, but he said (5) *it wasn't necessary, because he was getting out at Nuneaton*.

He saw I was working, but he wanted to talk, and he needed an audience.

(B) 'Have you ever been to Disneyworld?' he asked, and before I had time to answer, added, (C) 'You should go. It's marvellous.'

After that (6) *he explained that he had been all over the USA*. He described New York and Niagara Falls, but he was obviously annoyed that I didn't show much interest.

(D) 'It's too hot,' he remarked suddenly. Then he got up and opened the window. The wind blew my papers all over the floor, but he didn't apologise. He just stuck his head out of the window. (7) *I warned him that that was dangerous*, but he took no notice. When I stood up after picking up my papers, I accidentally knocked his hat off the rack, but before I had time to replace it, he turned round and (8) *accused me of doing it on purpose*. Of course (9) *I denied it*, but he just stared at me angrily, and lay down on the three seats opposite.

(E) 'I'm going to sleep now,' he said, 'but don't shut that window, because I need fresh air. Wake me up at Nuneaton.'

Fortunately, the train was on time and about half an hour later, we were approaching Nuneaton. I could hear the man snoring underneath his hat. (10) *I wondered if I could get out of the compartment without waking him*. I had already put my papers back in my case, so I picked it up, climbed silently over his case, and slid the door to one side.

The train came to a halt and Mr Burgess, our client, came up and (11) *greeted me*. We stood talking on the platform and (12) *he asked me if I had had a pleasant journey*, but all the time I was expecting a furious man with a Texan hat on to come up behind me and (13) *demand why I hadn't woken him up*. But then the whistle blew, and as the train went by, I saw him still fast asleep in the compartment. I hope he went all the way to Glasgow!

## Comprehension

1. What essential information for understanding the story is given in the first paragraph? Why is the mention of Watford Junction important?
2. Why is the use of the word 'but' in the second paragraph important to the development of the story?
3. Find as many examples as you can of the man's rudeness.
4. Which of the following possible titles for the story seems most appropriate? Give reasons for your choice: (a) An unpleasant journey (b) The problems of young advertising agents (c) The rude man from Watford Junction (d) Julia's revenge. Consider the last line in the last two paragraphs.

## 14 Narrative

### Using direct and indirect speech in narrative

Look at the story on the opposite page again. You will see that there are five occasions where direct speech is used (A–E), and thirteen where it could have been used, but the writer has used an introducing verb and an indirect form; these are printed in *italics*. Transform each of the examples from one form to the other, as in the examples given. Where necessary, use Reference Section, p. 110 as a check to find the right introducing verbs and correct structure.

Examples:
(1) Our client there said: 'You should take the fast afternoon train to Glasgow. It only stops once...
(A) He said loudly that he had bought the hat in Texas, throwing it...

Now read the story again, decide which version you prefer, and give your reasons.

### Further Practice

In answering any of the following questions, try to use direct speech at the important points of the story, and use indirect forms with introducing verbs to explain the less important details that are necessary for the story to be understood.

1. You were travelling on a train when you met a person who told you about an interesting incident in his/her life. Explain how you met, what caused the person to tell the story, tell his/her story, and end with your reaction to it.
2. A few years ago, you met a young man/woman who was very ambitious. Describe what the person told you about his/her hopes for the future. Imagine that he/she has now become very successful, and you are explaining your meeting to a friend.
3. Write a letter to a friend explaining how you found two friends of yours quarrelling. Tell him/her what they told you of their reasons for quarrelling, and how you made peace between them.
4. An older relative of yours (e.g. grandfather, grandmother) likes to tell stories about his/her youth. Give an account of an occasion when he/she told you a story like this.
5. You have read an interesting book or seen a documentary about an explorer's adventures in a foreign country. Write a letter to a friend, giving him/her an idea of the content of the book or film and why you found it interesting.

# 15 Description: places

## ✍ Describing a city

Read the description of Bristol below, and then answer the questions.

### Bristol (Avon)
Population: 426,657
VISIT: Clifton Suspension Bridge
Theatre Royal
St. Mary Redcliffe Church
*SS Great Britain*
Cathedral
London 121 miles, Birmingham 91 miles

Bristol was for a long time the largest city on the west coast of England and the main port for transatlantic trade. It is still the main industrial centre in the south-west, and well worth visiting because of its historical monuments. Although the city lies on the river Avon, only a few miles from the sea, it is very hilly and the winds blowing across the Atlantic give it a higher rainfall than the national average.

The city was founded in the Middle Ages, but its prosperity grew with the discovery of America. During the seventeenth and eighteenth centuries it was the centre for trade with the West Indies and the American colonies, but the abolition of the slave trade and the development of the Lancashire cotton industry eventually caused it to be replaced by Liverpool. Efforts were made to maintain the city's position, however, and the great engineer, Isambard Brunel, was employed to design ships. One of them, the *Great Britain*, can still be visited today as a tourist attraction.

Brunel was also responsible for the most impressive sight in the Bristol area, the magnificent Clifton Suspension Bridge over the Avon river, which was completed in 1864. Apart from the bridge, Bristol has a number of other interesting monuments. The cathedral was built on the site of an abbey founded in 1142, and the church of St. Mary Redcliffe is regarded as one of the most beautiful in England. The university, built on a hill in Clifton, a district of Bristol, was founded in 1876 and has since become one of the most prestigious in the country.

Bristol is fortunate in possessing a splendid old theatre, the Theatre Royal, the home of the Bristol Old Vic, one of the best known provincial theatre companies, and is a lively centre for the arts. It has two professional football teams, a famous rugby club, and county cricket matches take place there in summer, as well as a Grand Prix tennis tournament.

The countryside around Bristol is very pleasant. The lovely city of Bath, which still preserves the atmosphere of its peak as a fashionable centre for aristocratic visitors in the eighteenth century, is only 13 miles away. To the north lie the Cotswold Hills, and to the south the fascinating caves at Cheddar Gorge and the delightful Somerset villages.

The people are friendly, slow-speaking and polite, helping to make Bristol one of the few large industrial cities in Britain that can still be said to have charm.

1 Where do you think this text comes from? Give your reasons.
2 Give each paragraph a topic heading. What other topics could be included in a description of a city?

# 15 Description

## Practice

Françoise is on holiday in England with her friends, Marie-Claire and Jean-Claude. Read her letter to her English teacher in Geneva. It would be much easier to understand if it were not continuous. Separate it into four paragraphs, giving reasons for starting new paragraphs where you decide. It should be possible to give each paragraph a topic heading. Then answer the questions that follow.

1. Compare your topic headings with those on the opposite page. In what ways is the letter a description of a place, and in what ways is it a narrative?
2. What facts do we learn about Stratford and about Shakespeare and his family from Françoise's account?
3. What do we learn about Shakespeare's plays that may surprise foreigners?

---

**FALSTAFF HOTEL**
Stratford-upon-Avon CX38 4PS

20th July, 1989

Dear George,

We're having a wonderful time in England. Yesterday we arrived here at lunch-time from Oxford and spent the whole afternoon exploring Stratford. We had heard so much about it from you that I was surprised it was so small, but of course it was full of tourists at this time of year. After lunch at the Hamlet restaurant – you can't escape from Shakespeare here – we visited the house where he was born, and then walked to Shottery to see Anne Hathaway's cottage. It was such a delightful old farmhouse, and it seems such a pity that part of it was burnt a few years ago. The house I liked best though was Hall's Croft, his son-in-law's house. I knew Anne Hathaway was his wife, but I had never realised that his elder daughter married a famous doctor. In the evening we went to the Royal Shakespeare Theatre to see Twelfth Night. That was the visit we had all been looking forward to, and we weren't disappointed. I was so glad that I took your advice not to read the play before seeing it because now I really believe what you have always told us about Shakespeare being a genius. I was expecting to see a classical play with a lot of actors solemnly reciting the lines but instead the performance was full of action all the time and I found it really interesting even though I didn't understand all the words. I must stop now, and post this before we get the coach to Chester. Marie-Claire and Jean-Paul send their kindest regards,

Love,
Françoise

---

## Further Practice

1. Collect a few facts about your own town or city or one that you know well, and then write a description of it for tourists. Plan the description in paragraphs, with one paragraph for each topic, like the description of Bristol.
2. Imagine that you are on holiday. Write a letter to a friend explaining what you have been doing in the previous two days and include any details describing the place that are necessary for him/her to understand you.
3. Write a short historical account of a place you know well.

# 16 Formal Letters: complaint, apology and explanation

## ✎ Complaining

Poul Nielsen and his wife Grete live in Copenhagen, but they booked a package tour to a Mediterranean island through a British tourist agent because it was cheaper. Read Poul's letter complaining about the poor service they received on their holiday, and complete the blanks with the appropriate connectors from the list given. Then answer the questions that follow.

above all    according to    although
at least    consequently    either    finally
in fact    in our opinion    in short
instead of    needless to say    secondly
therefore    to begin with
to make matters worse

1 What is the purpose of each paragraph?
2 List Poul's complaints. Who do you think was to blame in each case – the travel agent, the courier, the hotel or someone else?
3 Before looking at the travel agent's reply on the opposite page, think of an excuse for everything that went wrong, either by putting the blame on someone else or explaining the problem.

---

233 Sigurdsgade,
København,

Sunshine Holidays Ltd.,
119 Sidney St.,
London NW2 5CA

April 24th, 1989

Dear Sirs,
My wife and I have just returned from a ten-day Easter Break holiday organised by your company on the island of Mocosa. __(1)__ your brochure, the holiday offered 'the ideal holiday in delightful, unspoilt surroundings' and claimed that 'Sunshine Staff are available at all times to help our clients'. Our experience has been very different, and I am __(2)__ writing to draw your attention to a number of defects in your organisation that completely spoilt our holiday.

Our outward journey was a disaster. __(3)__, our flight from Luton was delayed for four hours. __(4)__, the Sunshine representative was not at the airport in Mocosa to meet us, and we could not find the coach that was supposed to take us to the hotel, so we had to hire a taxi. __(5)__, when we reached the Beach Hotel, __(6)__ we arrived in the afternoon, our room was not ready.

Our second cause for complaint was the hotel itself. The swimming pool pictured in your brochure was not open; __(7)__, it had not been cleaned during the winter, and __(8)__ it was unpleasant to sit beside it, and we could not have a drink on the terrace. __(9)__, we complained to the courier, but he said it was not his responsibility, and he could not do anything about the awful food, __(10)__.

The most misleading feature of your brochure is that the Beach Hotel is not on the beach, as we imagined; __(11)__, it takes ten minutes to walk along the main road to find a way down the cliff. When we reached the beach, __(12)__ finding 'unspoilt surroundings', it was crowded with people and covered with litter.

__(13)__, we consider that you owe everyone on the tour an apology. __(14)__, it is dishonest to make misleading statements in your brochure, and __(15)__ to advertise a courier service for your clients that you do not provide, __(16)__ in Mocosa.

Yours faithfully,
Poul Nielsen

# 16 Formal letters

## ✏ Apologising and Explaining

Read the reply Poul received to his letter of complaint, and complete it by choosing the most appropriate word or phrase from the alternatives given. The object is to be polite, but not to exaggerate. Then answer the questions that follow.

**SUNSHINE HOLIDAYS LTD.**
**119 Sidney Street,**
**London NW2 5CA**

Mr Poul Nielsen,
233 Sigurdsgade,
København, Denmark

May 5th, 1989

Dear Mr Nielsen,

Thank you for your letter of April 24th, which ___(1)___. In the first place, I would like to say that I ___(2)___ that your recent holiday in Mocosa was a disappointment to you. We have inquired into the circumstances surrounding this particular Easter Break holiday, and I will try to deal with the points you have raised.

We cannot, of course, accept responsibility for the delay in your flight, which was due to a go-slow by French air-traffic control, but we recognise that our representative should have met you at the airport. ___(3)___, he did not receive accurate information about the delay, and arrived with the coach-driver half an hour after your plane landed.

___(4)___ the hotel not being completely ready for the tourist season. The management ___(5)___ that the swimming pool would be available for our clients, but they ___(6)___ because ___(7)___. We are sorry that the food was ___(8)___. It ___(9)___ that the regular cook at the hotel was taken ill just before Easter.

We have written to the Mocosa Tourist Authority to complain about the state of the beach, which was no doubt due to ___(10)___, and trust that this situation will be remedied in future.

In conclusion, I ___(11)___ for any inconvenience you have been caused. We ___(12)___, and under the circumstances, I have noted your complaint and we are pleased to offer you a 10% discount on your next holiday with Sunshine.

Yours sincerely,
Maurice Sweet
(Marketing Manager)

(1) (a) has been passed to me for attention (b) I have got to answer (c) I have the greatest of pleasure in replying to
(2) (a) am deeply distressed (b) am sorry (c) very much regret
(3) (a) As a matter of fact (b) Luckily (c) Unfortunately
(4) (a) I'm afraid we can't do anything about (b) We certainly owe you an apology for (c) We must apologise most humbly for
(5) (a) assured us (b) dropped us a line to say (c) made a solemn promise to us
(6) (a) let us down (b) proved incapable of fulfilling their obligations (c) were unable to keep their promise
(7) (a) of a shortage of staff (b) of severe problems in contracting new employees (c) they haven't got enough staff
(8) (a) awful (b) not as excellent as usual (c) not to your taste
(9) (a) seems (b) was just your bad luck (c) was lamentably the case
(10) (a) dirty local people (b) so many local people being on holiday (c) local people having inadequate facilities for the disposal of litter
(11) (a) I humbly beg your forgiveness (b) must once again apologise (c) suppose I should say 'sorry'
(12) (a) get upset if our clients are not happy (b) pride ourselves on giving total satisfaction (c) take complaints from clients very seriously

1. Give each paragraph a heading. Do they coincide, more or less, with the headings you have given to Poul Nielsen's letter of complaint.
2. Look at the list you have made of Poul's complaints. How many of them are answered by putting the blame on someone else? How many of them does Mr Sweet apologise for? Does he make an excuse, and if so, what is it? Are there any complaints he ignores? Can you suggest why he ignores these?

# 16 Formal letters

## Practice

On this page you can see three skeletons of letters for you to complete. Study the information given in each case, and complete the sentences with suitable phrases. Invent a name and address for the bookshop in England and begin and end the letter in the normal way.

(a) You wrote to a bookshop in England in August requesting four books you needed for a university course beginning on October 2nd, and promising to pay for them on receipt by banker's order in pounds. You received the books in time but have not been able to obtain the banker's order until now. The bookshop has written to you to remind you. Write apologising and enclosing the banker's order. The date is now October 23rd.

I am writing with reference to your letter . . . concerning my order of . . . I . . . until now, because . . .

I am therefore . . . for £42.25 in convertible currency. I regret the delay in . . . and any inconvenience . . .

(b) In a similar situation, you have not received the books on October 23rd, and write complaining about the bad service and threatening to cancel your order.

I am writing with reference to . . . When I ordered the books, I . . . October 2nd. I wrote to you . . . ago, asking . . . but so far . . . a reply.

. . . opinion, you owe me . . . the delay, which has caused me . . . Would you please inform me whether . . . ? Unless I receive . . . November 1st, I will be obliged to . . . I look forward to . . .

(c) In this case, you did not receive the books in time, but found them in a local shop, and bought them. You wrote to England on October 2nd, cancelling your order. The books arrived on October 23rd, but you refused to accept them from the postman. It is now November 13th, and you have just received a standard computerised letter claiming the money from you and threatening you with legal action.

I am writing with reference to . . . and also to my letter . . . , cancelling . . .

I would like to draw your attention to the fact that when I . . . , . . . October 2nd. As . . . , I was obliged to look for them locally. Fortunately, I was able . . . and consequently . . . on October 2nd.

Your books arrived . . . but as I . . . , I did not accept . . . In due course, I am sure that you . . . I must add, under the . . . , that . . . opinion you should . . . addressed to you before threatening . . .

## ✍ Further Practice

1 You have ordered some goods from an English firm which have not arrived. You have already written to inquire about the goods but have received no reply. Write, pointing this out and threatening to cancel your order.
2 You went on a language course in England, organised through a local English-speaking representative in your country, and were not satisfied. Write a letter of complaint, listing the reasons for your dissatisfaction.
3 On your return to your own country, you found you had brought with you a library book you borrowed from the local library. Return the book with a letter of apology.
4 You work for a travel agent in your country, and receive a letter from an English-speaking tourist containing a number of complaints like Poul Nielsen's on p.40. Write a polite letter, apologising and making excuses for what went wrong.

# 17 Discussion: for and against (2)

## ✍ Listing the arguments

Before starting this unit, mark your instant reaction to the following statements in the columns on the right. ++ means strongly in favour, + in favour, 0 no strong feelings, − against, −− strongly against.

|  | ++ | + | 0 | − | −− |
|---|---|---|---|---|---|
| The state should not use lotteries and football pools to collect money. |  |  |  |  |  |
| It is much better to go to a foreign country by yourself than on a package tour. |  |  |  |  |  |
| Professional sportsmen and women are paid too much; all sport should be amateur. |  |  |  |  |  |

Now note down all the arguments you can think of *for* and *against* each of these statements, *whether you agree with them or not*.

Compare your list for the first topic with the list of points made below. If you have thought of points not included, decide how important you think they are. If points are listed there that you have not thought of, decide whether you think they are relevant and should be mentioned. Then put the points in order of importance, for and against, including your own.

**FOR**
1. Gambling is immoral. The state should not encourage it.
2. It is unwise. The state should persuade people to save money, not waste it.
3. It is an unfair system of taxation, because the poor are more likely to gamble than the rich.
4. It is unfair to those who gamble, because the state takes a big profit and very often only half the money is distributed in prizes.
5. It does not depend on skill, but on luck.

**AGAINST**
1. Gambling is popular. If the state does (did) not have lotteries, people (would) gamble, anyway, and private individuals (would) get the profits.
2. In this way, the money is spent on hospitals, education etc.
3. People hate paying taxes, and this is a good way of getting money without them objecting.
4. No one cares how much of the money goes to the state, provided there are big prizes.
5. It is fair because it does not depend on skill. Everyone has an equal chance.

Note that in each case a reason is given for the point made. It is not convincing in an essay of this kind to say, for example, 'Gambling is unfair/popular' unless you explain why or comment on it.

Before writing the essay, consider which is the best way to begin. Choose from the three alternative first paragraphs given here, and decide which you like best, giving reasons.

(a) In many countries, the state uses lotteries and football pools to collect money. This is wrong, because gambling is immoral. Instead of that, the state should tell people to save their money and only tax the rich. Lotteries are unfair to the poor.

(b) In many countries, the state uses lotteries and football pools as an alternative means of collecting taxes. It is much easier to get the money in this way than by direct taxation. However, many people consider it is wrong because it encourages gambling and is unfair because the poor are more likely to buy lottery tickets than the rich.

(c) In many countries, the state uses lotteries and football pools to collect money, but in some it does not, because the Government thinks the state should not encourage gambling, even though people gamble anyway and instead of the money going towards hospitals and education, private individuals get it, which is not a good thing because a lot of them may be gangsters.

Now write an essay on this topic, basing it on the important points you have chosen. Use your choice of the three paragraphs above to begin; then write second and third paragraphs making the points for and against. If you feel strongly about the subject, it is a good idea to put the opposite point of view first, in the second paragraph, and the view you agree with in the third.

# 17 Discussion

## Practice

You may respond to a general statement in entirely personal terms, but you should take other people's behaviour into account. For example, in this case, most people go abroad by package tour. Why do they do this? What sort of people do it – age, holiday interests etc.? What sort of package tours do they prefer and why? Discuss these questions with others in the class, and then complete the essay below, choosing appropriate connecting words and phrases from the alternatives given. Then answer the questions below.

**It is much better to go to a foreign country by yourself than on a package tour**

___(1)___, most people would agree with this statement. Travelling abroad by yourself has an immediate appeal because it suggests freedom to go where you like and choose what you want to do. ___(2)___, package tours suggest cheap holidays in the sun where people try to make you have a good time even when you don't feel like it. ___(3)___, you are not only taken everywhere by a guide who organises everything, but you are told what time to get up and how long you can spend over lunch. ___(4)___, most people who go abroad go on package tours. Why do they do this?

___(5)___ we must take into account the age and interests of the people who are travelling. Young people are not so interested in comfort. ___(6)___, they enjoy the challenge of finding their own way, meeting the people in the country and learning the language. Older people, ___(7)___, have more luggage, and prefer to have an experienced person with them who speaks the local language and resolves all their problems. ___(8)___ making friends among the local population, they tend to look for companionship among people of the same background on the coach. The principal advantage of package tours for people who go to the Mediterranean islands is cost and speed. ___(9)___, people who go on them are not very interested in the place; all they want to do is to get as much sun and entertainment as possible in the time available. The reason ___(10)___ such holidays are cheap is that there are so many of them.

___(11)___, I would like to find out what other countries are really like, and get to know the people, but I would rather travel with a friend than go by myself, ___(12)___ if I did not know the language. It is not much fun being alone in a foreign country with no one to talk to. ___(13)___, if I went to a big country a long way away, like the USA or Mexico, ___(14)___ the first time, it would be helpful to have a guide, and so I would probably go on a package tour, ___(15)___ even then I would prefer to have a friend with me, rather than go alone.

(1) (a) Actually (b) At first sight (c) In fact

(2) (a) But (b) In consequence (c) In contrast

(3) (a) Also (b) As well (c) To make matters worse

(4) (a) Although (b) In spite (c) Nevertheless

(5) (a) In conclusion (b) In principal (c) To begin with

(6) (a) Also (b) Apart from that (c) As well

(7) (a) on the contrary (b) on the one hand (c) on the other hand

(8) (a) Instead of (b) Rather than (c) While

(9) (a) Besides (b) However (c) Nevertheless

(10) (a) because (b) for (c) why

(11) (a) For me (b) In person (c) Personally

(12) (a) above all (b) over all (c) specially

(13) (a) But (b) However (c) While

(14) (a) at least (b) personally (c) to a certain extent

(15) (a) although (b) however (c) in spite

1. Make a list of all the reasons given for and against (a) travelling abroad alone (b) package tours. Indicate where they are to be found in the text. Is the writer more in favour of (a) than (b)? What third possibility does she suggest?

2. List the advantages of package tours for (a) older people (b) young people (c) the writer. What sort of package tour is referred to in each case?

3. Each paragraph is constructed around a different contrast. What is it, in each case? Give each paragraph a heading.

# 17 Discussion

## ✍ Points of view

Another way to deal with a balanced composition topic is to consider it from different points of view. If you answered + + to the third topic on p.43, did you do so for both parts of it? If all sport were amateur, there would be no professional sportsmen and women at all. If your objection is really to the first part, how much is too much, and why? How does the question appear to (a) those who believe in the original ideal of the modern Olympic Games (b) professional sportsmen and women (c) you yourself. Assume these will be Paragraphs 2–4 of your essay. Look at the list of points given for Paragraphs 2 and 3, decide which are the most important and add any of your own. Base these two paragraphs on the most important points.

### PARA 2
1. Governments encourage sport because it is healthy, but professionals even take drugs to improve their performance.
2. The important thing in sport is to take part, but professionals are only interested in winning, and often cheat.
3. When the Olympic Games were revived, they were strictly amateur, but now professionals can take part and earn money directly or indirectly for it.
4. It is ridiculous that people should be paid enormous sums just to kick a ball or hit it with a racket when others work much harder for little money.
5. Professionals set a bad example to young people, because they behave badly; this is because they are only interested in money.

### PARA 3
1. Professionals have a hard life, demanding a lot of practice as well as skill, and their career only lasts about 10–15 years, so they need big rewards in return for their sacrifices.
2. Professional sportsmen took part in the ancient Olympic Games.
3. Those who took part in the revived Olympic Games at first were rich people who could afford it; if sport were amateur, only the rich could compete.
4. Everyone knows that the reason why people play games is to try to win.
5. Modern sport is a show and the public pay to watch the best, the same as they pay actors and singers. Professionals are worth what they can get, the same as other people.

As before, choose which of the first paragraphs given here is the best way to begin, giving your reasons. Then complete the essay, as indicated above.

1. At one time all sport was amateur, but now professional sportsmen and women earn millions of dollars. Is that fair? There are a lot of people who work hard, and never earn much. On the other hand, professionals only have a short career, so of course they want a lot of money.
2. The idea that sport should be amateur comes from the Olympic Games, that is to say the modern Olympic Games, because in the ancient Olympic Games there were professionals, but nowadays only the rich could afford to take part if that were the case. So it is a good idea to pay sportsmen and women, but there are a lot of people who think they get paid too much.
3. In effect, there are two separate questions here. Should sportsmen and women be paid at all, and if they are, how much should they earn? Those who believe all sport should be amateur base their arguments on the Olympic ideal that what matters is to take part. In the modern world, however, sport is so popular with the general public that it is like a show. Consequently, professionals expect to be paid well, like actors or singers.

## ✍ Further Practice

Use the techniques indicated here to write a balanced essay on one or more of the following:
1. 'Exams are unfair and do not serve a useful purpose.'
2. 'Computers have brought more disadvantages than advantages to our lives.'
3. 'If young people get into trouble with the law, it is usually their parents' fault.'
4. 'Tourism should be aimed at encouraging foreigners to learn about the country, not just to spend their money.'
5. 'The United Nations Organisation is a waste of time and money.'

# 18 Guided Writing:
## using a diary

## ✏ Letters and postcards

When writing postcards, people often leave out words because of the lack of space, but they seldom do this in writing personal letters. Compare what Julia says in the postcard to her friend Cathy (left) with the presentation of the same information in part of her letter to her boy-friend Andrew (right). Note the linking words, the use of tenses, the order in which the information is given and any additional descriptive details. Then complete the paragraph in Julia's letter by rewriting the last few lines of the postcard in the form of a letter.

> Arrived here today from Toronto, and saw the famous Falls from a boat. The American ones looked small, but Canadian Falls really exciting. Anne got wet through — waterproof provided didn't fit her. Serves her right for being so tall! She sends her love. Spending a quiet evening. Long trip ahead tomorrow, all the way to Washington. Looking forward to seeing the Capitol, Kennedy memorial etc. So far have enjoyed trip very much. New York hot, sticky, violent, but interesting. Boston delightful. Toronto very modern. Tell you all about it when we get home.
>    Love Julia (and Anne)

> We stayed in Toronto last night, and arrived here in the morning to see the famous Falls. We got a boat, and put on waterproofs. The American Falls seemed small, and we wondered what all the fuss was about, but when we reached the Canadian ones, it was really exciting. Poor Anne got wet through, because the waterproof they provided for her was too small! It serves her right for being so tall!
> We're spending a quiet evening here, because we have a long trip ahead of us tomorrow, all the way to Washington. We're looking forward to seeing the Capitol and the principal monuments and we plan to visit the Kennedy memorial in Arlington Cemetery

## Practice

Now read Susan's postcard from Rome to her pen-friend, Margarita, in Spain. Imagine what Susan wrote about her experiences in a letter to her parents in England. Use the information given to construct complete sentences, and be careful to use the right tenses, and include such words as *the*, wherever necessary. There is no need to begin and end the letter in the usual way, as this would only be one paragraph from the whole letter.

> Have been here two days. Weather marvellous since arrival. Have been exploring city with Rachel. Yesterday visited Colosseum and Forum. In the evening, had dinner in typical restaurant off Via Veneto. I love pasta, but will put on weight in week here. So much to see in short time. Today walked in Villa Borghese in morning — lovely park. All afternoon at St Peters. Michelangelo ceiling in Sistine Chapel incredible. Could spend days looking at it
>    Love,
>    Susan

46

# 18 Guided writing

## Transforming a diary

Many people keep a diary on journeys to remember what happened. In writing letters about their experiences, they use the same techniques as you have practised in transforming a postcard into a paragraph from a letter.

Ronald Beamish has been invited by the British Council to give some lectures on literature in Italy. Compare his diary for a typical day with the extract from a letter he wrote to his wife.

**MARCH 14 MONDAY**

- 9.00 Briggs (Council) picked me up, drove to university
- 9.30 Met Benetti – very nice, excellent English.
- 10.00 Benetti introduction, Jane Austen talk, v. flattering. Audience good, asked interesting questions.
- 12.30 Early lunch
- 5.00 Arrived Padua. Checked in. Beautiful city. Pity no time to do sight-seeing.
- 7.00 Lecture at university on Wordsworth. Difficult. Next time do Keats. Excellent dinner with Professor Mancini, Briggs. Mancini expert on Romantics. Prefers Byron. Had long discussion over whether Byron is really Romantic. Very enjoyable. To bed at 12.30.

> Robert Briggs from the Council called at my hotel to drive me to the university, where I was introduced to Professor Benetti and his colleagues. Benetti is a charming man, who speaks excellent English. He introduced me to the audience when I gave my talk on Jane Austen, and said some flattering things. There was a good audience, and they asked some interesting questions.
>
> We had an early lunch, because we had a long drive to Padua in the afternoon. We arrived there about five and checked in. It is such a beautiful city that it was a pity I had no time to do any sight-seeing, because I had to give my lecture on Wordsworth at the university at seven. I always find him difficult, and next I will do Keats.
>
> Afterwards, I had an excellent dinner with Professor Mancini and Robert Briggs. Mancini is an expert on the Romantics, and we had a long discussion over whether Byron, his favourite, really is one. I didn't get to bed till 12.30, but it was most enjoyable.

**JULY 21 THURSDAY**

- 8.00 Breakfast. Met other members of course. Nine different nationalities. All speaking English. Only way to communicate.
- 9.00 Course began. Introductory talk. Full schedule. 9.30–12.30, 2–4. Some visits in afternoon
- 12.45 Over lunch, met friend of Janet's, Kristin Anderson, Swedish. Met each other when Kristin on year's study leave in Boston. Long talk about problems of Spanish/Swedish students.
- 2.00 Videos and computers. Very interesting. Try to persuade school to equip us with them. Not very likely. Headmaster old-fashioned, shortage of money.
- 5.00 Walked round Oxford with Kristin. Has been here before, knows it well. Colleges beautiful. Am sure I will enjoy my month here.

## Further Practice

Use the diary entries, together with the information given about the writer, to write an extract from a letter, as in the example above.

Carla Navarro is a teacher attending a summer course at Oxford. Afterwards she uses her diary to write a letter to her friend, Janet, in the USA.

# 19 Descriptive Narrative: human scenes

## ✍ Describing a scene

Read the description of Oxford Street, comparing it with the picture on the right, and answer the questions that follow.

Oxford Street is the central stretch of a long road joining the City of London to the West End on the north side. At the western end is Marble Arch, and from there the fashionable thoroughfare of Park Lane, facing Hyde Park, runs south. Halfway along Oxford Street is Oxford Circus, linked to Piccadilly Circus to the south by the elegant shopping street, Regent Street.

Oxford Street is also famous as a shopping street but it is a more popular one. It is incredibly busy during the day, but relatively quiet at night when the shops are shut. It is particularly attractive to foreign tourists, and if you stand on the pavement for five minutes in summer you will probably hear at least a dozen different languages spoken.

At the same time, it is a street of contrasts. On the north side stand most of the great stores, like Selfridges and John Lewis, and the pavements are full of people staring in the shop windows and going in and out. Yet opposite these stores, where most of the shops are smaller, you can see all kinds of street traders, some with stalls selling fruit, others with souvenirs and cheap toys laid out on the pavement to attract passers-by.

Essentially, it is a street that attracts people who like crowds. Apart from the continuous movement of the shoppers during the day, it is the route for a number of London buses, and there are four underground stations for the people who are travelling underneath it. Personally, I have never liked it, because I hate having to stop every few yards to avoid bumping into people, but it is certainly the London street that conveys most obviously the atmosphere of a great cosmopolitan city.

1 Give each paragraph a heading. What is its purpose, in each case?
2 Which aspects of Oxford Street are shown in the picture?
3 Where does the writer express his personal opinion of Oxford Street?

## Practice

Write a similar description of Trafalgar Square. Plan four paragraphs, relating to (a) situation (b) buildings and monuments (c) atmosphere in summer (d) atmosphere at Christmas and New Year. Add personal comments to Paragraphs (c) or (d) if you have been there.

For (a) use the map; for (b) the picture, which is taken from the south, with the National Gallery in the background, and St. Martin's in the Fields on the right, and also the notes; for (c) and (d) the notes.

Notes   Trafalgar Square marks junction of cities of London and Westminster. National Gallery (1838) houses national art collection. St. Martin's in the Fields, church built 1726 (what does the name tell us about the area at that time?). Nelson's Column (1842), four lions, two fountains, built in honour of hero of naval victory of Trafalgar (1805). Centre of square empty; summer, thousands of pigeons; tourists resting; sometimes large political meetings. Christmas, crowds of people; giant Christmas tree, present from Norway; celebration of New Year, bathing in fountains etc.

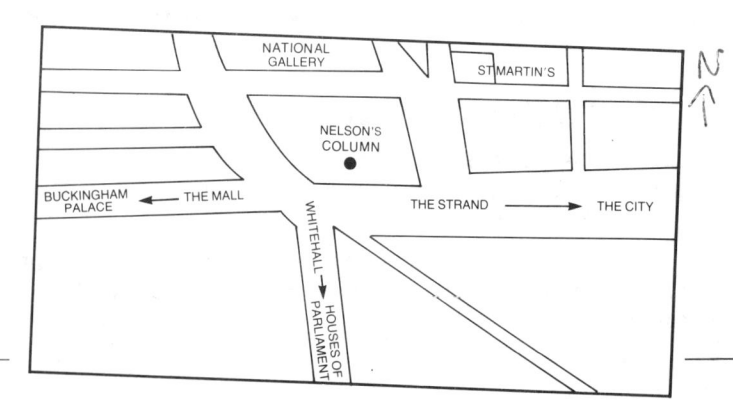

# 19 Descriptive narrative

## ✍ Describing a day

A composition like 'A Day at the Seaside' is not pure description, like those on the opposite page, but contains a narrative structure. Read the composition below, and decide which parts of it are narrative, which are descriptive, and how it is organised into paragraphs.

---

A Day at the Seaside

Last Sunday was a beautiful day, and my brother and sister and I were up early, impatient to go to the beach, but as usual my parents had watched the late-night film on TV, and in any case my father hates getting up on Sundays. I think every family in the city must be the same because by the time my mother had packed the lunch and my father had had breakfast, it was 10.30, and when we got to the outskirts of the city the road to the beach, ten miles away, was full of cars. We took two hours to get there.

When we arrived, we could hardly see the sand or find a place to spread our towels. There were thousands of people there, lying on the sand under brightly coloured umbrellas, or standing on the edge of the water, or bathing in the sea. Boys and girls were trying to play games, but there was no space because of all the people lying down. There were ice-cream sellers and drink-sellers wandering in and out between the bodies, and I could not hear the sound of the sea because of the shouts and screams and the noise of hundreds of radios playing different kinds of music. The only way to escape was to run into the sea and swim out for twenty or thirty metres beyond all the little children and their parents in the shallow water. At last I could lie on my back in the water and feel the sun on my face, away from the noise.

About three o'clock, everyone had lunch, and my mother wouldn't let us go back into the water again till six. I wanted to stay there all evening, but my father insisted on going home at seven because he wanted to see the football match on TV. Every other father obviously had the same idea. When we started our journey, there were already hundreds of cars on the road. We took two hours to drive the ten miles home, and my father missed most of the football match. When I am grown-up I will have my own car and I will always go to the beach on weekdays.

---

## ✍ Further Practice

1 Describe an interesting street or square in your town, or one you have visited.
2 Describe a typical scene at a market, a railway station or an airport.
3 Write about a day you spent either (a) at the seaside (b) in the country or (c) in the mountains, either in summer or winter.
4 Write about a day trip you made to a famous place.
5 Write about a picnic with friends in the country.

# 20 Making and Reporting Speeches: informal

## Making a speech

Julie Livingstone is a teacher on a summer course for foreign learners of English in England. Before the course begins, she meets all the students to give them necessary information about the timetable. Study the notes she made of the information she had to present, and then read her speech, and answer the questions below.

1 Find all the information from Julie's notes in her speech. Is it given in the same order as it is presented in the timetable?
2 Now look at the rest of the speech, and decide (a) which parts are additional information; (b) which parts are asking for help or offering it; (c) which parts are informal phrases to make people feel at home.

---

**Morning Sessions**
9.00-10.00
10.15-11.15
11.30-12.30

**Afternoon Sessions**
2.00-3.00
3.15-4.15

*Lang. Lab. Computers, Video, etc.*

**Meal times**
Breakfast: 8.00-9.00
Lunch: 12.45-1.45
Dinner: 6.00-7.00

*Morning Coffee
Afternoon Tea*

Outings on Tuesdays and Thursdays

*Oxford, Stratford*

Bar open: 12.30-2.00 and 5.30-10.30
Tennis courts and squash courts. Please book times at Secretary's office.

---

Well, I think everyone's here now, so we might as well start. I expect you've all seen the programme already, but I'd just like to remind you of a few things. First, the course itself. There are three sessions in the morning, from nine till ten, ten-fifteen to eleven-fifteen, and half-past eleven to half-past twelve. We give you a break in between, you see, in case you get tired, but it's really so that you'll have a chance to get to know each other. After the second session, at a quarter-past eleven, there's a coffee break in the bar.

The afternoon sessions are from two till three, and from three-fifteen to four-fifteen, but these are a lot more flexible because they take place in the Self-Study Centre, where we have a language laboratory, computers, videos, all kinds of reading material, and so on. But please ask me for advice on things to do that will suit your particular needs. After that, there's afternoon tea in the bar from four-fifteen till five.

I can see some of you are wondering when you get a chance to eat. Breakfast is from eight to nine, lunch from a quarter to one till a quarter to two, and dinner from six to seven. We'd like to ask you to co-operate here, please, and not leave it too late. You may arrive late for classes, and it's a bit awkward for us with the catering staff if people arrive for breakfast at five to nine!

There are outings on Tuesday and Thursday this week. On Tuesday we'll be going to Oxford to look at the colleges, and on Thursday we've booked seats for *As You Like It* – that's at the Shakespeare Memorial Theatre in Stratford. The cost is included in your fee, and of course you'll miss dinner on those days, but the catering staff will provide sandwiches. If you'd rather stay here, having a drink in the bar or playing tennis or squash, would you please let me know?

And on the subject of the bar, it's open at lunch-time and in the evening till half-past ten. You can play tennis or squash in the afternoons and evenings, too, but please book your court in advance at the secretary's office, or you may be disappointed.

I think that's everything. Are there any questions?

## Practice

At the end of the course, the other students ask you to make a short speech thanking Julie for her work. The group have bought her a small gift and you must present it to her. Use the notes below to construct an informal speech.

Notes End of course. All enjoyed ourselves. Very grateful to Julie for help. Wonderful teacher. Always calm and kind when anything went wrong (Suzanne left camera in Oxford, made enquiries, got it back). On behalf of everyone, like to thank Julie. Students have bought a little present to remind her of us. Hope you like it. Look forward to seeing her again.

# 20 Making and reporting speeches

## Giving a talk

Ingrid Frederiksson is a guide in Stockholm. Compare the information contained in a guide book with the way she presents it when she is talking to a group of English-speaking tourists.

The warship *Wasa* was built for King Gustav II Adolf of Sweden in 1628. It was 62 m. long, weighed about 1300 tons, and carried 64 bronze cannon. The main mast was 52 m. above the keel. The poop was magnificent, decorated with 700 sculptures in wood, originally painted or gilded with gold-leaf.

On its maiden voyage on August 10th, 1628, however, the ship suddenly turned over and sank in Stockholm harbour, where it remained for over 300 years.

In 1961 a private researcher, Anders Franzen, found the ship at a depth of 30 m. and the task began of raising it to the surface and restoring it. Over 24,000 objects have been recovered, including cannon, tools, clothing, food, and the skeletons of many of the crew. The ship has been preserved with a substance called polyethylene glycol since it was raised, and you can see it now in Stockholm, very much as it was on its single, fatal voyage.

> We're now going to see the warship *Wasa*. The *Wasa* was built for the king of Sweden at the time of the Thirty Years War, King Gustav the Second Adolf. That was in 1628. It was a very big ship for those days. It was 62 metres long, weighed about 1300 tons, and had 64 cannon, made of bronze. If you look up you can see the main mast – that's 52 metres above the keel. As we go around, you'll also see the magnificent poop. Originally, there were 700 sculptures made of wood on it, and they were painted and some of them gilded with gold-leaf.
>
> Before we go over the ship, however, I'm going to tell you something about its history. The fact is that the ship was top-heavy, and so on its maiden voyage – that was on August 10th, 1628 – it suddenly turned over and sank in the harbour here. It lay on the bottom for over 300 years, and then a private researcher called Anders Franzen found it, 30 metres down. That was in 1961. After that, they decided to raise it to the surface – at that time, it was the oldest identified warship ever raised – and to restore it. They've brought up over 24,000 objects from the ship – cannon, tools, clothing, even food, and the skeletons of many of the crew. Of course, the ship has to be preserved, and so for many years, they sprayed it with a substance called polyethylene glycol. Let's go and have a look at it now.

## Practice

Arturo Lombardi is a guide in Rome. Use the information given about the Colosseum and transform it into what you imagine he would say to a group of tourists about it in an informal talk, like Ingrid's about the *Wasa*.

The Colosseum was built as an amphitheatre in the reign of the emperor Vespasian. It was begun about AD 70, and officially dedicated by the emperor Titus ten years later in a ceremony that included 100 days of games. The top storey was added in AD 82 under Domitian. Most earlier amphitheatres had been dug into hillsides for additional support, but the Colosseum, built of stone and concrete, stands by itself. It is oval in shape, measuring 190 m. by 155 m. and originally seated 50,000 spectators. It was used for gladiatorial contests, fights between men and animals, and even for spectacular imitation battles. During the Middle Ages the Colosseum was damaged by lightning and earthquakes and all the marble seats and decoration disappeared, smashed or stolen by vandals.

## Further Practice

1 You are going to welcome a group of English-speaking people attending a course on your country's language, life and customs. Work out a timetable of events and write an informal speech.
2 Do the same thing for a group of English-speaking tourists on a coach trip through your country, lasting a week. Imagine you are their guide.
3 You work in a multinational company in your country, where English is used as a common language. Make an informal speech, giving a goodbye present to one of the foreign staff.
4 Some English-speaking people are visiting your school, university or place of work. Make a short informal speech describing it and its history.
5 You are a tourist guide in your city. Give an informal talk to English-speaking tourists about an important building, monument or work of art.

# 21 Discussion: for or against

## ✎ Developing an argument

Read the two articles below on the same subject, and then answer the questions on them on the opposite page. Whether or not you personally agree with one side or the other, or think they are both mistaken, pay particular attention to the way in which the writers develop their arguments.

## Freedom of choice for parents

In what is supposed to be a free country, it is remarkable that parents have no control over what their children are taught at school. It is even more remarkable that up till now, unless they could afford to pay for their children's education, they have had no real choice over the kind of school the children went to. In theory, parents can state a preference, but in practice it is the local educational authority that decides where the child should go, and its main concern is usually to ensure equality in terms of ability and social background.

Of course, those who defend the system that has developed in the post-war years argue that it would be irresponsible to allow parents to interfere with the curriculum. Few parents are qualified to argue with teachers about the merits of doing different subjects or how they should be taught. However, the curriculum is not the main concern of those parents who have demanded a choice. As long as teachers were respected professionally, parents trusted them, but nowadays there is an understandable reaction against a generation of semi-literate teachers who use the classroom as a political platform.

Teachers frequently blame parents for children being rude, undisciplined and unwilling to study, and in general they are right to do so. It is therefore inconsistent for them to deny parents the responsibility for deciding which school the children should go to. Parents who care about their children's education naturally object to them being forced to go to schools with a bad reputation.

The Government's proposal to allow parents freedom of choice is very welcome. It will not only satisfy those who are concerned about their children being handicapped by attending badly-run schools; by introducing an element of competition it will force those schools to improve or risk being closed down if they are unpopular. A further valuable proposal is to allow schools to opt out of the local educational authority's control and request funds from the Department of Education and Science. In this way, too, parents will be able to express their disapproval of local authorities who have turned education into a field for political action.

## Freedom to do as you like

'It's a free country, isn't it?' No doubt there was a time when that rhetorical question, taking our agreement for granted, was a source of pride. In my view, however, it is too often an excuse for doing what you want to do, whether or not it upsets or inconveniences someone else. The Government's proposal to give parents freedom of choice in picking the state school their children go to, and subsequently for schools to opt out of local authority control and apply to the Department of Education and Science for funds, has the immediate attraction of the popular phrase. In fact, however, it will provide a wonderful opportunity for people to do what they like in a way that will divide the country even more clearly into 'haves' and 'have-nots'.

It is quite true that up to now parents have not always been able to send their children to the school they preferred. Local authorities have had to balance their wishes against the need to provide adequate schools throughout the area. It is also true that in a few extreme cases, which have been exaggerated out of all proportion in the right-wing press, local authorities have appeared to make educational decisions for political reasons. The Government's proposals, however, will not solve these problems but will almost certainly disrupt the whole educational system.

Parents are not necessarily the best people to judge which school will be the best for their children, and even if they were, freedom of choice will ensure that some schools are much more popular than others. Those that are popular will soon be overcrowded, and will in many cases opt out of local authority control. Those that remain the authority's responsibility will be the unpopular ones with all the factors that already count against good education – bad housing, parents who are unemployed or poorly paid – and on top of that they will get worse, with fewer pupils and less money available to support them.

In short, there is not likely to be 'healthy competition' between schools, where the weakest go out of business, because schools are not supermarkets. The gap between the well-educated and those who are hardly educated at all will grow. This kind of competition between schools means a 'rat-race', where the already underprivileged sections of the community will be certain to lose from the start.

52

# 21 Discussion

1 Find references to the following in both articles, and compare what the writers say: (1) 'a free country' (2) local authorities disregarding parents' wishes (3) political influences on education (4) parents being capable of choosing the best school for their children (5) the possibility of schools being able to opt out of local authority control (6) competition between schools.

2 Each of the sentences here summarises a paragraph from one of the articles on education. Which sentence summarises which paragraph?
   (a) If parents are responsible for children's behaviour, as teachers say, they should be free to choose which school they go to.
   (b) Local authorities have to disregard parents' wishes in some cases to ensure that all their schools function; freedom of choice will lead to chaos.
   (c) It is surprising, but true, that parents are not allowed to choose the school their children will go to.
   (d) The result of the Government's proposals will be to make it almost impossible for under-privileged children to be educated at all.
   (e) The reasons why parents want to choose schools for their children are not academic, but have to do with politically motivated, incompetent teachers.
   (f) The word 'freedom' can be misused to mean 'the freedom to be selfish', so the Government's proposals are not as attractive as they seem.
   (g) If parents have complete freedom of choice, they will all choose the same schools and the weaker ones will get worse.
   (h) The Government's proposals will reassure parents and improve the weaker schools by forcing them to improve their standards.

3 Having put the sentences into the correct order, decide whether the writer in each case justifies his opinion by an example or by appealing to the prejudice or sympathy of readers. Find phrases to support your analysis.

4 How do the titles of the two articles summarise the two writers' different arguments?

5 In the first paragraph, both writers introduce the subject, but clearly indicate which side they are on. Which phrases indicate this?

6 In which paragraph do the writers mention opponents' arguments. Which word shows that the writer does not agree with them?

## Practice

Use the phrases given below to make this paragraph more convincing. They are printed in the correct order, but in some cases may require capital letters to begin a sentence.

> The problem of violence in our society is in danger of getting out of hand, and people react violently against it, and demand more police, bigger prisons and heavier punishments. There is no proof that this sort of simple solution will work. We should look at the causes of this violence, and they are not hard to find. Crime arises mainly in the inner city areas, where young people are brought up in poverty and ignorance. Without the hope of a better future, they behave violently to express their frustration. Prison is supposed to correct such attitudes, but they seldom benefit from the experience. Contact with professional criminals often turns them into criminals themselves. The answer to the problem lies in altering the living conditions of the inner cities.

it is understandable that   however
it is essential that   certainly
in the majority of cases   consequently
in fact   on the contrary   only sensible
however much it costs

## Further Practice

Use the techniques you have studied in this unit to write about any of the following topics that you feel strongly about.

1 Capital punishment should be re-introduced for violent crimes.
2 'A woman's place is in the home.'
3 Military service should be abolished (or re-introduced, if it has been abolished).

# 22 Summary: fact

## ✍ Selecting important points

Read the text, and then answer the questions that follow.

### Halley's Comet

There can be few people who have not heard of Halley's Comet, but there are still a great many non-scientists who have no real idea of what a comet is. The most popular mistake is to assume that a comet streaks quickly across the sky, disappearing in a few seconds. In fact all comets are very distant – far beyond the top of the Earth's atmosphere – and they do not move perceptibly against a starry background. If you see an object moving visibly, it certainly cannot be a comet. It will be either an artificial satellite, of which thousands have been launched since the Space Age opened with the ascent of Russia's Sputnik 1 in October, 1957, or else a meteor (unless it is something much more mundane, such as a weather balloon or a high-flying aircraft).

Comets are members of the Sun's family or solar system, but they are quite unlike planets. They are not solid and rocky; a large comet consists of an icy central part (or nucleus), a head (or coma) and a tail or tails made up of tiny particles of 'dust' together with extremely thin gas. Though comets may be of immense size – the head of the Great Comet of 1843 was larger than the Sun – they are very flimsy, since the nucleus, the only relatively massive part of a comet, cannot be more than a few miles in diameter. Even a direct collision between the Earth and a comet would do no more than local damage.

Comets move around the Sun, but in almost all cases their paths (or orbits) are elliptical, and with one exception – Halley's – all the really bright comets take hundreds, thousands or even millions of years to complete one circuit. This means that we cannot predict them, and they are always liable to take us by surprise. During the last century several were seen but in our own time they have been depressingly rare, and the last really 'great' comet was that of 1910, though there have been many others which have become bright enough to be seen with the naked eye.

In addition there are many short-period comets which reappear after only a few years. But these short-period comets are faint, and usually remain well below naked-eye visibility. Moreover, they often lack tails, and appear as nothing more than tiny, fuzzy patches. Halley's Comet is in a class of its own. It has a period of 76 years, and it has been seen regularly since well before the time of Christ; there is even a Chinese record of it dating back to 1059 BC, though it was not until more modern times that astronomers realised that there was anything particularly unusual about it.

From *Catching Halley's Comet* by Patrick Moore, *Illustrated London News*, November 1985.

A  The first stage in preparing a factual summary is to decide which items of information are most important. Study each paragraph in turn, and choose from the alternatives given which offers the most accurate summary of it.

1 (a) Most people who think they see a comet do not really know what comets are like, and are actually looking at satellites or balloons. (b) Almost everyone has heard of Halley's comet, but most people do not know what comets are. They think they are bright objects that move quickly across the sky, and then disappear, but in fact you cannot see them moving. (c) Since the Space Age began with the launching of Russia's Sputnik 1 in 1957, many people have imagined that they have seen comets moving across the sky, but they are mistaken because you cannot see comets moving.

2 (a) Comets have an icy central part (or nucleus), a head (or coma), and a tail or tails made up of tiny particles of 'dust'. They are members of the Sun's family. (b) Comets belong to the solar system, but are quite different from planets. Though they can be very large, they are not solid and if they crashed into the Earth, they would only do local damage. (c) Comets are sometimes enormous – the head of the Great Comet of 1843 was larger than the Sun – but do not do much damage because they are not solid.

3 (a) Bright comets, apart from Halley's, take a very long time to go round the Sun, so we cannot predict when they will be visible. (b) Bright comets have an elliptical orbit, and are likely to take us by surprise because we do not know when they will reappear. (c) It is disappointing that there have not been very many bright comets in this century. This is because they take such a long time to go round the Sun.

4 (a) There are a lot of short-period comets, but we can't see them clearly, like Halley's. (b) Halley's Comet is in a class of its own, because it has a period of 76 years, and has been seen regularly since before the time of Christ. (c) Short-period comets cannot often be seen with the naked eye, so Halley's Comet is unique, because records of its appearance every 76 years go back to before the time of Christ, though they were not calculated until more modern times.

# 22 Summary

B  In writing summaries of the main points of the paragraphs, I have followed certain rules, which you should follow in attempting summaries yourself.

(a) The original text contains about 450 words, and a summary of its content should be expressed in about 120. Direct quotations from the text like 2 (a) and 4 (b) can only suggest part of the original meaning, and quickly use up the number of words allowed.

(b) It is unwise to repeat words and phrases that you do not fully understand – e.g. in this passage you may not have seen adjectives like 'flimsy', or 'fuzzy' before, but can guess they mean 'light' and 'not clear' from the context. On the other hand, do not try to replace precise nouns like 'comet' with words of your own.

(c) Do not waste space on repeating details that will not affect the reader's understanding of the main points, as in 1 (c) and 2 (c).

C  Now write out the correct answer, and check (a) whether it has continuity (b) how many words it has. In this example, I have done it for you.

Almost everyone has heard of Halley's comet, but most people do not know what comets are. They think they are bright objects that move quickly across the sky, and then disappear, but in fact you cannot see them moving. Comets belong to the solar system, but are quite different from planets. Though they can be very large, they are not solid and if they crashed into the Earth, they would only do local damage. Bright comets, apart from Halley's, take a very long time to go round the Sun, so we cannot predict when they will be visible. Short-period comets cannot often be seen with the naked eye, so Halley's Comet is unique, because records of its appearance every 76 years go back to before the time of Christ, though they were not calculated until more modern times. (138 words)

D  If we rewrite the final version to connect these ideas together we should have something like this:

Almost everyone has heard of Halley's comet, but most people do not know what comets are. They think they are bright objects that move quickly across the sky, and then disappear, or would be dangerous if they crashed into the Earth. In fact, you cannot see them moving, and although they belong to the solar system, they are different from planets because they are not solid and could only do local damage. Halley's Comet, which appears every 76 years, is unique because other bright comets take a long time to go round the Sun, so we cannot predict when they will be visible, while short-period comets cannot often be seen with the naked eye. (114 words)

Check your choices for question 1, and make sure that those you have picked keep within the rules suggested. The best way to do this is to read the four choices one after the other and see if they make sense, and have some continuity. If you read all four (a), (b) or (c) answers, you will see that this continuity is missing.

Before going any further, ask yourself what you consider to be the main points the writer is making about Halley's Comet in the article as a whole. You should find two. Make a note of them in your own words.

It would not be difficult to reduce 138 words to 120 here, but it is much wiser to take out whole clauses than to try to use complex structures to link sentences together – for example, the last clause (nine words) is not essential.

What is missing for this to be a very good summary is complete continuity. Refer to the two main points you have picked out for the article as a whole and answer the following questions:

(a) What is the connection between the popular error that comets 'move quickly across the sky, and then disappear' and 'if they crashed into the Earth, they would only do local damage'?

(b) Why is Halley's comet unique? What makes it different from other bright comets and from other shor-period comets?

Note that in the final version, the two main connecting ideas – 'most people do not know what comets are' and 'Halley's comet . . . is unique' appear in sentences that are followed by an explanation.

# 22 Summary

## ✍ Further Practice

Read the text and then summarise it in your own words, following the techniques indicated on p.55, and using the guidance given below.

### The Channel Link

There is nothing new about the idea of a fixed link across the English Channel, but it has continued to make news for nearly 200 years. For all of this time, men have been designing bridges, tunnels, tubes, submerged railway lines and other ingenious and sometimes lunatic schemes to establish a direct and permanent line of communication between Britain and Europe. But in spite of their enthusiasm and the support of many distinguished statesmen, from Napoleon to Winston Churchill, the Channel has remained unbridged and unbored.

War was for many years the main deterrent. The fact that Napoleon was keen explained the lack of enthusiasm on the British side when it was first suggested. A direct link was regarded as a threat to the island's natural defences, and there was a graphic portrayal of a sea and land invasion at the time of the Napoleonic wars, with the French army marching through a tunnel under the Channel, to demonstrate the point. Though public interest in the idea grew during the later nineteenth century, the requirements of defence continued to inspire official British rejection. Lord Palmerston was against any plan to shorten a distance which was, he said, already too short.

Winston Churchill later rejected this view, maintaining in the 1930s that resistance to a tunnel on strategic grounds was no longer valid. A tunnel would have been the greatest value to Britain's support of France in the First World War, he believed, and if danger had threatened it could always have been closed. Later strategists have supported this view, and there are today no serious military objections to the construction of a fixed link.

The more recent problem has been lack of political determination. The last Anglo-French tunnel project, which in the early 1970s seemed likely to go ahead, was abruptly cancelled in 1975 by a Labour government less committed to Europe than Edward Heath's administration. But the idea was given yet another breath of life in 1984, when Mrs Thatcher and President Mitterand committed their respective governments to support the construction of the fixed link, provided that it could be totally financed by private means. The two governments then issued an 'Invitation to Promoters' for the development, financing and operation of a fixed link, with detailed proposals to be submitted by the end of October 1985, enabling them to decide by the end of January 1986.

From *The Race to Cross the Channel* by James Bishop, *Illustrated London News*, November 1985.

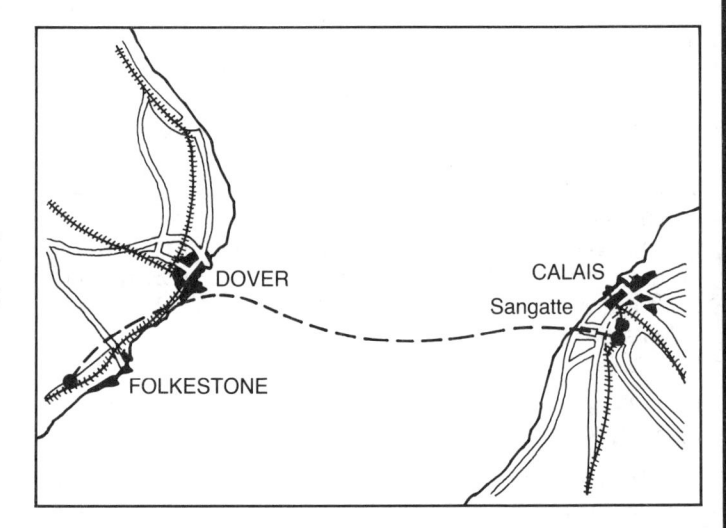

Summarise the main ideas expressed in each paragraph in a sentence or two. In considering the links between them, consider the answers to the following questions:
1 How long have engineers been working on projects for a link across the English Channel and why?
2 What objections were raised to the link when it was first suggested, and why?
3 How were they different from more recent problems, and why?
4 What conditions have been attached to the most recent attempt to establish a link?

Then summarise the whole passage in not more than 120 words.

# 23 Formal Writing: reports

## Products

Brian Cunningham owns a restaurant, and wants to add some new wines from the Rioja to his list. His wine waiter, Charles Lucas, tries four different red wines and submits a report on them. Look at Charles's notes, and compare his notes on the first wine with his report on it.

> Marqués de Cuenca (1984, 12°, £2.30) rich, dark red; low acidity; smooth, warm; fair amount of body; pleasant aroma (grapes); suitable – meat, espec. roast, game, cheese. Price reasonable. Recommended.
>
> Conde de Oviedo (1983, 12.5°, £2.22) cherry coloured; low acidity; smooth, fruity (cherries), fair amount of 'body'; very noticeable aroma (cherries); suitable – meat, espec. veal, cheese. Price reasonable. Recommended, but will not please all customers.
>
> Monte Arenas (1984, 12°, £3.70); dark red; fairly high acidity, but smooth and with a lot of 'body'; very fruity, and noticeable aroma (blackberries); individual flavour; suitable – meat, cheese. Will not please all customers, and price rather high. Like it personally, but cannot recommend it.
>
> Rey Alfonso (1983, 12.5°, £2.10) dark red; high acidity; bitter, but without much 'body', strong, but not warm; noticeable aroma (cherries); best served with beef, but definitely not recommended, although price reasonable.

> Marques de Cuenca. This is the 1984 vintage. It is of average alcohol content (12°) and costs £2.30. It is a rich dark red in colour, and has low acidity. A very smooth, warm red wine, with a fair amount of 'body', and a pleasant aroma of grapes. It would be suitable with meat, especially roast beef or veal, and would also go well with game and with cheese. The price is reasonable and I recommend it. All our customers should like it.

Use Charles's notes to write reports on one or more of the other wines.

## Further Practice

1 Write a short report on a soft drink you like or don't like. Take into account cost; when you would like to drink it (weather, time of day, before, after, during meals); taste (sweet, too sweet, not sweet enough, bitter, acid, fruit?); what sort of food goes best with it. Do you recommend it?

2 Write a short report on a record or cassette by a well-known singer or group. Take into account words (lyric) and music; quality of playing (are all instruments equally good); accompaniment to singer (? piano, guitar, backing of other singers); where you would prefer to listen to it (at home, in a disco etc.); how it makes you feel (happy, sad etc.). Do you recommend it? If so, would it suit everyone, or especially young people, older people etc.?

3 Write a short report on a perfume or after-shave. Take into account cost; scent – what does it remind you of – violets, roses, pine woods etc.? Is it pleasant, fresh, agreeable, or too strong, unpleasant? Do any of your friends use it? Do you prefer it to others? If so, why? Do you recommend it?

4 Write a short report on a computer program. Take into account cost; purpose; effectiveness – does it do what you want it to do, is it useful?; is it entertaining, enjoyable? Is it suitable for everyone, or only for experts? Would it be useful for children, their parents? Do you recommend it?

## 23 Formal writing

### Personal

International company requires young people fluent in English to work on stand during International Exhibition in Athens, June 27th – July 10th. Previous experience of similar work desirable. Pleasant manner and high standard of personal appearance essential. Telephone: 1 462 6226

The personnel officer for the company, Irene Kapsos, interviewed four candidates for the job, using a standard form and making notes on it for her final report. Look at the table and then read her reports on the first two candidates.

| Name | Elena Gangas | Alexis Pilava | Christos Mina | Vanessa Loizides |
|---|---|---|---|---|
| Age | 18 | 22 | 34 | 20 |
| Married/single | single | single | married | single |
| Profession | student | student | translator | student |
| Experience | none | tourist guide, trade fair | travel agency, translation | trade fair, teaching |
| Qualifications | CPE | university courses | translating diploma | CPE, university course |
| Travel | UK (2 summers) | Europe, USA | | UK (6 months) |
| Spoken English | fair | fluent, but erratic | accurate, but slow | fluent |
| Manner | quiet, shy, pleasant | aggressive, extrovert | serious, correct | pleasant, self-confident |
| Appearance | well-dressed | untidy, jeans | suit, formal | attractive, natural |

```
ELENA GANGAS This candidate is rather young for the job, and has no
previous experience. She has good written qualifications in English
and has visited Britain twice on summer courses, but her spoken
English is only fair, possibly because she is quiet and shy and does
not express herself confidently. She has a pleasant manner, and was
well-dressed, but my general impression is that she would not be
mature and extrovert enough for this kind of job.

ALEXIS PILAVA This candidate is the right age for the job, and has
worked before as a tourist guide and at a trade fair, although he did
not produce references from previous employers. He has studied two
or three different courses at the university but has not finished any
of them. He has travelled all over Europe and has also been to the
USA. His English is typical of an extrovert who has no difficulty in
communicating, but has had little formal training, and so he makes
frequent mistakes. I am sure he would be active on the stand, but his
manner is rather aggressive and he looked very untidy at the
interview. He was wearing the oldest pair of jeans I have ever seen.
I cannot recommend him.
```

### Further Practice

1 Write what you imagine that Irene wrote about one or both of the other two candidates. Consider whether the information given is good or bad *for this job*. Which one is closer to what is required in the advertisement? Why? Which one would be more confident and make English-speaking visitors to the stand feel welcome?
2 Imagine that someone you know well has applied for a job as (a) an English-speaking secretary; or (b) a guide to tourists; or (c) a private teacher of English to a small group of children. Write a personal reference, explaining why you think the person would be suitable. Use the table above as a guide, but note that you must include details of name, age and previous experience etc. You can invent any qualifications or previous experience that will help the application.

## 23 Formal writing

### Events

There was an accident in Market Road last week. When PC Grimes arrived, he took the names and addresses of the drivers and a shopkeeper, whose shop window had been broken, and wrote down what they said.

Read their statements, but before reading his report, draw a simple diagram to show what happened.

When you have read the report, look for the evidence for what PC Grimes says in the statements. Compare his way of reporting it. Note anything that he has supplied himself, and what he leaves out.

Then complete his report, based on the statements of Mr Higgins and Mr Porter.

Michael Winston, 34, sales representative, driver of Ford van AM 271 X.

I'd just delivered some goods to Mr Porter, you see. I was parked opposite his shop. And then he came out on to the pavement, and shouted to me. But I couldn't hear him, so I just opened the door, and suddenly this motor-cycle came up, smashed into the door, and then skidded across the road into Mr Porter's shop-front. If I'd stepped out into the road, he'd have hit me, and he only just missed Mr Porter ... Well, yes, I'm sure I looked in the mirror, but he was coming so fast.

Mark Higgins, 19, student, motor-cyclist, Ducati, registration BZ 463 Z. I was coming along Market Road. I'd just passed a parked car on the left, so I suppose I was in the middle – it's not very wide, you see – and as I came up to this van, this chap opened his door without any warning. I had no time to brake. The next thing I knew I was lying on the pavement here with my face cut. If he'd looked in his mirror, the accident wouldn't have happened ... Well, perhaps I was doing more than 30, and I was a bit over to the right, I suppose, because of the parked car I told you about.

Henry Porter, 58, shopkeeper, witness. I'd just come out of my shop because I wanted to speak to Mr Winston before he drove off. I called out to him, but I suppose he couldn't hear me with the noise of that motor-cycle coming up. It was going so fast, and I called out 'Be careful', but he didn't hear, and then this young fellow crashed into the van door, and came straight across the road. He only just missed me. Look at all that broken glass! ... Well, I suppose he looked in his mirror. I don't know. But the young man was going at least 50 miles an hour, in my opinion ... No, I don't drive myself.

```
              ACCIDENT REPORT 4378/6 (June 22nd,1989)

     Market Road. I was called to the scene at 10.45 a.m., by Mr Henry Porter,
     grocer, 37 Market Road. A Ducati motor-cycle, registration BZ 463 Z,
     ridden by owner, Mark Higgins, 19, student, had crashed into the door
     of a Ford van, registration AM 271 X, parked opposite, as the driver,
     Michael Winston, 34, sales representative, was opening it. The motor
     cycle had swerved across the road, mounted the kerb and crashed into
     the front of the grocer's shop, breaking the shop window. Apart from
     the damage to the shop window, the front wheel of the motor-cycle was
     damaged and the left door of the van. Mr. Higgins, who was wearing
     a crash-helmet, suffered cuts and bruises, but was otherwise unhurt.

          I took statements from the drivers and from Mr. Porter, who
     was standing in the shop door when the accident occurred and therefore
     witnessed it.

     Mr. Winston claims that he was just going to drive off, after
     delivering goods at the shop, when Mr. Porter shouted to him. He could
     not hear, so he opened the van door. He claims that he looked in the
     mirror before doing so.

     Mr Higgins claims that he had just passed ...
     Mr Porter confirmed the details of the accident. He could not say
     whether ...
```

### Further Practice

1 Write an account of an accident from the point of view of (a) a driver, (b) a passenger, or (c) a witness.
2 Imagine that you are a policeman investigating an accident, and have interviewed the drivers and a witness. Write an official report of it.

# 24 Guided Writing: using graphs

## ✍ Interpreting graphs

Basing a report on the information provided by a graph is partly a matter of interpretation, but also requires correct use of the technical terms.
Study the notes on vocabulary in the Reference Section, and then look at these graphs, which show the total attendance at football matches in England between 1976 and 1987, and the average weekly attendance for five teams at home.
Note the symbols used: L League champions; C Winners of a cup competition; P Promoted to the First Division; R Relegated to a lower division.

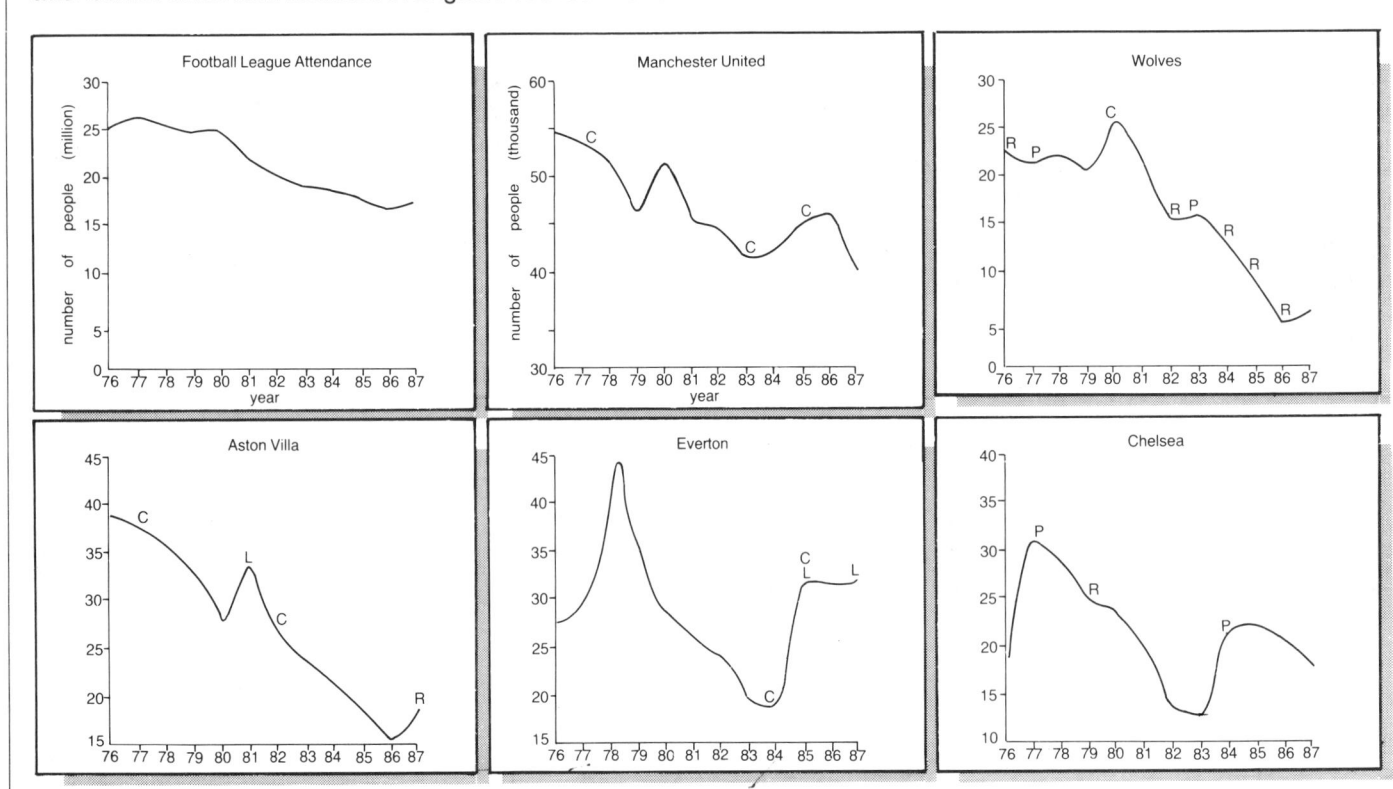

Read the following report, interpreting the first three graphs, and then complete the sentences relating to the last three.

During the period 1976–87, attendance at Football League matches showed a steady decline from just under 25 million spectators in 1976 to 17 million in 1987. Attendances rose slightly in 1977 and 1987, but from 1980 to 1986 there was a consistent fall. The experience of individual clubs depended in part on their varying success.

The most popular club, Manchester United, with a high average attendance throughout this period, reflected the general pattern. The club won the FA Cup on three occasions but each rise in attendance was followed by a more noticeable fall, and in total averages fell from nearly 55,000 a week to just over 40,000.

Wolves were a clear case of a team whose support fell sharply as their fortunes declined. On two occasions they were relegated and immediately promoted, which enabled them to maintain the same level, and there was a considerable increase in attendance in 1980, when they won the League Cup, but when they were relegated three times in succession from 1984 to 1986, their failure was reflected in steeply falling attendance figures.

Aston Villa began this period with average attendances of nearly ........................, but their successes in the League Cup in 1977, the League in 1981 and the European Cup in 1982 only had a temporary effect in preventing ........................, which ended with their being relegated in 1987.

Everton's attendance ........................ from 1976 to 1978, but then ........................ until they won in the FA Cup in 1984. This led to ........................, rewarded by more success in winning the League and European Cup-Winners Cup in 1985. Since then ........................, although they won the League again in 1987.

Chelsea's attendance ........................ in 1977, when they were promoted to the First Division, but they were relegated again in 1979, and attendance then ........................ until their promotion year of 1984, when ......................... Since their return to the First Division, their attendance .......................... .

# 24 Guided writing

## Practice

The two graphs on this page show (a) the proportion of votes received by the main three parties at British General Elections since 1935 (b) the proportion of MPs elected. Because members are elected individually in constituencies (voting areas) only the winning party's vote in the constituency matters; consequently, the system favours the Government and main opposition party at the expense of others.

Study the graphs, and then answer the questions that follow.

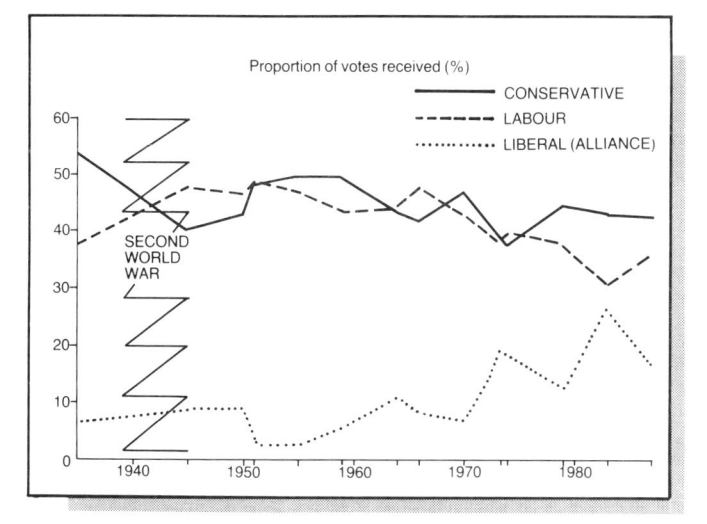

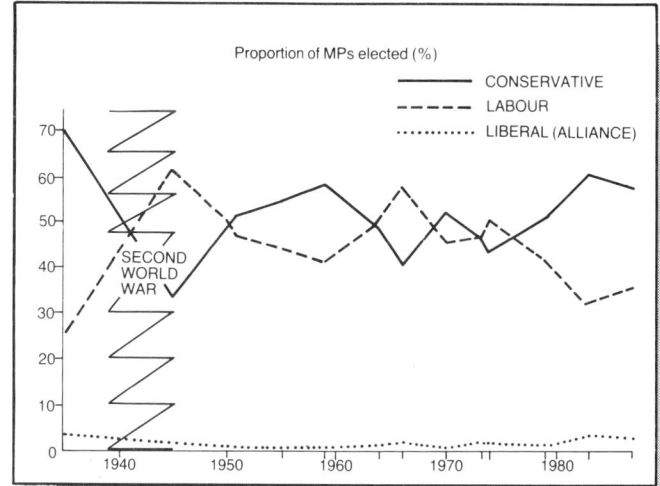

### Graph 1

1 What happened to the Conservative vote immediately after the Second World War?
2 When did it show a noticeable rise?
3 How would you describe the pattern since 1950 – (a) fluctuating considerably (b) fairly consistent (c) steadily declining?
4 How would you describe the Labour vote between 1935 and 1950, 1950 and 1965, and since 1965 – (a) steadily declining (b) fairly consistent (c) steadily rising?
5 What was the effect on the Liberal vote of the formation of the Alliance at the beginning of the 1980s?
6 How would you describe the Liberal vote since 1970 – (a) steadily rising (b) fluctuating considerably (c) fluctuating but rising?

### Graph 2

1 How was the proportion of votes reflected in terms of the number of MPs elected?
2 Does the system accentuate the trend in voting? Look at the Conservative and Labour MPs elected before and after the Second World War, between 1945 and 1960, and since 1975?
3 What effect has the rise in the Liberal/Alliance vote since 1970 had on the number of MPs elected?

## Further Practice

Write a short report (a) describing the pattern of voting for the three parties since 1935 (b) comparing this to the number of MPs elected to Parliament.

# 25 Descriptive Narrative: biography

## ✍ A biographical account

Read this biographical account, and then answer the questions that follow. Note the use of time phrases (in **bold**).

1 Give each paragraph a topic heading.
2 In general the information about Camus's life is given in chronological order, but there are some exceptions to this. Find them.

### Albert Camus

Albert Camus, the great French writer, was born in Algeria **in 1913**. **Less than a year later**, his father was killed in the First World War, and Camus was brought up by his mother, who was of Spanish origin, in a working-class district of Algiers.

Camus won a scholarship to the Algiers high school **in 1923**, and was an excellent student, as well as taking a great interest in sport, especially football. **At the age of 17**, however, he had the first attack of the tuberculosis that troubled him **all his life**, and this interrupted his studies and ended his sporting career. **After he had recovered**, he registered as a student at the University of Algiers, paying for his studies by working at a number of jobs.

A further attack of tuberculosis prevented him from becoming a university lecturer, but **while he was at the university** he had become an important figure in left-wing intellectual circles and had taken an active part in a workers' theatre group. He became a journalist **in 1937**, and **during the Second World War** ran a news-sheet called *Le Combat* for the French Resistance. **At the end of the war**, Camus was the editor, but he resigned **two years later**, disillusioned by party-political manœuvring.

Camus's reputation as a writer rests primarily on his novels, *L'Étranger* (*The Outsider*), published **in 1942**, and *La Peste* (*The Plague*) (1947), an account of an epidemic in Oran that symbolises the struggles of the French people under the Nazi occupation. He also wrote an interesting play, *Caligula*, first performed **in 1945**, short stories and philosophical essays. Camus won the Nobel Prize for Literature **in 1957, when he was only 44**.

Camus became the spokesman of his generation in Europe. Although he sympathised with the left politically, he was too independent to accept orthodox Marxist dogma. In the same way, although he understood the disillusion of the post-war generation, his liberal humanism constantly made him the defender of truth, moderation and justice.

Camus's brilliant career was ended tragically early by his death in a motor-accident near Sens in France **on January 4th, 1960**.

---

## Practice

Read the information given below about Ernest Hemingway, and use it to construct a biographical account. Use the Camus account as a model to order paragraphs, and note that you will have to re-order some of the information to do this.

**Ernest Hemingway.** Born Oak Park, a suburb of Chicago, July 21, 1899. Father a doctor fond of hunting and fishing, like Hemingway himself; mother artistic.

Outstanding student at high school, wrote stories. Left school, 1917, became a journalist in Kansas City. Enlisted as ambulance driver in American Red Cross, badly wounded in Italy in 1918, decorated as a war hero.

Married four times. Lived and worked as journalist and writer in Paris in 1920s, made frequent visits to Spain, war correspondent during Spanish Civil War (1936–9), active supporter of Republican side. Went to live in Cuba (1939), and remained there till 1960, but war correspondent in Second World War.

Novels reflect own experiences and interests: *The Sun Also Rises* (1926), about expatriates in Spain, *A Farewell to Arms* (1929), First World War in Italy, *For Whom the Bell Tolls* (1940), Spanish Civil War, *The Old Man and the Sea* (1952), deep-sea fishing in Cuba. Also wrote books about bullfighting, big-game hunting, and memorable short stories. Won the Nobel Prize for Literature (1954).

At first identified with 'Lost Generation', post-First World War generation of disillusioned people in 1920s, but later more concerned with idea of personal courage of men alone facing death and danger. Attempted to make private life a reflection of values expressed in novels.

Committed suicide by shooting himself, depressed by knowledge that he had cancer, at his house in Ketchum, Idaho, July 2nd, 1961.

# 25 Descriptive narrative

## Linking the phrases

Study the use of relative clauses and phrases in apposition in the Reference Section (p.103), and then complete this account of the life of Guglielmo Marconi by choosing the most appropriate phrase from those given below.

### Guglielmo Marconi

Guglielmo Marconi, ___(1)___, ___(2)___ in Bologna in 1874, is famous as the inventor of a system of radio telegraphy and for his later work on shortwave wireless communication, ___(3)___ of most modern radio transmission.

Marconi, ___(4)___ was Irish, studied in Italy and began his experiments on his father's estate in 1894, but in 1896 went to England, ___(5)___ by the chief engineer of the Post Office, ___(6)___. He was soon able to send signals several kilometres, and three years later, set up a wireless station capable of transmitting across the English Channel.

His greatest achievement, however, came in 1901, ___(7)___ signals across the Atlantic, ___(8)___ that the Earth being curved would limit radio communication to a few hundred kilometres. Marconi gradually perfected his system in the following years until he was able to send the first radio message from England to Australia in 1918.

Meanwhile, he also carried out research on shortwave wireless communication ___(9)___ in the 1920s, and later, in 1932, installed the first radio telephone between Vatican city and the Pope's palace at Castel Gandolfo.

Marconi, ___(10)___ during his life, ___(11)___ in 1909, was also the Italian delegate to the Versailles Peace Conference in 1919, ___(12)___ the peace treaties with Austria and Bulgaria. He died in Rome in 1937 at the age of 73.

where he was assisted
which disproved the theory
which forms the basis
Sir William Preece
whose mother
who received many honours

where he signed
that led to the establishment of radio stations
when he succeeded in transmitting
the Italian physicist
among them the Nobel Prize for Physics
who was born

## Practice

The account of the life of Alexander Graham Bell, in the left-hand column, is incomplete without the additional information given on the right. Use relative clauses or phrases in apposition to join sentences or phrases from the two columns together, and include commas where necessary.

| | |
|---|---|
| Alexander Graham Bell was born in Scotland in 1847. | the inventor of the telephone |
| Bell became his assistant in 1868, and two years later the family moved to Canada. | his father had invented a system for teaching the deaf |
| While teaching the deaf in Boston, he met Thomas Watson | a young mechanic<br>he helped him to construct an electrical apparatus for transmitting sound. |
| After two years of experiments, Bell and Watson developed the telephone | It was patented in 1876. |
| The experiments were conducted with two deaf students, George Sanders and Mabel Hubbard | Bell married her the following year. |
| Throughout his life, Bell worked on a number of inventions | They included a machine for recording sound, flying machines and a hydrofoil. |
| He died in 1922 in Nova Scotia | He had lived there since 1885. |

# 25 Descriptive narrative

## Describing what might have happened

Some people's lives are memorable because of a crucial decision or turning-point. Compare the biographical account of Captain Scott with those on the previous two pages. Note (1) the amount of space devoted to the end of his life (2) the use of the conditional (in **bold** type) to indicate what would or might have happened if the decision had been different.

### Captain Scott

Captain Robert Scott, born in Devonshire in 1868, was the leader of the ill-fated British expedition that set out to explore Antarctica in 1910. Scott was an experienced naval officer who had previously commanded an expedition to Antarctica in 1901–4, and on this occasion his main objective was to be the first man to reach the South Pole.

Scott and eleven others began their overland journey to the Pole in October 1911, equipped with motor sledges, ponies and dogs. **If he had relied on dogs**, like the Norwegian explorer, Roald Amundsen, **Scott would probably have survived**, but the motor sledges broke down and the ponies had to be shot. On December 31st, Scott sent seven men back to base, and went on on foot with four companions to the Pole, which he reached on January 18th, 1912. The exhausted men were disappointed to find that Amundsen had been there a month before.

On the return journey the weather grew worse, and two of the men died. One of them, Oates, deliberately walked out into the storm in the hope of giving his companions a better chance of reaching their depot, where they would have found food and fuel. Towards the end of March, only eleven miles from the depot, the three survivors met another storm, which lasted nine days and confined them to their tent, where they died of exhaustion. Scott's diary, recording these events, was found with their bodies several months later.

Modern judgements of Scott suggest that he was a heroic, but stubborn man. **If he had listened to the advice of others, he might not have reached the Pole first, but he would probably not have died such a tragic death.**

## Practice

Use the information given below to construct a similar biographical account of the life of Scott's rival, Roald Amundsen.

**Roald Amundsen** (born near Oslo, 1872). Before leading expedition to South Pole, Amundsen had spent a winter in the Antarctic and sailed through the Northwest Passage, north of Canada (1903–06).
In 1909, Amundsen planned to be the first to reach the North Pole. Discovered that Peary had reached it, and changed plans. Sailed from Norway in June 1910. Set out for South Pole five days before Scott (October 19, 1911) with smaller, faster expedition (five men and 52 dogs).

Reached Pole, December 14, and returned safely.
Later tried to reach the North Pole by air. Flew over it in 1926 with American explorer, Lincoln Ellsworth, and Italian engineer, Umberto Nobile. In 1928, Nobile's expedition, in airship, crashed on ice near island of Spitzbergen. Amundsen tried to rescue him, died when plane crashed. Nobile later rescued by other explorers.
Personal reputation – single-minded, thoroughly professional man, determined to succeed.

# 25 Descriptive narrative

## ✍ A personal biography

A biographical account of a living person may be like those you have already read in this unit, except that there will be changes in the use of tenses. If it is an account of the life of someone known to the writer, he/she is likely to include more personal details. Read Elizabeth Markham's account of her grandfather's life, written in 1965, and then answer the questions below.

### My Grandfather

My grandfather, Henry Markham, was born near London in 1890. His father was a builder and decorator, and Henry, who was the only son, was trained to follow him in the business. In 1913, however, when my grandfather had just got married, his father's partner cheated our family, running off to Australia with the firm's money, and before Henry could re-establish the business, the First World War broke out and he had to go to fight in France.

During the war, my great-grandfather died, and the business collapsed, so when Henry came back from the Western Front, he had to make a new start. He **has always been** a resourceful person, so he tried various jobs before eventually finding one that suited him, working in an advertising agency. He was quite successful and had saved enough money to open his own agency when the Second World War started and advertising virtually disappeared. As a result, he was too old to carry out his plan after the war and remained with the same firm until he retired **five years ago**, at the age of 70.

In his retirement, he **has rediscovered** the skills he **learnt** as a young man, and **spends** most of his time decorating houses in the neighbourhood and making toys for my children. I **have always been** grateful to him for his kindness to me, and **admire** him for his common-sense and his refusal to be discouraged by the difficulties of his career.

1 Suppose this account was printed as an obituary in the local newspaper after Henry's death in 1970. Make all the changes necessary. Note that you will have to take out references to 'My grandfather', for example, and Elizabeth's personal opinion of Henry. You will also have to change the tenses and time references in **bold** type. Begin: 'Mr Henry Markham, a well-known local figure who died last Wednesday, was born . . .' End the obituary: 'Mr Markham was very popular in the town and will be very much missed by his many friends.'

2 How do you think Henry's life would have been different if (a) his father's partner had not cheated his family (b) the First World War had not broken out the following year (c) his father had not died when he was in France (d) the Second World War had not started in 1939 (e) he had not been trained as a builder and decorator?

## ✍ Further Practice

1 Write a biographical account of a famous person, now dead.
2 Write a biographical account of a famous living person that you admire.
3 Write an account of a person in history whose life was changed by circumstances.
4 Write a biographical account of an older member of your family, still living, or of one of your ancestors, whom you have heard about.

# 26 Making and Reporting Speeches: formal

## ✏️ Preparation

Robert Naylor has to make a speech on behalf of the Organising Committee at the opening of a film festival. Before reading it, note down what you imagine he will need to say.

Then compare your list of points with the general rules given here for almost all formal speeches of this kind.
1. Say who you are, and give the reason for your speech in appropriate language.
2. Convey your main message, using facts and examples, where necessary.
3. Mention anyone you want to draw attention to, either to introduce them or thank them.
4. Repeat the main message, and thank the audience for their attention.

Now look at the headings Robert wrote down as reminders for his speech. Compare them with the speech, and then divide the speech up into sections, according to the four rules listed above.

---

1. Welcome – committee
2. Occasion, now well established.
   Entries 29 – 113 – 242
   Categories 4 – 9 – 11
   3rd World – UNO.
3. Distinguished guests – UNO rep. Carlsson,
   Jury: Milton, Igoa, Altobelli, Kaligis.

---

Ladies and Gentlemen,

Good evening. My name is Robert Naylor. I am the Chairman of the Organising Committee, and it is a great pleasure for me, on behalf of the Committee, to welcome you to the fifth International Documentary Film Festival. I am sure you will all agree with me when I say that the Festival is now well established. The proof of its success is that when it was first held here, four years ago, we had 29 entries for the four categories of documentary film originally laid down; last year, the figures were 113 entries for nine categories, and this year there are two additional categories, and the entry has risen to a record number, 242!

The additional categories are in our opinion of great interest. One is a prize for the best documentary about the problems of third-world countries, and the other, donated by the United Nations, is for the documentary film that in the opinion of the jury does most to promote understanding between the different countries of the world. We are very grateful to the United Nations for making this prize available, and honoured to have with us the Secretary of the United Nations Communications Sub-committee, Mr Sigurd Carlsson, who will present the award.

Among our distinguished guests I must single out the jury, who will be the group working hardest during the following week, especially in view of the great increase in entries. They are well known to you and need no introduction but I would like to thank them for having agreed to form part of the jury: Mr Walter Milton, one of the most creative directors in the Australian film industry; the Academy Award winning actress from Mexico, Señorita Carmen Igoa; the Italian producer, Signor Carlo Altobelli; and last but not least, last year's winner of the critics' prize, Mr Nikos Kaligis from Greece.

Now all that remains for me to do is to say once again how happy we are that so many of you have come to the festival. We are sure that it will be a success. I will now hand over to my colleague, Neil Andrews, who will give you some more detailed information on the programme.

# 26 Making and reporting speeches

## Practice

At the end of the film festival, there is a dinner. Nikos Kaligis has been chosen by the other members of the jury to make a speech thanking the organisers and commenting on the standard of the films entered. The five paragraphs of his speech are printed below, but they are not in order. Put them in the right order. In some cases, the expression he used is left out. Complete the speech by choosing from the alternatives given below.

A  If I ___(1)___ everyone who has helped to make our task easier, I would ___(2)___ all night, but in particular I ___(3)___ ___(4)___ Mr Robert Naylor, who, together with the members of the Organising Committee and their staff, has ___(5)___ to making the festival a success.

B  ___(6)___ would also like to thank everyone who entered films at this festival. The number of entries was exceptionally high, but ___(7)___, and that gave us a very difficult job. We have done our best and we ___(8)___ that our decisions have reflected the opinion of the majority here, ___(9)___ in such circumstances many people are bound to be disappointed.

C  ___(10)___, I can only ___(11)___ our thanks to everyone concerned. We hope that you have enjoyed participating in the festival, and ___(12)___ seeing films of the same standard next year.

D  ___(13)___ my ___(14)___ on the jury and myself, I would like, ___(15)___, to thank the Organising Committee for their hospitality and for the smooth organisation of the festival. You have made us very welcome here and we are very ___(16)___ to you for making our task so pleasant.

E  As evidence of the high standard of the entries, I would like to draw attention to the fact that in four categories the prize was shared. ___(17)___ encouraging sign, ___(18)___, was that 26 different countries entered prize-winning films. This is good news for the film industry ___(19)___ and helped to make this a ___(20)___ festival.

(1) (a) thank (b) thanked (c) bother to thank
(2) (a) be here (b) keep you here (c) be saying 'thank you'
(3) (a) have to (b) can't help (c) would like to
(4) (a) single out (b) pick (c) choose
(5) (a) troubled (b) tried (c) contributed
(6) (a) I (b) The jury (c) The jury and me
(7) (a) the standard wasn't (b) so was the standard (c) the standard was
(8) (a) hope (b) expect (c) want
(9) (a) but (b) so (c) although
(10) (a) At last (b) Finally (c) Last but not least
(11) (a) say (b) tell (c) repeat
(12) (a) expect (b) wait for (c) look forward to
(13) (a) Talking to you for (b) On behalf of (c) In the opinion of
(14) (a) colleagues (b) workers (c) critics
(15) (a) first of all (b) in principle (c) at first sight
(16) (a) thanked (b) grateful (c) kind
(17) (a) Other (b) Another (c) Also
(18) (a) without a doubt (b) probably (c) perhaps
(19) (a) on the whole (b) I suppose (c) as a whole
(20) (a) quite good (b) real good (c) truly international

## ✌ Further Practice

Use the guidance given here to write a speech for one or more of the following occasions:

1  A group of English-speaking visitors have come to your school or place of work on an exchange visit. Welcome them, and give them general information.

2  You have attended an international conference, and must make a speech, thanking the organisers and commenting on its success.

3  Your country is the host for an international folk music festival and you must make a speech welcoming the English-speaking groups.

4  A distinguished speaker from abroad has given a lecture or short course at your school or university. Make a speech thanking him/her and explaining how much you have learnt.

# 27 Summary: opinion

## ✎ Making notes

Summarising a passage expressing an opinion requires a similar approach to the summaries you have already done in Unit 22. You must remember, however, that your task is to reproduce the writer's ideas, not your own, even if you disagree with them.

First read the article below, and make a note of the main points.

### How Serious is the Problem of Unemployment?

In most European countries, unemployment was low for many years after the Second World War, and the bitter memories of parents and grandparents who had been out of work for long periods in the 1930s gradually faded from people's minds. But in recent years it has once again become a serious problem.

How serious the problem is depends on one's perspective, in particular when it becomes a question of blaming someone for it. Newspapers usually quote the number of people 'unemployed' as a percentage of the registered working population. On the basis of these figures alone, they make comparisons with past experience and also between different countries. Such simplified calculations do not take into account technological developments that have made a large number of unskilled jobs unnecessary. Apart from that, they do not allow for the increase over the past fifty years in the number of people who want to work or the effect of different social attitudes.

When we compare our unemployment figures with those of the 1930s, we must remember that far more women work nowadays, and consequently register as unemployed if they lose their jobs, so governments have a greater task and responsibility. International comparisons are complicated by the fact that the number of women who are registered varies from one country to another. In Denmark almost as many women are registered as men, in other Common Market countries only half as many. It is therefore more difficult for the Danish government to provide jobs for everyone and its record in international terms is better than it appears.

Comparisons between countries are also unreliable because of the percentage of people who are not registered. Are they housewives or students? In West Germany, most young people stay at school until they are 18; more of those not registered are likely to be students than in other countries in the Common Market, and they will not count in the unemployment figures.

For these reasons, comparisons with the past and with other countries are unfair. Yet in human terms, although this places more responsibility on governments in countries where everyone wants to work, the percentages quoted by the newspapers are the only reliable measure of a government's success in dealing with the problem of unemployment. The question a government must always face is: 'How many people in this country at this point in time want to work but cannot find jobs.'

Decide which of the following best expresses the meaning of each of the five paragraphs in the article:

1. (a) Unemployment is as serious a problem today as it was in the 1930s.
   (b) Unemployment is once again a serious problem.
2. (a) Newspapers simplify the problem of unemployment because they do not take all the relevant factors into account.
   (b) Newspapers deliberately distort the true facts about unemployment in order to blame governments.
3. (a) The main reason for unemployment today is that so many women go out to work, and this problem is much more serious in Denmark.
   (b) Comparisons with the past do not take into account the number of women working today, and international comparisons are unreliable because this figure varies from country to country.
4. (a) Nobody knows how many of the people not registered are students.
   (b) The difference in school-leaving age also makes international comparisons unreliable.
5. (a) Nevertheless, a government's success in dealing with unemployment must be measured in terms of the number of people who want to work and cannot.
   (b) Nevertheless, it is a government's duty to find jobs for everyone.

# 27 Summary

Which of the following summaries best expresses the meaning of the passage? Give reasons for your answer.

1  Unemployment is a big problem in Europe again, but it is a matter of perspective, especially when it comes to blaming governments for it. Newspapers compare the figures to the 1930s and compare different countries, but this is not fair because more women are working now, and in Denmark as many women are registered as men. A lot of people do not work. Some of them are housewives, and some of them are students, but there are more students in Germany because young people stay at school till they are eighteen. I think the only thing that matters is that everyone who wants to work should have a job and it is the Government's duty to provide jobs. (116 words)

2  Unemployment is a serious problem in Europe, but newspapers simplify it because they do not take all the relevant factors into account. It is difficult to measure the size of the problem by comparing modern figures with the past or making international comparisons. More women go out to work now but in different countries the number who work and register as unemployed varies. In some countries, too, young people stay at school longer, and so they are not registered. Nevertheless, although governments in countries where everyone wants to work have a more difficult task in controlling unemployment, the only measure of their success is how many people who are looking for jobs are out of work. (116 words)

## Further Practice

Summarise the following passage in not more than 120 words. List the main points of the argument and the writer's proposals, ignoring details, and construct your summary from the notes you have made.

### The Right to Walk

I belong to a rare species. I am a pedestrian who does not drive in a city full of cars. The worst of it is that motorists regard me as a nuisance or behave as if I did not exist. I try not to irritate them. I keep to the pavement and only cross at traffic lights, waiting for the green light, but that is not enough, because they want to invade my territory.

One of the main problems is parking. In my city, people often park half-way onto the pavement, and sometimes block it altogether, so pedestrians have to walk in the road. All scooters are parked on the pavement and the young riders never think of getting off at the kerb to park. They ride along the pavement until they reach their house or school.

Another problem is traffic lights. A recent study by the city council shows that every time the lights change in the city, two motorists go through when they are red. I am used to the idea that as the lights change, motorists accelerate, instead of stopping; what I cannot get used to and prepare for is that at many corners the lights are green for the pedestrian but yellow for the motorist coming off the main road. As far as he (or she!) is concerned, yellow is green, and they turn the corner without slowing down. They even blow their horns impatiently if they have to stop because I am walking across.

Of course the solution would be to enforce the law. The city council should provide more car parks and tow away vehicles obstructing the road. As it is, they only do so if someone telephones to complain. They should fine people who park on the pavement; at present, only 30% of fines are paid, but the council do not take drivers' licences away unless they fail to pay several fines. More traffic wardens should be employed, even though the city council study says that last year traffic wardens on duty were the victims of 422 serious physical attacks by motorists.

At a time when the newspapers are full of articles about the right to work and the right to prevent other people from smoking, when are the authorities going to concern themselves about the right to walk?

# 28 Discussion: solutions to problems

## ✏ Planning a discussion

Composition topics asking you to provide a solution to a problem in modern life require planning.
First, look at the planning of the composition that appears below on the topic: 'What can be done to reduce the pollution of the environment in modern cities?'

Stage 1  List the nature of the problem and its causes, like this:
(a) air – contamination of the atmosphere, 'smog' (smoke and fog), sulphur: factory chimneys, chimneys in houses, car exhaust
(b) water – pollution of rivers: factory effluent, rubbish
(c) streets – inefficient rubbish disposal, dogs fouling pavements, litter.

Stage 2  List possible solutions to these problems:
(a) remove factories from cities; install clean air equipment; use alternative sources of energy (solar, nuclear?, smoke-free coal, electric cars or lead-free petrol)
(b) control of factories, pumping oxygen into rivers
(c) well-organised rubbish collection, making citizens aware of responsibilities.

Stage 3  Consider what *should* be done. What *would* be the result? Limit yourself to possible, not ideal, solutions, and take problems into account, such as cost, penalties for companies or private individuals and enforcement of the law.

Now compare the stages of this plan with the composition below. Decide on the purpose of each paragraph, and see which stage contributes to it.
Composition topics of this kind also demand confident use certain structures. Read the notes in the Reference Section (p.113) on *should* and *would*, and put the verbs in the last two paragraphs in the correct forms.
Note that some of these verbs will be passive: e.g. ... some action (take) will become *some action should be taken*.

---

Everyone agrees that modern cities are polluted and something must be done about it. The air we breathe is not pure, the water we drink has to be purified with chlorine, and our streets are often dirty because of rubbish that has not been collected, paper bags and cans thrown away and pavements frequently fouled by dogs.

Factories are responsible for most of the pollution. Their chimneys pour out smoke, contaminating the atmosphere, and also produce harmful chemicals like sulphur that are invisible and also dangerous. In many cases, they contaminate rivers with effluent, even though the factories themselves are outside the city. But private individuals are also responsible. Many citizens add to the smoke with coal fires from their chimneys; almost all of us have cars that fill the air with poisonous exhaust fumes; a large number of us are guilty of throwing litter away in the streets, or allowing our dogs to foul them.

Although some cities are more industrialised than others and have more serious problems, some action (take). *In the first place*, companies (encourage), with the aid of Government grants, to move their factories outside the city, and they (install) clean air equipment or (close down). They (force) to dispose of effluent without contaminating rivers, and (fine) if they break the law. *Secondly*, people using coal fires (give) electric fires or (tell) to use smokeless fuel. *Thirdly*, taxes on lead-free petrol (reduce) to encourage motorists to buy it, and eventually, only cars using this petrol (allow) on the roads. *Finally*, most cities have laws to punish citizens who make the streets dirty or allow their dogs to do so, and these (enforce).

Naturally these proposals (oppose), because such improvements (cost) money. The authorities (have to deal) firmly with companies and (help) householders and drivers. But *above all* people (have to co-operate) and (*learn*) to respect others because it (be) impossible to arrest everyone who *threw* rubbish *away* or *owned* a badly-trained dog. There is really no alternative, however. If we *do not find* a solution to the problem of pollution, our cities *will become* uninhabitable.

# 28 Discussion

**Comparative National Statistics**

| Country | BR | DR | IMR | IPC | Cal. | Arms Imp. | Arms Exp. |
|---|---|---|---|---|---|---|---|
| United States | 15.5 | 8.7 | 10.5 | 15490 | 3641 | 500 | 10600 |
| U.S.S.R. | 19.4 | 10.9 | 16.5 | 7000 | 3360 | 1600 | 9800 |
| United Kingdom | 13.3 | 11.7 | 9.6 | 8510 | 3249 | 650 | 1600 |
| France | 13.9 | 10.0 | 8.2 | 9880 | 3529 | 60 | 4300 |
| Japan | 11.9 | 5.1 | 5.5 | 10400 | 2852 | 750 | 200 |
| Bangladesh | 43.3 | 16.6 | 128.0 | 120 | 1837 | 60 | 0 |
| Chad | 43.0 | 21.0 | 139.0 | 100 | 1762 | 5 | 0 |
| Ethiopia | 49.7 | 23.1 | 155.0 | 110 | 1793 | 525 | 0 |
| Haiti | 35.6 | 13.0 | 117.7 | 330 | 1905 | 0 | 0 |

KEY
BR = Birth rate per 1000 population
DR = Death rate per 1000 population
IMR = Infant mortality rate per 1000 babies born
IPC = Income per head of population ($)
Cal. = Calories consumed per person per day. According to climate, the United Nations establishes the daily nutritional requirement between 2200 and 2400.
Imp./Exp. = Import/Export (million ($))

## Practice

Another major problem with compositions of this kind is that emotional statements are not convincing unless they are based on facts. For example, imagine you have to write on the topic: 'Solving the problem of hunger in the Third World'. It is not enough to know that 40,000 children under five years old die of hunger every day in the Third World, and to accuse 'them' (the governments of developed countries) because they spend money on arms.
The table of comparative national statistics and the additional notes given here will help you to plan and write such a composition.
Look at the table, answer the questions related to it, and then look at the notes, with the questions that follow.

## Table

1 What conclusions can be drawn from the birth rate and death rate in advanced industrialised countries and in those of the Third World? If you compare the two for each country, where is the population growing fastest?
2 What chances has a baby born in the industrialised countries of surviving compared to those of a baby in the Third World countries?
3 What proportion of the people in the two groups is likely to be hungry, taking into account the UN nutritional requirements?
4 Expenditure on arms does not take into account what the industrial countries spend on those they manufacture for their own use. What conclusions can be derived from the export figures for these countries and the imports for Ethiopia, for example?

## Notes

What conclusions do you derive from the following statements of fact?
1 In 1986, Africa earned $19,000 million less than in 1985 from its exports because prices fell. In the same year, interest payments on loans to banks amounted to $15,000 million (total loss = $34,000 million).
2 Aid to Africa in this year amounted to $16,000 million from governments and $2,000 million from private sources (total gain = $18,000 million).
3 In 1970, in the United Nations, developed countries agreed to pay 0.7% of their income every year to aid the poorest from 1975 onwards. Only three countries, the Netherlands, Norway and Sweden, have kept this promise.
4 The stores of such foods as milk and butter in the Common Market countries are so enormous that they eventually have to be sold at cheap rates to the USSR and other countries or destroyed.

## Planning

Look at the two plans presented here, both employing four paragraphs, choose the one you consider most likely to be convincing, and write a composition on the topic.

A  1  Developed countries should act immediately to solve the problem of hunger in the Third World. (Table q.4, Notes 3–4)
   2  The size of the problem. (Table q.2,3)
   3  Action suggested. What should developed countries do?
   4  How could the situation be permanently improved? – agricultural methods, birth rate etc. Results of action.

B  1  The nature of the problem (Table q.3,2). Population growth (Table q.1), lack of money (Notes 1–2), local problems (drought in Africa, floods in Bangladesh, political instability in Haiti).
   2  Aid resources available. Table (IPC), Notes (4), Table (q.4).
   3  Short-term action suggested. Notes (3), (1), (2), Table (q.4).
   4  Long-term action suggested. All these + points in A 4.

## 28 Discussion

### *Further Practice*

In attempting to answer any of these questions, study the vocabulary in the Reference Section (p.116).

1 Most robberies are committed by young people. What would you do to solve the problem of juvenile delinquency?
2 Smoking is now considered dangerous to other people apart from smokers themselves. What would you do to reduce its effects?
3 A large number of accidents involve young people on scooters. What would you do to reduce the number of such accidents?

# 29 Formal Writing: commenting on a book or film

## ✍ Choosing the tense

Before attempting these exercises, study the Reference Section (p.117) for the examples of the changes in tenses required in writing about a book, play or film.
The two passages below are written as if they were narrative, with the Past Simple tense the main tense. Change the tenses in *italic* type, so that the story is told as it should be in a synopsis or essay on a book or play.

### The First Scene of *Hamlet*

It *was* night in the castle of Elsinore, in Denmark. A sentry *was* on guard, and another one, Bernardo, *came* to take his place. Both men *were* nervous, as if they *expected* something terrible to happen. Soon afterwards, an officer, Marcellus, *arrived* on the scene with a gentleman called Horatio. The soldiers *began* to tell Horatio about a strange vision they *had seen* on two previous occasions. Horatio *did not believe* in ghosts, but while they *were talking*, the figure of a ghost suddenly *appeared*, dressed like the dead king of Denmark. Everyone *was* frightened but Horatio *spoke* to it. It *did not answer* him, apparently angry at his tone of voice. When it *had gone*, Horatio *admitted* that the figure *had been* just like the king. Everyone *felt* sure that this *meant* that something important *was going to happen* in Denmark. The ghost *returned* and Horatio *begged* it to tell them what it *wanted*. Then a cock *crew* because it *was* dawn and the ghost *disappeared*. The men *decided* to tell Prince Hamlet, the son of the dead king, what they *had seen* because they *were* sure the ghost *would speak* to him.

## ✍ Choosing the vocabulary

Study the notes on vocabulary in the Reference Section (p.117), and then complete the passage below with appropriate words. In each case, the first letter of the word needed has been given to help you.

On the whole, the greatest n_____ do not make the best f_____. *Gone with the Wind* won several Oscars, but everyone criticised *War and Peace*. In some cases, this may be the fault of the director, or the actors and a_____s, and the person who usually gets most of the blame is the one who wrote the s_____, a very difficult job, because it may mean condensing 30 or 40 c_____s of a book into a dozen s_____s.

Another reason why such adaptations usually fail is because we already have a clear idea of the main c_____, the h_____, the h_____and the v_____, and we may be disappointed if the faces on the s_____ do not resemble our conception of them.

### *The Spy that Came in from the Cold*

In the first chapter of the novel, Leamas, a British secret agent, *was waiting* at a check-point in Berlin for one of his agents, Karl Riemeck, to cross over from the Russian zone into the American zone. All his other agents in East Germany *had been captured* and executed by the chief of the East German secret police, Mundt. A woman *crossed* the border in a car and Leamas *recognised* her as Riemeck's girl-friend. She *told* him that Riemeck *was going to escape* on a bicycle and Leamas *was* horrified that his agent *had trusted* her with his plans. However, he *gave* her the key to a flat and *told* her that he *would telephone* her when Riemeck *arrived*. At last Leamas *saw* Riemeck at the East German check-point. He *was behaving* very calmly. Then he *got on* his bicycle and *started* to ride across the bridge between the two sides, but when he *was* half-way across, a searchlight *was turned on*, and the East German sentry *shot* him.

The most important reason of all, however, is probably that the n_____ can explain at length why a character behaves in a certain way, but in a film the actor must do this with a few words and facial expressions. At least film actors have an advantage over actors in the t_____ taking part in s_____ adaptations of books, because the director can use a close-up, and we can see their facial expressions clearly.

## 29 Formal writing

# ✍ Describing a Character

Note the following points in planning a composition of this kind:
1. list the character's main actions, and think of adjectives to describe them. Is the character consistent throughout, or does he/she change? If so, why? Is he/she compared to or contrasted with other characters?
2. list his or her opinions. Are they justified?
3. list other characters' opinions of the character, taking into account whether they are friends, enemies, or impartial.
4. find three or four adjectives to express your general opinion of the character.

Use the example of the plan and essay below on the character of Brutus in Shakespeare's *Julius Caesar* as a basis for your own work.

1 Decides to assassinate Caesar to prevent him from becoming a dictator – accepts the leadership of the conspirators – does not agree with Cassius' suggestion that they should also kill Mark Antony – joins the rest in killing Caesar – agrees to meet Mark Antony, and allows him to speak after him at Caesar's funeral, against Cassius' advice – makes a speech to the people justifying the assassination – once driven out of Rome, following Antony's speech, quarrels with Cassius, but forgives him – resolves to fight at Philippi against Mark Antony and Octavius, against Cassius' advice – loses the battle, and commits suicide. Character consistent. Compared to Cassius, Mark Antony and Octavius.

2 Admires Caesar, but hates tyranny – is not personally ambitious or envious – believes Caesar must die to save the Republic – is convinced that he was right and the people will understand his arguments – does not regret any of his actions and dies convinced that he did what he had to for his country.

3 *Cassius*: 'noble', 'honourable'; *Casca*: loved by the people; *The people* (before Antony's speech) 'noble' (after) 'traitor', 'villain', 'murderer'; *Antony* (after his death): 'This was the noblest Roman of them all'.

4 'honourable', 'sincere', 'idealistic', 'self-righteous', 'politically naïve'.

---

When Brutus first appears on the stage in the play, he is clearly contrasted to Cassius. Cassius's motives in wanting to assassinate Caesar are mainly personal, because he is envious and knows Caesar dislikes him; Brutus, on the other hand, is one of Caesar's favourites and admires him, but he has a strong sense of duty and hates the idea of Caesar becoming a dictator. He does not immediately agree to take part in the conspiracy, but after thinking about it decides that Caesar must be killed for the good of the Republic.

Although he is not personally ambitious, he has an unattractive feature in his character. This is that he is so sure of his own nobility and virtue that he is always convinced that he is right. In moral terms, he *is* right, and no one doubts his sincerity, but for the same reason he is politically naïve and refuses to listen to Cassius's advice. He believes that the people will understand his motives and uses logical arguments, but Antony's emotional appeals and skilful oratory convince them that he is a traitor and a murderer. Throughout the play, even in making the decision to fight at Philippi, he does the wrong thing for the right reasons.

Antony's final tribute to him emphasises that he was the only one of the conspirators who acted unselfishly. At the same time, in contrasting him with Mark Antony and Octavius, Shakespeare seems to be suggesting that self-righteous political idealists like Brutus do not understand the nature of the people and of the world as it is well enough to succeed against less honest but more realistic opponents.

---

Study the three paragraphs here and by referring to the notes, decide how they are organised and related.
Are Brutus's actions commented on in chronological order?
At what point are the adjectives relating to him introduced?
At what point are the comparisons with other characters introduced?

## 29 Formal writing

### ✎ Writing a Review

Use this check-list for a review of the film *Casablanca* as a starting-point for your own work (Further Practice).
The review itself is printed with the paragraphs in the wrong order. Decide on the most appropriate order, giving reasons for your choice.
Then study the check-list to see which information is given in which paragraph, and make a plan of your own on this basis.
Use the table in the Reference Section (p.117) if you write about a book or a play.

| | |
|---|---|
| Title: | *Casablanca* |
| Director: | Michael Curtiz |
| Screenplay: | Julius J and Philip G Epstein and Howard Koch |
| Date: | 1943 |
| Type: | adventure film |
| Music: | Max Steiner; song 'As Time Goes By' (Frederick Hollander) |
| Setting: | Casablanca, in 1941, during the Second World War, governed by the Vichy French government, subservient to the Nazi regime in Germany, before the USA entered the war |
| Characters (and actors/actresses): | Rick (owner of the Café Américain) (Humphrey Bogart); the girl (Ingrid Bergman); her husband (resistance leader) (Paul Henried); the Vichy chief of police (Claude Rains); the Nazi major (Conrad Veidt); the boss of the underworld (Sidney Greenstreet); black pianist (Dooley Wilson) |
| Main events: | Rick was in love with a girl he met in Paris at the beginning of the war. She appears in his café in Casablanca with her husband, whom she previously thought was dead. They are among the many refugees hoping to escape to Lisbon, and from there to the USA. The chief of police has the power to grant exit permits, but he is influenced by the Nazis, who want to arrest the husband. |
| Theme: | Basically, Allied propaganda against Hitler, suggesting that free people everywhere will rise against him. |
| Opinion: | memorable film, superbly written, a series of unforgettable scenes and lines of dialogue, characters a series of simple types, well acted. |

(Note that if you were writing an essay on a book, play or film you would include knowledge of all the events, but in a review you would not say how the film ended)

### Casablanca

(1) The film was obviously made to encourage resistance against Hitler, and to persuade neutrals to take sides against him, as the USA had done by the time it was made. Its continuing attraction, however, depends on a series of unforgettable scenes and the creation of characters who are immediately recognisable as 'types' but are so well acted that they seem like individuals.

(2) *Casablanca* was made during the Second World War. It is set in Morocco, at that time governed by the French Vichy government, subservient to the Nazis. The hero is an American café owner called Rick, played by Humphrey Bogart, who is neutral, because the USA has not yet entered the war, but sympathises with the Allied cause.

(3) A good deal of the credit for this must go to the screenwriters, as well as to the director, Michael Curtiz. People who have never seen the film know the song 'As Time Goes By', sung by the black pianist (Dooley Wilson), and the famous line spoken by Ingrid Bergman: 'Play it again, Sam.' Among the actors, of course, all perfect in their roles, Bogart stands out. As Rick, he created a new kind of hero, tough and independent on the outside, but also sentimental, capable of falling in love and making sacrifices.

(4) *Casablanca* is full of refugees trying to escape to Lisbon, and from there to New York. Rick protects them, and uses his influence with the French Chief of Police (Claude Rains) and the boss of the underworld (Sidney Greenstreet) to help them. He is eventually forced to take sides, however, when a girl he was in love with in Paris (Ingrid Bergman) arrives with her husband (Paul Henried). When Rick left Paris in 1940, he expected her to go with him, but at the last minute she received the news that her husband, a Resistance leader, was not dead as she had thought. Rick does not know this, and has never forgiven her.

### ✎ Further Practice

1. Tell the story of a chapter from a novel you have read, or a scene from a play or a film.
2. Write about a character in a novel, play or film.
3. Describe a book you have read or a play or film you have seen, and give your opinion of it.
4. Write a review of a book, play or film.

# 30 Guided Writing: classified advertisements

## Abbreviation

Abbreviations are often used in classified advertisements to save space and money. Look at the following advertisements and decide whether they are for flats to be rented or for flats to be shared. Then look at the two columns on the right and match the abbreviation with the appropriate full form. Finally, write out the information in each advertisement in full.

**NR. HAMPSTEAD HEATH** Available immediately. Furn. flat recently redec. Dble bed, Sgle Bed, Recep., K/b. £150 pw. 01 268 9595.

**DOCKLANDS** Room in hse. use of k/b, all mod cons. Suit Prof F. £66 pw. Tel: 01 241 7795.

**HIGHBURY**, nr. tube, 1 dble bed, s/r., k/b., CH. £120 pw. Refs. rqd. Suit couple. 01 838 1371.

**BALHAM** Prof n/s lge rm in flat. All mod cons., CH, gdn. £45 pw. Tel: 01 528 5091.

**CHELSEA** Pleasant, flat. Bed., s.r., k/b. CH £140 pw. 01 141 9116 evgs.

**DULWICH** Well furn hse, 2 receps., 4 beds. Gas CH. Family only. £150 pw. IV Ltd. Tel: 01 115 5249.

| | | | |
|---|---|---|---|
| A | bed. | 1 | furnished |
| B | CH | 2 | redecorated |
| C | dble. | 3 | bedroom |
| D | evgs. | 4 | double |
| E | F | 5 | single |
| F | furn. | 6 | reception room |
| G | gdn. | 7 | kitchen/bathroom |
| H | hse. | 8 | per week |
| I | k/b. | 9 | professional |
| J | lge. | 10 | house |
| K | Ltd. | 11 | modern conveniences |
| L | mod cons. | 12 | female |
| M | n/s | 13 | telephone |
| N | nr. | 14 | underground |
| O | pw. | 15 | sitting room |
| P | prof. | 16 | near |
| Q | recep. | 17 | references |
| R | redec. | 18 | required |
| S | refs. | 19 | non-smoker |
| T | reqd. | 20 | large |
| U | rm. | 21 | garden |
| V | s.r. | 22 | room |
| W | sgle. | 23 | central heating |
| X | tel. | 24 | evenings |
| Y | tube | 25 | limited |

## Practice

Suppose you own one of the properties described below, and want to let it to English-speaking people. Write out a concise classified advertisement, using abbreviations wherever possible, for each of the following. Invent a telephone number and/or address.

1 A villa on the Costa del Sol, Spain, with three bedrooms, a garden, a swimming pool, two reception rooms, a kitchen, central heating, near the beach. To be let for two weeks at Easter and two months in summer. Price: £180 per week.
2 A fisherman's house in a picturesque village on the Portuguese coast, with two double bedrooms, a reception room, kitchen and bathroom, recently redecorated. Available for weekly rent in July and August. Price: £120 per week.
3 A large flat in a village in the south of France, with one double bedroom, one single bedroom, all modern conveniences, gas central heating, to be let by the month in July and August. Price: £400 per month. You are only at home in the evenings.
4 A large house on a Greek island, with three bedrooms, two reception rooms, near the beach. It would suit a family or three couples, but you would require references. Available for weekly rent all through the summer. Price: £160 per week.

## 30 Guided writing

## Replying to an advertisement

You are a post-graduate student and have been awarded a scholarship for a year to study at Cambridge University. You are attracted by an advertisement in an English newspaper inserted by a Cambridge lecturer, and wish to offer your flat in exchange; assume that it will be suitable for her in every way. Read the advertisement, and complete the letter replying to it, beginning and ending it appropriately. Note that you must (a) refer to the advertisement and indicate your interest (b) describe your flat in attractive terms (c) end by asking for information about the proposed method of meeting expenses etc.

> Cambridge lecturer, owner pleasant two bed flat nr colleges, s/r, k/b, CH, seeks exchange for academic yr beginning Sept. 1989 in agreeable European city during sabbatical leave. Would suit postgraduate student M/F with similar flat own country. Write to Dr. Angela Cookson, 96c Hills Street, Cambridge CU12 5MA.

I was very interested to see your advertisement in ........................ on ........................ offering ........................, and think that I may ........................ .
I am planning to come to ........................ because ........................, and I was looking for ........................ .
At the same time, I believe I can offer you ........................, since I have ........................ here in ........................ .
I don't know whether you have ever visited ........................, but I am sure ........................ . It is a very interesting city to work in or to spend a long holiday in because it ........................ . My flat is ........................ . It is ........................ floor, and has a view ........................ .
There are ........................ rooms, ........................, ........................ and ........................, and it has ........................, so you would not be cold ........................ .
It is quite near ........................, and very convenient for ........................, because ........................ . I think you would be ........................ here, and hope that we ........................ an agreement.
If you ........................, please write and ........................ .
I would also be interested to know how we would ........................ respective countries. I look ........................ you.
   Yours ........................,

## Further Practice

1 You are planning to go to England to work or study next year. Answer an advertisement from an English firm offering to find accommodation in the place where you want to live, indicating what you would like and what you would be willing to pay.
2 You have a house or apartment near the beach or in the country and would like to sell it. Insert an attractive classified advertisement for it in an English newspaper.
3 Imagine that you answered one of the advertisements for holiday accommodation on the opposite page, and paid a week's or a month's rent in advance, but when you arrived found that the house/flat was not as advertised. Write from the place where you are staying to an agency in England (who let it to you on behalf of the owners) complaining, listing what is wrong, and demanding all or part of your money back.

# 31 Descriptive Narrative: changes in people and places

## ✎ Choosing the correct tense

Before reading the text, study Reference Section (p.117) carefully, noting the examples given of the sequence of tenses. Complete the passage by putting the verbs in brackets in the correct tense, making sure that the adverbs appear in the right position, and then answer the questions that follow.

My parents (move) away from London in the year I (leave) school and I never (live) there since, but about a year ago, when I (be) there on business, a curious coincidence (lead) to my going back to the suburb where I (grow) up. I (stand) outside my hotel, waiting for a taxi, when a man on the opposite side of the road (catch) sight of me, (stop), and suddenly (cross) the road to speak to me. He (come) straight up to me, (hold) out his hand, and (say): 'Hello, Martin! You (be) Martin Scott, (be) not you? You not (change) much in thirty years!'

He (be) tall and thin, almost bald-headed, with grey hair and deep lines across his forehead, but I (recognise) him from his eyes and expression. Something (remind) me of a boy with thick, black, curly hair who (be) one of my closest friends at school. 'Peter Lindsay!' I (exclaim).

We (stand) talking on the pavement for a few minutes, briefly telling each other the story of our lives since we last (meet). He still (live) in the house he (inherit) from his parents, and before we (part), I (promise) that I (visit) him the next time I (come) to London. When I (tell) him that I not (be) to Woodbury, the suburb where we (grow) up, for nearly thirty years, he (say) I (be) amazed at the changes that (take) place.

A few weeks later, I (catch) a train to Woodbury. When I (be) a boy, Woodbury station (be) still a ruin, because it (be) bombed during the war, but it already (be rebuilt) before I (leave) the neighbourhood. In those days, trams *used to run* along the High Street outside, but now there (be) no longer any signs of the tramlines. The first thing I (notice) when I (come) out of the station (be) that the row of little shops where my mother *used to buy* meat, fish and groceries (disappear); there (be) an enormous supermarket in their place. Another prominent landmark that (vanish) (be) the Capitol Cinema, where children *used to go* on Saturday mornings. On the site (be) a multi-storey car-park.

On the way to Peter's house, I (notice) fewer changes, though some old Victorian houses (be knocked down) and (replace) by modern flats. But when I (turn) the corner into his road, I (see) the first real improvement. The saplings that (be planted) just after the war (grow) into splendid trees. As I (reach) Peter's house and (open) the front gate, I (have) a shock that (make) me think for a moment that I (travel) back thirty years in time. A young man with black, curly hair (park) his car in front of the house, and when he (look) at me, I (see) Peter as he *used to be* when we (be) at school together.

He (smile) and (say), 'You must be Martin Scott. My father (expect) you.' It (be) Michael, Peter's son.

1 Why has Martin not lived in the Woodbury district of London since he left school, and when did he last visit it?
2 What was he doing when Peter saw him?
3 How had Peter changed since their last meeting? What had not changed in his face?
4 What did Martin and Peter talk about at first?
5 What did Martin promise that he would do the next time he was in London?
6 What did Peter think would surprise Martin?
7 Martin mentions three things that *used to take place* in Woodbury when he was a boy. Why couldn't they take place now?
8 What buildings had replaced those that were there when Martin was a boy?
9 What improvement had taken place in Peter's road?
10 Why did Martin think for a moment that he had travelled back thirty years in time?

# 31 Descriptive narrative

## Practice

Study the two photographs of Clapham Junction (in south London), taken almost from the same position, one about seventy years ago, the other recently.

First, make a list of all the features that remain the same: – buildings, the name of a shop, the shape of the road.

Then, list as many changes as you can: – buildings knocked down, and put up, public and private transport, amount of traffic, street lamps, traffic lights, bus stop.

Do you notice any changes in the way the people are dressed?

Now write two paragraphs about Clapham Junction.

In the first paragraph describe Clapham Junction as it was seventy years ago.

Begin, 'Seventy years ago, Clapham Junction...' Make points in comparison to the present with phrases like: 'In those days, ... used to...'

Begin the second paragraph by mentioning some features that are still the same, and then go on to describe the changes that have taken place, like this: 'The trams and tramlines have disappeared. In their place, there are...'

79

# 31 Descriptive narrative

## ✏️ Describing the past

Read the passage and complete it by filling the gaps with the most appropriate phrase from those listed below.

**Timetable**
| | |
|---|---|
| 6.00–9.00 | Lessons |
| 9.00–9.15 | Break |
| 9.15–11.15 | Lessons |
| 11.15–1.00 | Lunch |
| 1.00–3.00 | Lessons |
| 3.00–3.15 | Break |
| 3.15–5.30 | Lessons |
| 5.30 | Prayers |

## The Elizabethan Grammar School

Schoolchildren have always grumbled about having to go to school, but they have an easy life .....................¹ compared to their ancestors in Shakespeare's time. .....................², as the timetable for a typical Elizabethan grammar school indicates, children *used to get up* very early to be in their places in class .....................³ for the first lesson at six o'clock. .....................⁴ the day they had three breaks, but .....................⁵ they spent over nine hours a day at their lessons, six days a week, .....................⁶ Saturdays, and had only one afternoon off for games. To us, it seems incredible that .....................⁷ teachers found it necessary to justify the rest periods to parents, who often thought they were a waste of time!

When they first went to school children were taught to read, write and count, but .....................⁸ teachers *used to devote* almost all the time to two subjects, Latin and rhetoric, the art of self-expression in one's own language. .....................⁹ the monotony of the teaching method, modern educationalists, .....................¹⁰ children .....................¹¹, *would* also *have been horrified* by the competitive nature of the school and its discipline.

Teachers encouraged children to arrive .....................¹² in the morning. When they arrived the teacher *would place* the first to appear at the top of the class, and the last at the bottom. But the children *used to change* places in the course of each day, because those who failed to answer a question were sent to the bottom. Discipline was a controversial subject among teachers, but the argument was not about .....................¹³ children should be physically punished, as it *has been* .....................¹⁴, but about .....................¹⁵ they should be beaten and for what reasons.

We do not know .....................¹⁶ what Shakespeare, the most remarkable pupil of one of these schools, thought about the subject. In one play, .....................¹⁷, he has a Latin lesson, where the pupil, a small boy called William, shows more common-sense and imagination than the teacher. .....................¹⁸ his friend, Ben Jonson, Shakespeare was not very good at Latin or Greek, but he *must have been* exceptional at rhetoric. .....................¹⁹, he *would* surely *have been* happier in a modern school, where children are encouraged to develop their gifts for self-expression, .....................²⁰ learning all the names of the rhetorical techniques by heart.

according to   afterwards   altogether
apart from   as well as   during
even then   for certain   how often
however   in recent years   in those days
in time   including   instead of
nevertheless   on time   these days
today   whether

1 Give each paragraph a heading.
2 *Used to* is used in each of the first three paragraphs. What is the modern equivalent of the practice which is being contrasted to what happens nowadays?
3 The construction *would have* + Past Participle is used in two places. What is the 'impossible' condition in each case that has been omitted.
4 How could we rewrite the form *would place* correctly?
5 Why does the writer suppose that Shakespeare *must have been* exceptional at rhetoric? Why does he think he *would have been* happier in a modern school?
6 List all the differences you can see from the text between the Elizabethan grammar school and the school you went to or are going to, and make sentences like this: In Elizabethan schools ... *used to* ... but *nowadays* ...

# 31 Descriptive narrative

## Practice

The four paragraphs of the text below are not in order. Put them in the right order, giving reasons for your choice, and give each paragraph a heading. Then make a list of all the contrasts the writer mentions between the world he was born in and the world as it is today.

### The World I was Born In

(a) Nothing very dramatic happened in the world on that day. The main news item at home was about a railway accident in London; abroad, there was an account of a war going on on the borders of Afghanistan, but the soldiers involved were not from the Soviet Union but British forces stationed in what was then the Indian Empire, since Pakistan did not exist! In the London theatres, there were plays starring promising young actors like Laurence Olivier and Alec Guinness. The newspaper lists all the BBC radio programmes – there was no independent broadcasting – and the one television programme, shown between 3.00 p.m. and 10.00 p.m.

(b) The world I was born in was apparently a very peaceful place, or seemed so in Britain. As Londoners prepared for the coronation of King George VI, the only news item that hinted at the trouble to come was one about people joining the Nazi party in South-West Africa (now Namibia). I wonder how today's newspaper will appear to people in the twenty-first century.

(c) Perhaps the advertisements in the newspaper give the clearest idea of how people lived in those days. Until I looked at the pictures, for example, I had almost forgotten that in my childhood everyone wore hats. There were a lot of advertisements for servants, too, which would not appear nowadays, and no one would work for the wages offered (£1 a week plus keep). Houses were on sale for a hundredth of the price they would command today, but the cost of the paper itself was correspondingly low, just over 1p in the decimal system used these days, threepence in the old currency of pounds, shillings and pence.

(d) What do you imagine the world was like on the day you were born? What changes have taken place since then? Obviously, the older you are, the greater the changes, but I had not realised how different the world has become in my lifetime until someone gave me a copy of *The Times* for the day of my birth.

## Further Practice

1 Write a story about meeting someone again that you had not met for several years. Describe the changes in the person's appearance and personality.
2 Write about a place you knew as a child which has changed considerably since that time. Describe it as it was and as it is now.
3 Write about the life of people at some period of history in the past, comparing it with the life we lead nowadays. You can concentrate on one aspect of the subject, for example dealing with the situation of women or the life of people in the country or working in factories.
4 If there have been considerable changes in educational methods since you were at school, compare your schooldays with those of children today.
5 Compare life as it was when you were born or your earliest memories of it with life today.
6 Write about the news in today's newspaper or about modern life in general from the point of view of someone in the 21st century, imagining the changes that will have taken place in the meantime.

# 32 Making and Reporting Speeches: newspaper reports

## ✍ Reported speech

The Government is planning to extend a small airport near the market town of Clopton so that jet aircraft on charter flights can use it. At a public meeting, the Minister for Aviation, Mr Nicholas Browning, MP, explains the proposals to local people.

First, read the speech, and list the *advantages* for the local people that Mr Browning mentions.

Secondly, put the speech into reported speech: 'Mr Browning told the audience that/said that...', but ignore everything in *italic* type.

Finally, compare your version in reported speech with the newspaper report printed below, and answer the questions.

---

*I would like to say first of all how pleased I am to have this opportunity of putting the Government's case before you.*

To begin with, speaking in general terms, air traffic in this country is increasing. Every year more people fly abroad for their holidays – *I am sure that many of you do so* – and they need an airport near their homes. At present, the nearest airport is Loxton, sixty miles away, so there is clearly a need for an airport in this area. Experts from the Ministry have inspected a number of sites and have reached the conclusion that Clopton is the most appropriate. It is much easier to expand an existing airport than to build a new one.

Nevertheless, *although you may agree that Clopton is the best site from a technical point of view*, you may still ask *yourselves – and you are welcome to ask me questions afterwards* – what advantages it will have for local people.

In the first place, unemployment has been growing in Clopton in recent years. The airport will create new jobs in the short term, while it is being expanded, but also in the long term, because when it is completed, staff will be needed to maintain the aircraft and for the shops and other services.

Secondly, if the airport is developed, people will pass through Clopton on their way to it, and this will benefit trade in the shops and hotels in the town. In fact, several new hotels will have to be built.

Thirdly, access roads will be built to the airport from the larger towns in a radius of forty miles around Clopton. This will create more jobs for the local people, and also attract new industries to the area. At present, *as I am sure you realise*, Clopton is a little bit off the map. The airport will bring it into the twentieth century – or, rather, I should say, *into the twenty-first century*!

In conclusion, in the Government's view, the expansion of the airport can only be of benefit to the people of this town.

---

The Minister stressed the need for an airport in the area, and pointed out that experts had chosen Clopton as the most appropriate site because there was already an airport there.

Turning to the advantages for local people, he mentioned the unemployment problem in Clopton. The airport would create new jobs while it was being expanded but also in the long term, because staff would be needed to maintain the aircraft and for shops and other services. The airport would also benefit trade in the town.

Finally, access roads would be built from the larger towns around Clopton. This would attract new industries, and put Clopton on the map. The minister's conclusion was that the expansion of the airport could only be of benefit to the people of the town.

---

1 What do you think is the purpose behind the different comments the speaker makes that are printed in *italic* type?
2 Can all the arguments used be summarised in terms of one advantage? If so, what is it?

# 32 Making and reporting speeches

## Choosing the appropriate connectors

Mr Sam Hislop, a local farmer, has led the opposition to the Ministry's proposals and formed the Save Clopton Committee.

First, complete the speech he made in reply to the Minister by choosing the appropriate connectors from those given.

Secondly, write a continuation to the newspaper report on the opposite page, making use, where possible, of alternative expressions to 'said' and 'told'.

___(1)___, all the advantages the Minister has mentioned in connection with the airport ___(2)___ add up to one: creating more jobs. But I don't think the Minister understands the local situation.

Clopton is a market town serving a farming community in some of the finest countryside in England. Expanding the airport will change that.

___(3)___, there will be noise from the planes. That will be a permanent nuisance for everyone who lives near the present airport and also affect farmers. ___(4)___, building new main roads all over the countryside is bound to destroy it, and ___(5)___, on the subject of traffic, if we are going to have a lot of tourists passing through the town, the town itself will suffer. The Council will ___(6)___ have to widen the High Street and knock down the beautiful old buildings or build a ring road, and ___(7)___ the tourists won't benefit local trade.

The Minister claims the airport will create jobs in Clopton and bring the town into the twentieth century. ___(8)___, I am not sure that the jobs will be permanent, as he says, I don't think local people will get them, and ___(9)___, I'm not sure they are the sort of jobs local people want.

We already have tourists in Clopton, who come for peace and quiet and buy souvenirs of the English countryside. Is that the sort of tourist the Minister wants to attract here? ___(10)___! His tourists are waiting to get onto planes to buy souvenirs abroad!

___(11)___, if we agree to the extension of the airport, it will mean destroying the countryside, destroying the town, and, ___(12)___, destroying our way of life.

(1) (a) Personally (b) In my opinion (c) From a personal point of view
(2) (a) in fact (b) it's a fact (c) indeed
(3) (a) Principally (b) In principle (c) In the first place
(4) (a) Also (b) As well (c) Secondly
(5) (a) apart from that (b) in contrast (c) too
(6) (a) either (b) or (c) as well
(7) (a) in some cases (b) in this case (c) in that case
(8) (a) But (b) However (c) Though
(9) (a) above all (b) over all (c) consequently
(10) (a) On the other hand (b) On the contrary (c) Certainly
(11) (a) For all this (b) To sum up (c) At last
(12) (a) worse and worse (b) even better (c) worst of all

## Further Practice

1 You have been chosen to represent the students at your school to explain to the board or to parents a number of improvements they require. Write a speech, basing it on a series of points.
2 In your school, university or firm, you believe there is discrimination against girls or women. Write a speech suggesting changes in the system.
3 In your area, the local authorities want to build a ring road. This will involve destroying houses, a park etc. Write a speech for a public meeting.

# 33 Discussion: choosing an approach

## ✍ Planning

Writing a good composition on a general topic requires a plan. An effective plan depends on choosing an approach. Here, the topic is 'It is better to live in the country than in the city'.

First, look at the list of positive and negative points for each in the table below. Place them in order of importance, good and bad.

Secondly, look at the points in the right-hand column and answer the questions below.

| Country | | City | | Questions |
|---|---|---|---|---|
| + | − | + | − | |
| fresh air | no jobs | jobs | pollution | personal |
| neighbours | no services | services | loneliness | experience |
| houses | no cinemas etc. | entertainment | flats | who? |
| slow pace | bad weather | comfort | rush | hard work? |
| peace | isolation | communications | noise | travel? |
| beauty | boredom | excitement | ugliness | neighbours? |

1. What is your personal experience? Have you lived in both the town and the country? Which did you prefer? Why?
2. Do you think people in the country envy people in the town because they think they have easy jobs, and people in the town envy people in the country because they think they always work in the fresh air in the sunshine? Is this a true picture?
3. Do you think people in town live closer to their friends than people in the country and travelling is easier for them?
4. Is it an advantage or a disadvantage to have neighbours who take an interest in your life and what you do?

## ✍ Approaches

There are four basic approaches to this sort of composition: (a) balanced (b) in favour (pro-country) (c) against (pro-town) (d) contrast.
The same first paragraph, given here, could be used in all four cases, but on the opposite page you will see four different combinations of second and third paragraphs. In each case:
(a) complete the passage with appropriate connectors from the list given
(b) decide which approach is being used
(c) give each paragraph a topic heading, and decide on its purpose; in arguing in favour or against, what is the order chosen?

Finally, write the last paragraph for the composition you prefer (or, for further practice, for all four), using the beginning provided.

### Paragraph 1

There is nothing new about the argument between town and country. Some people point to the advantages of the country, with its fresh air, beauty and peace and quiet, while others praise the excitement of the town and stress the advantages it offers in terms of opportunities for employment, schools, hospitals and entertainment.

# 33 Discussion

1) These advantages are the ones that attract people from the country, because it must be admitted that ....................¹ country districts lack essential services, and ....................² life can be dull for young people. ....................³, the city can offer them opportunities, though ....................⁴ they often have to accept boring jobs in factories of offices. They imagine that the city is full of bright lights, and they will easily make friends, but they usually have to live in a room in the suburbs and may be very lonely.

In the country, ....................⁵, everyone knows everyone else, and so neighbours are more willing to help. ....................⁶, even in bad weather the country is beautiful and the air is much healthier than in the city. ....................⁷, the pace of life in the country is slower and there is an atmosphere of peace and quiet, while the city is full of people in a hurry, rushing about and making a noise.

Consequently, in my opinion...

2) Very few people, ....................⁸, have experienced life in the city and in the country in similar conditions. Country people who move to the city usually do so because they need work; those who move out of the city often go on working there. Most people see the other way of life on holiday, and imagine they would like to live there because they only see the best side of it.

....................⁹, the farmer who gets up early to milk the cows thinks it would be pleasant to work in an office and get home at six, but he wouldn't like to stand in queues with thousands of other people and waste two hours a day travelling to and from work. ....................¹⁰, the city worker goes out to the country at weekends in summer, breathes the pure air and imagines working in the peace and quiet, but doesn't think of the hard life farmers have in winter, or how bored he would be in a village with only the TV to entertain him.

My conclusion is, therefore, that...

3) The country and the city each have advantages and disadvantages. People in the country live in more beautiful surroundings. They enjoy peace and quiet, and can do their work at their own pace because no one is in a hurry. ....................¹¹, they live in larger, more comfortable houses, and their neighbours are more friendly, and ready to help them when they need it. ....................¹², their life can be boring, and they may be isolated, a long way from the nearest town, which is a serious problem if they are ill or have to take children to school.

The city, ....................¹³, has all the services the country lacks, but it also has a lot of disadvantages. ....................¹⁴, cities are often ugly and polluted; ....................¹⁵, they not only have bad air but are also noisy; ....................¹⁶, everyone is always in a hurry, and this means that people have no time to get to know each other and make friends.

To sum up, ...

4) It is quite natural for people to enjoy the countryside and want to go there at weekends. The fresh air and the peace and quiet are perfect for relaxation. The situation for people who live there, ....................¹⁷, is different. ....................¹⁸, there is very little entertainment. Most city people would soon get bored if they had nothing to do in the evenings but talk to the same neighbours. People in the country are supposed to be more friendly but ....................¹⁹ they are just more inquisitive. ....................²⁰, when the weather is bad, it is much better to live in a warm flat with central heating than in a cold, draughty farmhouse.

Cities are noisy, dirty, full of people rushing about, and often ugly. But cities have a lot of practical advantages. They offer a choice of jobs, a choice of services, a choice of entertainment. There is no reason for anyone to be bored or lonely in a city.

Consequently, in my opinion, ...

Some connectors can be used in more than one space, but do not use any of those in the list more than once.

above all   actually   apart from that
finally   for example   for one thing
however   in contrast   in fact
in general   in particular   in practice
in theory   in the first place
in the same way   nevertheless
on the whole   on the other hand
secondly   worst of all

## 33 Discussion

### ✏ Further Practice

Study the table of positive and negative points below, decide which are the most important, and answer the questions.

Then choose an approach and adopt the appropriate technique to write a composition on '*Travelling by air is preferable to travelling by train*'.

| Air | | Train | | Questions |
|---|---|---|---|---|
| + | − | + | − | |
| speed | limited seats | more room | slowness | distance? |
| cleanness | discomfort | comfort | dirt | real time? |
| timekeeping | cancellation | reliability | delay | risk? |
| no luggage | danger | safety | luggage | |
| modern airport | bad food | choice of food | old station | |
| package tour | more expensive | cheaper | own arrangements | |

1 How far do you have to travel before flying becomes much quicker?
2 In answering that, have you taken into account the time that it takes to reach the airport as compared with the station and how long you have to wait before the flight is called, and on arrival, to collect luggage etc.?
3 Is it really more dangerous to travel by plane – crashes less frequent, but almost always fatal, hijacking?

In many cases, you will not be asked to compare two possibilities with advantages and disadvantages but consider the advantages and disadvantages of one thing or idea. Use the plan given below in the same way, and answer the questions.

Then choose an approach and adopt the appropriate technique to write a composition on '*It is an advantage for a country to have a strong tourist industry*'.

| + | − | Questions |
|---|---|---|
| Earns foreign currency | Not a stable source of income | tourists? |
| Makes country better known | Destroys national identity | welcome? |
| Shares cultural heritage | Heritage not appreciated | profit? |
| Encourages business | Encourages souvenir shops | |
| Maintains national customs | Cheapens national customs | |

1 What sort of tourists would you like in your country, and what sort do you get? Why would you like them to visit your country? Why do they visit it?
2 Are tourists really welcome, or only welcomed by those who earn money from tourism?
3 Does the country as a whole benefit economically, or only a small group of people?

In the same way as for the previous topic, write a composition on '*Women with children should not go to work*'.

| + | − | Questions |
|---|---|---|
| Children better looked after | Increases family income | motive? |
| Woman cannot do two jobs well | Life more rewarding | who? |
| Home neglected | Justifies studies | how long? |
| Woman's real purpose in life | Impossible to resume career | |
| Respect for family | Self-respect | |

1 Why is the woman likely to go on working? Because she has to or because she enjoys it?
2 Who is most likely to put forward the + and − arguments, a man or a woman?
3 Does the question mean only young children or until they are grown up?

# 34 Summary: dialogue

## ✏️ Comparing a dialogue and a summary

Read the dialogue, and make a list of the points Terry makes in favour of the Post Office being privatised and those that Fiona makes against it. Put them in order of importance.

Then compare your list with the summary below, and compare the summary with the dialogue.

Are the same points included in the summary as in your list?

Which parts of the dialogue are left out?

**TERRY:** I think the Post Office should be privatised. Firms are much more efficient. This letter has taken six days to reach me, and it's only travelled 100 miles.

**FIONA:** Well, letters usually reach me in two days, and sometimes on the same day. I doubt if the service would improve if companies took it over. At least the Post Office has a legal responsibility to deliver the letters sooner or later.

**TERRY:** Later rather than sooner! The newspapers and the milk are delivered on my doorstep every day, because the newsagent and the milkman want to make a profit. That's why so many firms use messengers to deliver their mail, instead of trusting the Post Office. The messengers have an incentive to deliver on time.

**FIONA:** But that isn't a fair comparison. They don't take the milk from a particular cow and address it to a particular person 100 miles away! Messengers are all right if you are in the same town, or for business circulars, where you deliver the same thing to every house. It's different if you're dealing with personal letters.

**TERRY:** Well, I think a private firm would make a better job of it!

**FIONA:** No, firms would take all the easy, profitable business, like the circulars, but if you lived in the country, and only got a few letters, they might take six weeks, because the company wouldn't make a profit unless you paid extra for the stamps.

Terry thinks that the Post Office should be privatised because firms are more efficient. He thinks many firms use messengers because they have an incentive to deliver on time, like the newsagent and the milkman.

Fiona does not agree. Letters usually reach her on time, and the Post Office has a responsibility to deliver them. Comparisons with the messengers are unfair because the Post Office has to deliver particular letters addressed to a particular person. If private firms delivered the mail, they would concentrate on the profitable business and people living in the country would suffer. (98 words)

Read the following dialogue, and summarise it in not more than 100 words.

First, make a list of the main points in each person's argument, and then write two paragraphs, expressing each point of view. Begin: Lucy thinks... Steve does not agree. He thinks...

**LUCY:** I think it's a pity that they're not going to teach Latin any more in most schools. I liked it. I found it very useful.

**STEVE:** Well, I didn't. I thought it was a total waste of time. What's the point of learning a dead language that no one speaks?

**LUCY:** Well, I enjoyed it. And because it's such a logical language it helped me with my English. I think a lot of the complaints about young people not writing English very well these days are due to the fact that they don't teach grammar any more.

**STEVE:** I can't see how Latin helps you with English. English doesn't follow the same grammatical rules. It's much more streamlined. You don't have to learn masculine and feminine and neuter, or conjugate verbs. I mean, why should a table be feminine? It's a thing!

**LUCY:** That's true, but it has a system behind it. Latin helps you to appreciate that there's a system behind English, too.

**STEVE:** I see what you mean, but I don't agree. English is a living language, and so it changes. We don't speak like our parents, do we? I think people should pay attention to the rules, but they should study modern English models, not pretend it has the same rules as Latin.

# 34 Summary

## Practice

Angela Brooks, Jordi Roca and Sofía Constantinides are attending an International Conference on traffic problems in European cities. Read the discussion, and then answer the questions and complete the tasks on the opposite page.

**ANGELA:** The main problem we have in London, I think, is simply that there are so many cars, and the roads haven't been developed enough to cope with the increase in the traffic. It takes the same amount of time to travel into the centre of London by car from the outer suburbs as it did fifty years ago.

**JORDI:** We have similar problems in Barcelona, because the number of registrations of new cars has doubled in the past year, but it's more serious. The city is much more compact, and more people go to work by car because they live nearer. We haven't enough parking space, and people are very careless about parking.

**ANGELA:** We discourage people from bringing cars into the centre of the city and leaving them there. You can only leave a car at a parking meter for two hours, and we have employed a lot of traffic wardens to fine people if they stay there too long.

**JORDI:** We have a lot of underground car parks now, but they're expensive and people don't use them. The main problem is that some people block the roads completely at certain times of day – vans delivering goods to shops and parents taking their children to school and collecting them in the afternoons.

**SOFÍA:** We have that problem, too, but the most serious problem in Athens is pollution. At times we have to limit the number of cars coming into the city, as we used to when petrol was so expensive.

**ANGELA:** How do you do that?

**SOFÍA:** Well, if the pollution reaches a certain level, and people are really ill, we say that only odd-numbered or even-numbered cars can go into the city. People obey this rule, because it's easy for a policeman to spot an odd number or an even number.

**JORDI:** I don't think people in Barcelona would accept a rule like that. It would be chaotic, because businessmen would only be able to go to work every other day if we used it as a regular system.

**ANGELA:** But surely they could use public transport, buses or the underground?

**JORDI:** Yes, but the underground and the trains do not reach all the outlying districts as they do in London, and it's also a matter of habit. If you are used to travelling by train, you don't mind so much.

**SOFÍA:** I think you have to be firm when people's health is at stake. Personally, I would like to see people going to work on bicycles, as they do in Denmark and the Netherlands.

**ANGELA:** You see quite a lot of people on bicycles nowadays in the centre of London, but of course it's very dangerous. I'd rather use the underground or a bus myself.

**JORDI:** Well, in Barcelona, it would be suicide! The streets are too narrow for us to introduce bicycle lanes, and with so many cars double-parked, and the motorists not being used to it, cyclists would be risking their lives every minute.

## Comprehension

1 List the main traffic problems in (a) London (b) Barcelona (c) Athens.
2 Give reasons for them.
3 What solutions have been adopted to solve these problems, and how successful are they in different cities?
4 Why does Jordi think that the solutions adopted in London and Athens would not work so well in Barcelona?
5 Why does Sofía propose that people should go to work on bicycles, and what are Angela's and Jordi's reactions to this?

# 34 Summary

## Summarising Information in Dialogue

There are a number of different ways of summarising the content of this discussion. We can contrast the situation in the different cities; we can concentrate on different problems and solutions; we can concentrate on different speakers. In each case below one paragraph has been completed for you. Write two more paragraphs along the lines suggested.

(a) The main traffic problem in London is the fact that the number of cars has increased, but the roads have not been developed enough to cope with the increase.

In Barcelona, the same problem exists, but...
In Athens the most serious problem is...

(b) The authorities have tried to limit the traffic in London by...

In Barcelona, there are a lot of underground car parks, but people do not use them and often block the traffic by double-parking. One solution is to take the drastic action favoured in Athens, where at times only half the cars are allowed into the city.

Other solutions are to...

(c) Angela Brooks says the main problem in London is that the roads have not been developed enough to cope with the increase in traffic. The authorities control the number of cars by using parking meters. If the problem were as serious as it is in Barcelona, she thinks that people should be persuaded to use public transport, but she considers that riding bicycles to go to work is very dangerous.

Sofía Constantinides says the main problem in Athens is... The only way the authorities have solved this is... She would like... because...

Jordi Roca thinks the parking problem in Barcelona is... because... He does not believe... the drastic solution used in Athens... He thinks Angela's suggestion... Finally, he thinks riding bicycles in Barcelona...

## Reporting a Discussion

If you had to report this discussion, as on p. 87, you would need to follow the course of it in the order in which people spoke, changing tenses, but use the techniques of summary to convey only the main points. Continue this report in the same style to the end of the discussion.

Ms Brooks said the main problem in London was that the roads had not been developed enough to cope with the increase in traffic. Mr Roca said there were similar problems in Barcelona, but they were more serious because the city was more compact, they hadn't enough parking space and people were careless about parking. Ms Brooks said the authorities controlled the number of cars in London by using parking meters. Mr Roca replied that...

Ms Constantinides said the main problem in Athens was...

# 35 Formal Writing: letters to the editor

## Responding to letters

In 1988 the Kingman report on the teaching of the English language in English schools was published. It caused many people to write to the newspapers. Read the first two letters, and answer the questions on them.

---

Sir,

As a businessman responsible for recruiting a large number of university graduates and other school-leavers every year, I was disappointed to read in the Kingman report that the Committee 'do not see it as part of our task to plead for a return to old-fashioned grammar teaching'.

Half of the young people interviewed by my firm make spelling mistakes in their applications; many more are not even given an interview because they are so illiterate that they cannot communicate their ideas clearly. The reason for this is that they have never been taught the rules, and by this time I wonder if their teachers know them.

The Kingman Committee have failed in their duty by not making it plain that the decline of the English language nowadays is due to sloppy teaching methods, allowing children to write what they like in the interests of what is called 'self-expression'. The present chaos will not be resolved until good old-fashioned methods are restored in order to teach good English.

**John Groby**
London SW1

---

Sir,

It was almost inevitable that the Kingman Committee would come up with the idea that children should be taught the difference between 'correct' and 'incorrect' English, and that it was desirable to teach them grammatical terminology. It is what one would expect of a body set up by the Government with a right-wing chairman.

English is a living language, changing every day, so what right has Sir John Kingman to tell me or anyone else what is correct and incorrect? I wonder if you, as a practising journalist, sir, can tell me if it has ever helped you in your profession to be able to analyse sentences and chop them up into subject-verb-predicate and so on. Good English is what the majority of people use today, not something you can learn in a lot of books based on dead languages

**Gary Trend**
Basildon

---

1. How does the way these two correspondents address the editor of the *Daily Post* differ from what they would say in a normal business letter.
2. Both writers criticise the Kingman Committee, but for different reasons. What are they?
3. What do you think is Mr Groby's idea of 'good English', and what is Mr Trend's?
4. Why don't they agree about the teaching of grammar?

These letters were published in the *Daily Post* on May 20th.

## Practice 1

Read Caroline Merchant's letter, published on May 24th, noting the way in which she draws attention to the publication of Mr Groby's letter, and refers to the points made in it.

Then write a letter to the Editor, using the same form of reference, expressing your opinion of Mr Trend's letter.

---

Sir,

Mr John Groby's letter attacking the work of the Kingman Committee (*Daily Post*, May 20) shows a complete failure to understand the nature of the problem. Mr Groby is right to be concerned about falling standards in English usage but wrong in my opinion in thinking that old-fashioned teaching methods based on formal grammatical exercises provide a satisfactory solution.

As an English teacher, I am well aware that there is such a thing as 'good English'. But it must be defined in terms of clarity and precise use of language, which is what concerns Mr Groby most. It does not help students to give them inexplicable rules based on Latin.

Abandoning traditional methods of memorising grammatical terms and analysing the parts of speech in sentences does not mean abandoning teaching of handwriting, punctuation, spelling, vocabulary and sentence or paragraph construction. It does not mean, either, that teachers allow students to write what they like. What matters is to make children aware of what they are saying and how they are saying it, so that they can express their thoughts clearly and recognise the advantages of 'good English' in their own writing.

**Caroline Merchant**
Kettering

# 35 Formal writing

## Practice 2

Read the following letters published on June 4th in the *English News*, an English-language newspaper in your own country, and write letters to the Editor, disagreeing either with (a) or (b), and with either (c) or (d). You can use ideas and vocabulary from other letters on the page, but should express your own opinions.

### (a)
Sir,

As the father of four children of school age, I am getting very tired of the one-day strikes called by teachers in support of their pay claims. These strikes do not affect all schools on the same day, so that in a family like ours, where the wife also goes out to work, we never know how many of our children are going to be at home, and what arrangements we must make to look after the younger ones.

The teachers' attitude is totally irresponsible. They have deliberately chosen to go on strike at a time when all children are concerned about their end-of-term examinations. How can they claim to belong to a responsible profession when they are obviously not concerned about the education, health and welfare of the children in their care? Their behaviour can only be compared to that of doctors and nurses refusing to treat people in hospital on certain days, and allowing them to die.

**Ralph Baker**

### (b)
Sir,

As a teacher unfortunately involved in strike action forced on us by the refusal of the Ministry of Education to consider our pay claim, I have frequently been insulted during the last few days by angry parents, and have twice been threatened with physical violence.

I would like to make use of your columns to point out to parents among your readers that teachers are underpaid and overworked. Many parents show no respect for the teaching profession, and think of us as people paid to look after their children while they can both go out to work and earn more money than we do. In my opinion, this is partly the result of teachers being poorly paid. Instead of threatening to attack us for taking the only action that remains in order to convince the Ministry, they should put pressure on the Ministry itself. The only way to resolve the problem is to pay us a fair salary, justified by our years of study to obtain qualifications.

**Anne Hart**

### (c)
Sir,

Last Wednesday evening, when my husband and I came home at ten thirty, after visiting some friends, we were shocked to find our three children, aged 11 to 15, watching a violent American film that not only contained horrifying scenes of gangsters killing and torturing one another, but also some explicit sex scenes.

My husband immediately telephoned the television service to protest at the film being shown at a time when children are likely to be awake, though in my opinion such films should not be shown at any time. The person who answered noted our complaint, but said that restrictions only applied up to ten o'clock.

I trust that you will publish this letter, since I am sure that there are may parents like ourselves who would like these films to be banned.

**Margaret Whitehouse**

### (d)
Sir,

I am writing to protest about the Government wasting money to set up yet another commission to inquire into broadcasting standards, with the power to monitor, and if necessary, censor television programmes.

It is quite clear that although the commission is supposed to be concerned with the increase of sex and violence in TV series, its real objective is to limit freedom of speech by banning programmes unfavourable to the Government. The old argument about children being exposed to violence on TV is complete nonsense, because such films are not shown before 10 o'clock when children should be in bed, anyway, and parents who object can easily turn off the set or change channels. In my view, the Government wants to use this as an excuse to censor news programmes that indicate the amount of violence in the real world so that people will remain ignorant of contemporary problems.

**Stanley Livingstone**

## Further Practice

Write a letter to the Editor of an English-language newspaper in your country on one of the following topics:

1 Suggest ways in which facilities for young people in the city or town could be improved.
2 Protest against the destruction of an area of natural beauty or of architectural interest in order to provide new houses.
3 Criticise the treatment of women at work or in public places.
4 Propose a peaceful demonstration in the centre of the city or town against something you consider unjust.
5 Draw attention to a dangerous crossing where a number of accidents have taken place, and ask for traffic lights to be installed.

# 36 Guided Writing: solving problems

## How did the thieves get in?

Paul and Julie Stewart live in Flat 18 of a block of flats. It is on the third floor, and there is no lift, so the only way to reach it is to climb the stairs and come through the front door. The door has two locks, one that shuts it from inside and another, also requiring a key, that locks from outside and bolts the door.

Apart from that, Julie always locks the glass door in the kitchen that leads to the small terrace at the back of the house, and bolts the kitchen door from the living-room side with a bolt about 50 cm. above the floor.

When Paul and Julie arrived home from two weeks' holiday abroad last week they were surprised to discover that the front door was locked but not bolted from the outside. When they opened the door, they saw that thieves had got into the flat. The only thing they had taken, however, was a cabinet from the living room containing a record player, radio and cassette player. The door from the living-room to the kitchen had been smashed with an axe, so there was a large hole in it, and it had been unbolted. The glass door in the kitchen was broken.

The flat next door, number 17, has not been occupied for six months, and there is a notice outside saying that it is for sale. When Paul and Julie went outside again, they saw that the door knob on the front door of number 17 had been unscrewed and the lock had been picked, but the door was shut. Then they realised how the thieves had entered their flat, and what they had done.

Write an account of how the thieves got into Flat 18. To do so, you must answer the following questions:
1. How did the thieves realise that they could not get into Flat 18 through the front door? Why did they think that Flat 17 was not occupied?
2. How did they get into Flat 17? What did they do with the door knob?
3. How did they get into Flat 18? What problems did they have? How did they solve them?
4. What did they do before leaving Flat 18?

Begin: 'When the thieves saw the front door of Flat 18, they must have realised they could not get in that way because . . . but they suspected Flat 17 was empty because . . .'

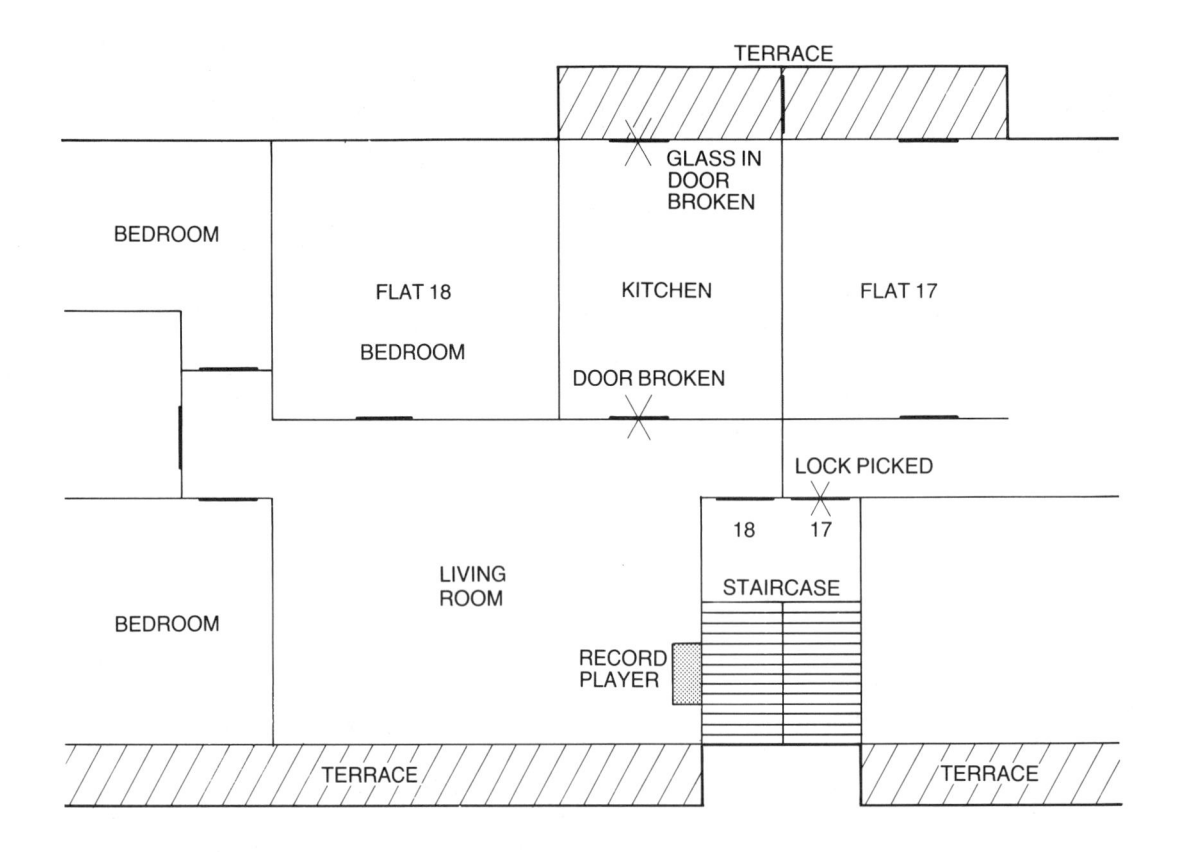

# 36 Guided writing

## Which route?

Paul and Julie spent two days' holiday in the Lake District last summer. Paul is very interested in the work of the poet Wordsworth, and he wanted to see his birthplace, Cockermouth, and the houses where he lived, Dove Cottage, Grasmere, and Rydal Mount, overlooking Rydal Water. Julie was more interested in the beauty of the lakes themselves, and in particular she wanted to hire a boat and sail on Ullswater or Windermere.

There are hotels in Cockermouth, Keswick, Grasmere and Ambleside. Paul and Julie wanted to find a way of seeing everything they wanted to see in two days without driving over the same roads.

Decide where they stayed, and plan the route for two excursions in different directions, enabling them to see all the lakes, visit Wordsworth's birthplace and houses and sail on one of the lakes where boats were for hire.

You should write two paragraphs, beginning like this:
1. Paul and Julie decided to stay at ... because ... On the first day, they drove towards ... They took the ... road to ..., passing by Lake ...
2. On the second day, they drove towards ...

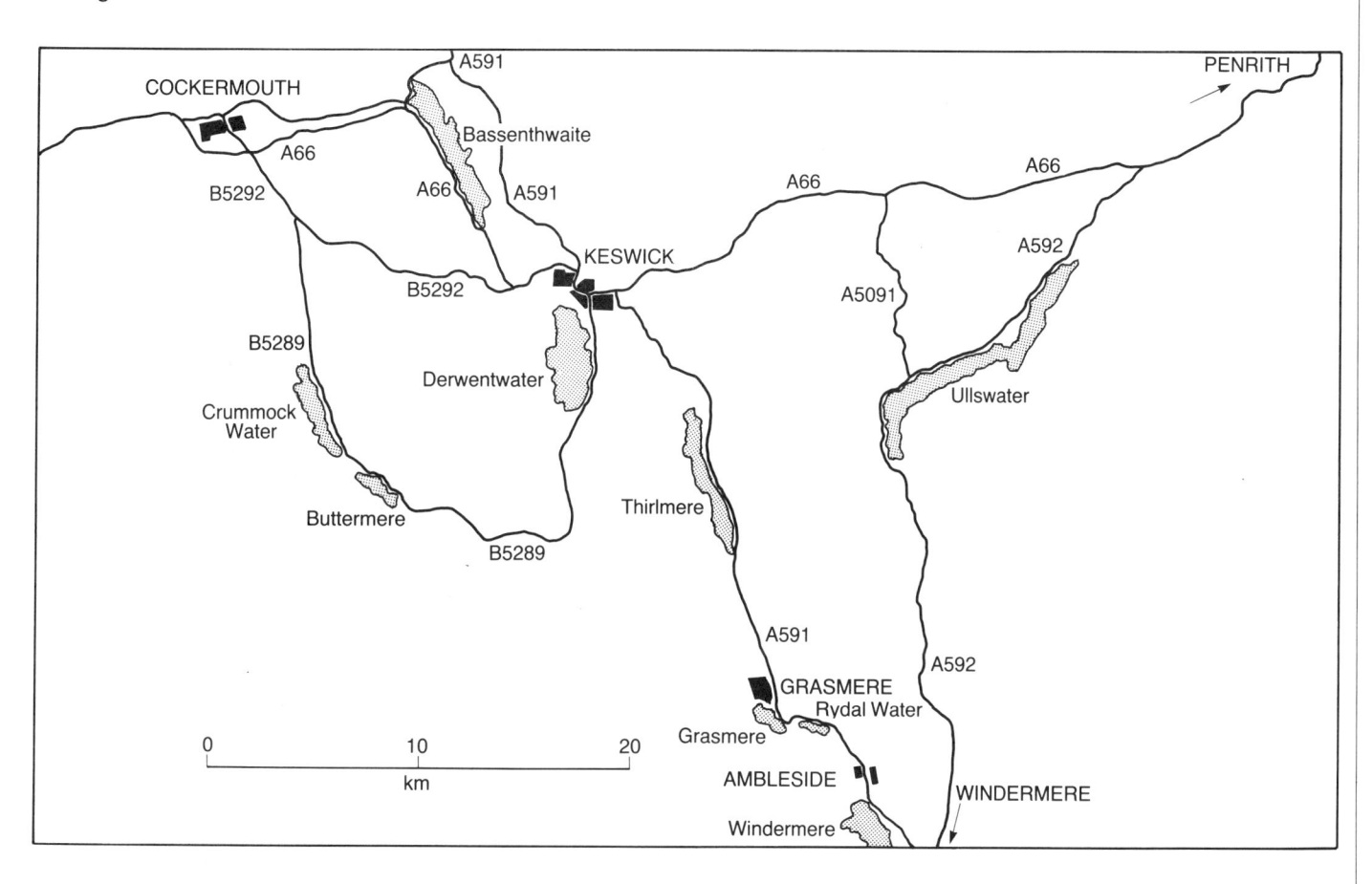

# Reference Section
## Unit 1

## A Personal Letters

Use the advice given here for reference when writing personal letters.

### 1 Address

Note the punctuation and layout of the address on p. 1. In Britain, people usually put their own address in the top right-hand corner. It is not usual to write the address of the person you are writing to in a personal letter. If you are asked to write a letter from your own address, do not translate it or change the order of words in the code.

### 2 Date

The date may be written **April 17**, **April 17th**, **17 April** or **17th April**. Note the abbreviations **1st** (first), **2nd** (second) and **3rd** (third). All others end in **th** (**4th**, **5th**) except **21st**, **22nd**, **23rd**, **31st**.

### 3 Beginning the Letter

The correct way to begin any English letter is to write **Dear** followed by what you would call the person addressed if you spoke to him/her: **Father**, **Aunt Jane**, **Richard**, **Mr Smith**, **Mrs**, **Ms** or **Miss Jones**. The choice in the last three cases is complicated by recent changes, but if you do not know the person or know if she prefers to be addressed as **Mrs** (a married woman) or **Miss** (a single woman), it is best to write **Ms**. *Do not* write 'Dear friend', because we usually call our friends by their names when we speak to them. English people use more affectionate variations such as **My dear**, **Dearest** etc., but although it is safe to imitate them in real life, it is not wise to do so in a composition task or examination.

### 4 Short forms

Many English people use short forms (*I'll*, *We've*, *You won't* etc.) in personal letters, and this is acceptable, but you should not get into the habit of using them in formal business letters or general compositions, except when you are writing dialogue.

### 5 Endings

Most English people end their letters to friends and relations as informally as possible: **Sincerely**, **Affectionately**, **Love**. **Yours sincerely** is the normal form to use in a personal letter to someone you address by name when the letter is more formal (see Richard Connor's letter on p. 2).

## B Tenses

A number of different sequences are likely to occur in personal letters. The following points are valid in all cases, but particularly important in such contexts.

### 1 Present Perfect/Past

The main problem in choosing between the present perfect and past tenses in British English can be overcome if you remember that the present perfect tense refers to fact, without a time reference, while the past tense refers to past time (in American English these distinctions are not always observed). So we say:
   *I **have written** to your parents.*
but
   *I **wrote** to your parents yesterday.*
In referring to a letter received, we can either talk about it in the past, thinking of when we read it, or in the present, if the facts are still true:
   *I **was/am happy** to hear that you are well.*

### 2 Future Plans and Intentions

We use the present continuous tense, with a future time expression, for plans we have already made. It is therefore commonly used with verbs of movement (*going*, *coming*, *arriving* etc.):
   *Katerina **is coming** to England in July.*
We use the *going to* form for personal intention:
   ***I'm going to** write to the Staffords to thank them for their invitation.*
We use the present simple tense for such future events as are contained in timetables – flights, train arrivals and departures, courses or holidays booked in advance:
   *Katerina's course in Cambridge **lasts** a month.*
The future with *will* appears most often in subordinate clauses referring to the future:
It also appears as the main clause with a time clause using a word or phrase like *when, as soon as, before, after, until*. Note the tense of the verb in the subordinate clause (present):
   *As soon as the wedding **is** over, we'**ll go** home.*
   *We'**ll go** home as soon as the wedding **is** over.*
The same combination of tenses and alternative order, where either clause can come first, is used in conditional sentences (Type 1):
   *If you (can) **come** this summer, we'**ll be** happy to put you up.*
The future continuous tense occurs when we are thinking about an action likely to continue for some time at a future date:
   *We'**ll be** thinking of you on the day when you **get married**.*

# Reference Section

### 3 Polite forms

When we invite people to our house or to a wedding, for example, we must give them the opportunity of refusing politely. We therefore use a conditional form: *would you like to...?*

If you haven't seen this play, **would you like** to join us?

We also continue to use the conditional in subsequent phrases referring to the invitation since it would be rude to assume that the other person will accept:

**It would be** lovely if you could come.
**Could (Would)** you let me know if you would like to come?

It is polite to use the imperative construction, too, provided we use the word 'please':

**Please** write soon and tell me if you can come.

### 4 Future reference in past time

Compare the use of tenses here to those used in Future Plans and Intentions (Section 2).

It **is thoughtful** of you to enquire whether we **are coming** down on the previous evening and to offer to find us somewhere to stay.
It **was thoughtful** of you to enquire (in your letter) whether we **were coming** down on the previous evening...

## C *For, Since, Ago, During*

We associate *for* and *since* with the present perfect tenses, *ago* with the past tenses, though *for* can also be used with the past tenses. For the difference between *for* and *since*, compare the following:

I **haven't written** to you **for** such a long time/six months/two years.
I **haven't written** to you **since** last Christmas/you got married.

*For* refers to the duration of time, with the present perfect tenses until now. *Since* refers to the time in the past when the action began. The main verb is always present perfect (or past perfect, but not past) though the clause that follows it may be in a past tense (got married) in which the time is indicated by the action.

*Ago* refers to a point in past time measured from now and is associated with the past tenses:

Your letter **arrived** two days **ago**.

*During* means 'at some time within a period of time'. Compare its use with that of *for* in these sentences:

Katerina **is coming** to stay **for** a few days in July. (duration of stay)
Katerina **is coming** to stay with us **during** the summer. (at some time in that season of the year)

## D *Expect, hope, look forward to, wait (for)*

*Expect* refers to what we think will happen (good or bad) in the future:

I'**m expecting** an answer to my letter soon.
I **expect** to receive/that I will receive an answer soon.

*Hope* refers to what we want to happen in the future (good), whether we think it will or not:

I **hope you'll** be able to come and see us.

*Look forward* to means 'expect to be pleased by...' so it combines the meanings of *expect* and *hope*. It is conventionally used as an ending in letters because we expect an answer for reasons of politeness and also hope for one, since we want to know what the other person will say.

I'**m looking forward to** your reply/**hearing** from you. (not 'hear' from you)

*Wait* is an activity, whereas the other verbs reflect states of mind:

I haven't heard from her yet. I'**m waiting** for her letter/the postman to arrive.

## E Useful Words and Phrases

### 1 Polite endings

(My) best wishes/kindest regards/love (to...); ... sends his/her best wishes/kindest regards/love (to...)

### 2 Thanks

Thank you (Thanks) very much for...; I'm very grateful to you for...; It is very kind of you to...

### 3 Apology, regret

I'm sorry (I can't)...; I regret (that I can't)... (more formal); it's (such) a pity that...

### 4 Congratulation

We wish you all the best (on the day/for the future); Our best wishes...

# Unit 2

## A Tenses

### 1 Past tenses in narrative

Narratives in chronological order are told mainly in the past simple and past continuous tenses.
We use the past simple tense for a series of actions in the order in which they occurred:

He **opened** the door, **went** into the room and **sat down**.

95

# Reference Section

The past simple and past continuous tenses are found in three basic combinations:
1 Sequence of actions (as in the example above)
2 Action taking place before, and possibly continuing after, the main action:
   *I **was writing** a letter **when** the lights **went out**.*
3 Actions continuing side by side in past time:
   *I **was writing** a letter, my wife **was reading** a book, and my son was watching a film on TV.*

Therefore in a question-and-answer situation, the sequence would appear like this:
*What **did** you **do when** the lights **went out**?*
*I **went** out onto the landing.*
*What **were** you **doing** when the lights **went out**?*
*I **was writing** a letter.*

## 2 Future reference in past time

As already shown in 1B4, future reference requires the conditional form (would):
*They were afraid that they **would miss** their flight.*
*They were wondering if the bus **would arrive** on time.*

## 3 Tense changes in reported speech

Use this table of examples for reference.

| Direct | Reported |
| --- | --- |
| I'm working very hard. | He said he was working ... |
| I earn £100 a week. | He said he earned ... |
| I'm going to change my job. | He said he was going to ... |
| I'll finish it soon. | He said he would finish ... |
| I've never seen her before. | He said he had never seen ... |
| I didn't break it. | He said he hadn't broken it. |
| I can run faster than Mary. | He said he could run faster ... |
| It may be too late. | He said it might be too late. |

## B Say and Tell

1 *Say* means 'speak words'. It has no personal object. *Tell* usually means 'inform a person', and with this meaning always has a personal object.
   *'Hello,' Paul **said**.*
   *Tell* cannot be used here because *Hello* is not information, and there is no personal object. Compare this with the following:
   *'It looks as if the whole city is affected,' I **told my wife**/**said**.*
   *I **told my wife**/**said** that it looked as if the whole city was affected.*
2 In reported commands we normally use *tell* with the infinitive:
   *My wife **told my son** to go to bed. (Go to bed!)*

## C Verbs of the senses with infinitive/present participle

With verbs of the senses like *see* and *hear*, the infinitive is used afterwards for a single or completed action, the present participle for an incomplete or continuing action.
*I **heard** him **say**: 'Help!'* (one word)
*I **heard** some people **arguing** in loud voices* (conversation continued)
*I **saw** the car **stop** at the traffic lights* (completed action)
*I **saw** the cars **moving** slowly up the hill* (incomplete action).

The verbs of the senses are often used with *can* and *could* in such sentences:
*I **could see** the light slowly **coming** towards us.*

## D Prepositions of time

Note the use of *at*, *on* and *in* in the combinations shown below:

**at**  for exact points of time: **at five o'clock, at dinner time, at this moment**.
festivals: **at Christmas, at Easter, at New Year**.
others: **at night** (but **during** the day), **at weekends, at the weekend**.

**on**  for days and dates: **on Monday, on June 10th, on Christmas Day, on a summer evening, on a Sunday morning, on Wednesday night**.

**in**  longer periods of time: **in August, in spring, in 1968, in the twentieth century, in the Middle Ages, in the past, in the future**.
periods of time within which or at the end of which something may happen; note the use of the apostrophe: **in five minutes, in a week's time, in three years' time, in the morning, in the afternoon, in the evening**.

\* **by** = 'at some time not later than'
*I'll pay you **at** the end of the month* (**on** the 30th or 31st)
*I'll pay you **by** the end of the month* (**at** some time **during** the month, but certainly not later than the end)

## E Time expressions

1 Study the use of time expressions in the following sentences:
*When the lights went out, I was writing a letter.*
*While I was writing a letter, my wife was reading a book.*
*As soon as the lights went out, I went out onto the landing.*
*I looked round, saw everything was in darkness, and then went back into the living-room.*
*As I stood looking out of the window, I saw lights beginning to come on again.*
*We had to spend an hour and a half in darkness before the lights came on.*
*We did not find out the reason for the failure until the next day.*

*After* the lights came on again, my son wanted to see the film on TV.
The lights went on in the next street, and **immediately afterwards**, in our flat.

2 Learn the following time expressions and when they are used. Use this list for reference in future narrative compositions.

**at first, in the beginning.** These are not used in making a list of points in an argument, where we say: *first, in the first place, to begin with*.
**in the end, finally.** The first is not used in argument. In describing places, we usually say *at the end* (of the street).
**eventually** = after a long period of time
**gradually** = slowly, over a period of time, little by little
**immediately** = without delay, without time passing, at once
**suddenly** = unexpectedly
**at last** comes at the end of a long series of events
**at the moment** = now; **at this moment** may mean 'now', but in context may mean the time referred to in a story, for example
**at once** = immediately
**at one time** refers to the past, contrasted to the present
**for the time being** = until things change
**in time** = not too late to do something (compare: *on time*)
**in the meantime** = meanwhile
**in due course** = in the future, at the proper time
**now and then** = from time to time, at irregular intervals
**on time** = at the time agreed, expected
**these days** = at the present time
**in those days** refers to the past
**nowadays** refers to the present in contrast to the past
**at present/at the present time** = now
**presently** (British English) = soon; in American English = now
**recently, lately** (usually with present perfect tense) = not long ago
**in recent years, during the last few years** (usually with present perfect tense) = not many years ago.

## F Vocabulary

In attempting the written tasks for further practice in this unit, you may need some of the words and phrases below. Look up their meanings in a dictionary if you do not know them already.
1 *flames*; *smoke*; *catch fire*; *set fire to*; *fire brigade*; *fireman*; *hose*.
4 (a) *ward, matron, sister* (in a hospital), *patient, night duty, emergency*.

# Unit 3

## A Adjectives, position and word order

1 Look at the use of *and* in these sentences. It is very seldom used to join adjectives before a noun, but it often appears when the adjectives are a complement, following *be*:
Aunt Barbara is a warm, friendly person.
Aunt Barbara is warm **and** friendly.
2 Note the use of commas when more than two adjectives are used together:
Gary Cooper was a tall, slim, handsome man.
Gary Cooper was tall, slim **and** handsome.
3 We usually put the more precise adjective nearest to the noun that follows but it is not always easy to decide which is more precise. Use the table given here as a guide for reference on adjective order.
 1 **both, all, half**
 2 **the**
 3 Ordinal number: **first, last**
 4 Cardinal number: **one, three**
 5 General judgement: **good, bad, nice**
 6 Measurement: **big, tall**
 7 Physical characteristics: **beautiful, slim**
 8 Mental characteristics: **intelligent, stupid**
 9 Age or temperature: **old, young, hot**
 10 Shape: **round, square**
 11 Colour: **red, green**
 12 Verb particle form: **carved, boiling**
 13 Material: **wooden**
 14 Origin, nationality: **French, Mediterranean**
 15 Noun used as an adjective: **steel, cigarette**
You are not likely to want to use many of these adjectives together, but here are some examples to show how the table works:
**All the first three** films he made were Westerns (1,2,3,4)
She has **large, green** eyes and a **lovely, slim** figure (6,11)(5,7)
He was an **honest young** man with a **round, smiling** face (8,9)(10,12)

## B Verbs describing appearance

*Look, seem* and *appear* are all used to describe what we think of people's appearance or what we imagine they are feeling. Note the different constructions used.
Barbara **looks/seems/appears** impatient.
She **seems/appears** to be angry.
She **looks like** her mother (general comparison – 'They are alike').
He **looks as if** he has ridden horses all his life. (He has probably ridden horses all his life.)

**Reference Section**

## C Verbs describing people's clothes

Note the use of *wear*, *dress*, *be dressed*, and *have (got) . . . on* in these examples:
*Barbara always **wears** high-heeled shoes.*
*She **dresses** well (chooses good clothes etc.)*
*He **was dressed** in (**wore**) a check shirt and jeans.*
*The bride **was dressed** in white.*
*She **had (got)** a white dress **on**.*

## D Tenses: present simple and continuous

We use the present simple tense for regular actions and personal habits. It is associated with adverbs like *always, often, sometimes,* and phrases like *every day, once a week, in the morning*.
*My wife **usually answers** the 'phone.*
*I **get up every day** about seven.*
The present continuous is associated with action in the present time, but not always at this moment:
*I **am doing** extra duty **this week** because I **am looking after** another doctor's patients while he is on holiday.*
But at the moment when the speaker says this, he is probably not looking after them, but talking to a friend.

## E Verbs not usually found in continuous forms

Certain verbs are almost never found in continuous forms. They are mainly verbs connected with senses, thinking, wishing, appearance and possession. Here is a list of the most common ones for reference:
**hear, notice, recognise, see, smell\*, taste; believe, feel** (that), **think** (that)\*; **know, mean, suppose, understand; forget, remember\*; care, dislike, hate, love, want, wish; appear** (= seem); **seem; belong to, consist of, contain, have** (= own, possess), **matter, refuse**
\* Note the following:
*That **smells** good.* (No object.)
*She **is smelling** the rose.* (with an object.)
*What **do** you **think**?* (What is your opinion?)
*What **are** you **thinking**?* (what thoughts are in your mind?)
*Do you **remember** the film we saw?* (Have you any memory of it?)
*Are you **remembering** the film we saw?* (are memories of it going through your mind?)

## F Word order: adverbs of frequency

Note these rules for the word order of adverbs like *always, sometimes, often, never*:
1 After be (including negatives and passives)
*I **am always** ready to visit my patients.*
*He **isn't usually** at home at midday.*
*Appointments **are generally** made by 'phone.*
2 Between auxiliary and be (including negatives and passives)
*She **has always been** kind to me.*
*She **may sometimes be** bad-tempered.*
*I **have often been** called out in the middle of the night.*
3 Before all other main verbs (including negatives and one auxiliary)
*People at surgery **generally have** coughs and colds.*
*We don't **usually have dinner** before nine.*
*I **have never felt** bored in her company.*
\* Note the word order in question forms:
***Do** you **ever get** impatient with your students?*
4 Between two auxiliaries:
*I **may sometimes have made** the wrong diagnosis.*

# Unit 4

## A Formal letters

In addition to the advice given on personal letters (1A), note the following when writing letters for an official purpose.

### 1 Address

It is normal to lay out the address of the person or company receiving the letter in the top left-hand corner, opposite your own address in the right-hand corner. The business address is normally positioned one line below the end of the home address. Most British addresses have a postal code, and addresses in the United States use a similar code, called a 'zip code' – e.g. The Director of Courses, Camford Polytechnic, Camford **CM2 8JT**.
In business letters, the date may appear on the left-hand side.

### 2 Beginning the letter

In formal or business letters, we write **Dear Mr Jones**, **Ms Smith** etc. if we are writing to an individual whose name we know. If we are writing to someone whose name we do not know, such as 'The Director of Courses', we begin **Dear Sir**, unless we know that the recipient is a woman, when we begin **Dear Madam**; if we are writing to a company, we begin **Dear Sirs**, using the plural form. In the United States, it is more common to address the company as **Gentlemen**.

# Reference Section

## 3 Endings

We end a letter to a person addressed by name **Yours sincerely**; a letter that begins **Dear Sir/Dear Madam/Dear Sirs** should end **Yours faithfully/Yours truly**. In the United States, **Yours truly** is preferred.

## 4 Polite forms

As in personal letters (1B3) we use conditional forms to be polite. Note the sequence of tenses in the following:
*I **would be** grateful if you **would (could) send** me further information.*
***Could (Would)** you also **give** me details of accommodation?*
*I **would like** to know how much time is spent on this option.*

# B Useful words and phrases

## 1 Beginnings

*I am writing to you* (not I write you) *with reference to/in connection with...; I was very interested to see your advertisement in...*

## 2 Requests for information

*I would be grateful if you would (could) send me...; Could (Would) you please give me details of...?*

# Unit 5

# A Comparison of adjectives

## 1 Comparative and superlative forms (one syllable and three syllables)

One-syllable adjectives form the comparative with -er and the superlative with est:
*The Tiziano is **cheaper** than the Michelangelo, but the Giotto is the **cheapest** (of the three).*
Adjectives with three or more syllables form the comparative with *more* and the superlative with *most*:
*The Tiziano is **more expensive** than the Giotto, but the Michelangelo is the **most expensive** (of the three).*
* Note the irregular forms:
good **better** **best**
bad **worse** **worst**

## 2 Two-syllable adjectives

Two-syllable adjectives usually form the comparative with *more* and the superlative with *most*, and it is wise to use these forms until a native speaker corrects you, but an important group of adjectives, those ending in -y (e.g. *happy, easy, lucky*) form the comparative with -er and the superlative with -est. Note that the -y changes to i in these forms:
*The Renault 5 was **easier** to park **than** the two cars we have had since, but the Ford Sierra is **the easiest** to drive.*
Other groups that usually take -er and -est are those ending in -le (*noble, gentle*), -ow (*narrow, yellow*) and -er (*clever, tender*). In some cases both forms are found – for example, those ending in -ly (*friendlier, more friendly*).

## 3 Comparison with as/so

When we compare two people or things that are equal, we use *as... as...*
*The Tiziano is **as** comfortable **as** the Michelangelo.*
A negative comparison of this kind can be made with *not as/so... as...* Compare these sentences:
*The Tiziano is **more** expensive **than** the Giotto.*
*The Giotto is **not as/so** expensive **as** the Tiziano.*

## 4 Comparison showing great differences

If we want to emphasise the difference between two things or people, we add the word *much* or *far* to the comparative form:
*The Giotto is **much/far** cheaper **than** the Michelangelo.*
In negative comparisons we add the word *nearly* to the adjective, using the construction, *not as/so... as...*
*The Giotto is **not nearly as/so** comfortable **as** the Michelangelo.*

## 5 Comparison showing small differences

Here we add the words *a little* (*a bit*, conversational) to the comparative form:
*The Tiziano is **a little more** expensive **than** the Giotto.*
In negative comparisons we add the word *quite* to the adjective, using the construction, *not as/so... as...*
*The food is **not quite as** good at the Tiziano (as it is at the Michelangelo).*

# B Comparison of adverbs

The comparative forms of adverbs are made with *more*, the superlative forms, which are rare, with *the most*.
*The staff at the Tiziano did everything **more** cheerfully.*
Exceptions are:

| | | |
|---|---|---|
| well | better | the best |
| badly | worse | the worst |
| hard | harder | the hardest |
| fast | faster | the fastest |
| much | more | the most |

## Reference Section

*The car started to rock when my father drove **faster**.*
*The Tiziano costs **more** than the Giotto.*

The constructions with (*not*) *as* (*so*) ... *as* ... are also used with adverbs:
*She works **as hard as** her brother.*
*He doesn't drive **as** (**so**) **carefully as** his father.*

## C The same ... as/different from

Note the forms used:
*The two hotels are not the same. They are different.*
*They offer the same service at different prices.*
*The service at the Giotto is not **the same as**/is **different from** the service at the Tiziano.*

## D Connectors and modifiers

Organising an argument to express a point of view in modern English depends primarily on the correct use of a number of expressions to connect or modify statements. Notes are provided for different units of the book; in this unit you should concentrate on the following.

### 1 Building up an argument

**In the first place; secondly; thirdly; finally** (list of points).
**Apart from that** (a further point of the same kind).
 *The room was very small and uncomfortable, and **apart from that** there was no bathroom.*
**Above all** (the most important point in the argument, which usually comes last).
**To sum up, in conclusion** (indicating that you are going to give a general opinion on all the points made).
**On the whole, considering all points of view, in general terms.**

### 2 Others

**However, nevertheless, all the same** (modifying what has been said).
**Especially, in particular** (emphasising a particular point or area where it is relevant).
 *I like the Sierra best, **especially** when we are on the motorway.*

# Unit 6

## A Imperative forms

The imperative forms (affirmative and negative) are as used here:
 ***Lock** the front door and **don't let** anyone in.*
If they are used with 'please', the phrase becomes a request, not an order:
 ***Please write** the name of anyone who 'phones on the pad.*

The imperative can take the place of a future tense in conditional clauses and time clauses:
 *If anyone rings, **write** the name on the pad.*
 *When Mr Scott arrives, **introduce** him to the staff.*

## B Future time clauses

The usual combination of tenses in future time clauses is the same as in conditional clauses (1), with a present tense in the clause containing the time phrase (*when, as soon as* etc.) and a future tense in the main clause (but see the note on the use of the imperative (6A).
 *Sheila **will stay** with the children until the Cranes **come** home.*
 *When she sees the children **are asleep**, she'**ll turn off** the light.*
If the action in the time clause must be completed before the other action takes place, we often use a present perfect tense:
 *When the Cranes **have gone out**, Sheila **will lock** the door.*

## C Can

### 1 ability

*Can* implies the ability to do something (in present and future time):
 *You **can do** all the shopping at the supermarket.*
It also implies knowing how to do something:
 *I **can play** the piano but I **can't play** the violin.*
It can be used in place of a future tense in time clauses and conditional clauses:
 *If/When the children get bored, you **can read** them a story.*

### 2 permission

It is more frequently used nowadays than *may* to give people permission to do things, referring to future time:
 *Gordon **can pay** the men overtime if it is necessary.*
The negative form is *can't*, and past forms (in reported speech) are *could/couldn't*.

## D Must

### 1 Orders

Orders can be given in the imperative, but frequently the speaker is explaining an order to a third person and in that case we use *must*:
 *Gordon **must make sure** they don't spend too much money.*

### 2 Obligation

In effect, Gordon has an obligation to obey orders. In the first person, *must* indicates an obligation we feel ourselves:

*I **must make sure** that the children are in bed by 8.30.*
In practice, *have to* has a similar meaning, but suggests the obligation is imposed on us by others:
*I **have to lock** the door because Mrs Crane says so.*

## 3 Prohibition

The negative form of the imperative can be used here, but we also use *mustn't* in such cases:
***Don't let** anyone in.*
*You **mustn't let** anyone in.*

# E Prepositions of place

## 1 *At, in*

*At* is used for particular points; *in* for larger areas:
*We don't expect anyone to call **at** the house.*
*There have been a lot of burglaries **in** the district.*
Confusion is only possible when the point of view of the speaker is different. Someone who lives in a city may say:
*My friend lives **at** Wellington (a small town).*
A farmer living in a village near the town may say:
*My friend lives **in** Wellington.*
A person answering the phone may say:
*Mrs Crane is having dinner **at** a friend's house.*
A person calling at the door may say:
*Is Mrs Crane **in** (inside the house)? but Is Mrs Crane **at** home?*

## 2 *In, out, on, off, into, out of, on to*

*In* almost always suggests 'inside' in English; *on* means 'on the surface'.
*The biscuits are **in** the cupboard **on** the second shelf.*
*Out* (of) is the opposite of *in*, and *off* is the opposite of *on*.
*She took her hat **off**.* (It was on her head.)
*The dentist took her tooth **out**.* (It was in her head.)
\* *On* or *at* the corner is used for corners outside (of a street, for example):
*The butcher's is **on (at)** the corner.*
*In* is used for corners inside (of a room, for example):
*The TV is **in** the corner of the room.*

## 3 Giving directions

Note the following phrases:
*on* the left-hand/right-hand/other side (of the road), the way to...; *at* the supermarket, the Post Office etc., an address (30 High Street); *in* a street, road etc.
*Go along the road, up/down the hill; cross the road.*

# F Polite requests

See 1B3 and 4A4, but also note the following, and compare the forms:
***Would/Could you call** at the library (, please)?*
***Would you mind calling** at the library?*
When asking someone's permission, note:
***Can/May/Could I come** to work an hour late tomorrow?*
***Would you mind if I came** to work an hour late tomorrow?*

# Unit 7

## A Purpose clauses

### 1 With infinitive

When there is no change of subject we normally express purpose by using the infinitive with *to*:
*We're having a party **to celebrate** moving into our new house.*

### 2 *So as to, in order to*

These are used in more formal sentences and often appear at the beginning of a sentence:
***In order to make** the tourists' visit worthwhile, we are organising sightseeing tours for them.*

### 3 Infinitive with *to* with double-object verbs

The infinitive with *to* can be used with verbs that can take two objects, like *give*, *show*, *send*, etc., although the subject changes:
*Mrs Marshall **sent** Julie to the baker's **to buy** some bread.*
In this case 'Mrs Marshall sent Julie', but 'Julie bought the bread'.

### 4 *So that*

With other verbs we use a clause with *so that* when the subject changes:
*I'm going to give you some instructions **so that** you can find your way to the flat.*

### 5 *So as not to, in order not to*

In negative sentences, the form with *to* cannot be used, and we must use one of these instead:
*He came in quietly **so as not to** wake the baby.*

101

**Reference Section**

## B  *Still, yet, already, no longer (not ... any more)*

*Still* implies continuation:
> She was born in Woodside Road, and she **still** lives there.

*Yet* (almost always negative or interrogative) refers to something that has not started:
> Has the 'phone been installed **yet**? No, it hasn't (been installed **yet**).

In a negative question, it suggests surprise:
> Hasn't the 'phone been installed **yet**? But you applied to the telephone company a year ago!

*Already* implies that something has taken place:
> You will **already** be in the station when you arrive at Victoria.

*No longer, not ... any more/longer* suggest that something has stopped after continuing for a period of time:
> They lived in Vine Road when they first got married, but they **don't** live there **any more**. They've moved to Walbury Park Road.
> They **no longer** live in Vine Road.

* *Still* is found in negative sentences as an emphatic form of *not yet*. Compare the sentences, and note the word order:
> We wrote to the telephone company last month, but they **haven't** installed the 'phone **yet**.
> We wrote to the telephone company a year ago, but they **still** haven't installed the 'phone.

## C  *Will be able to*

We use *will be able to* as an alternative to *can* in some future sentences:
> I'm very sorry that I **won't be able to** (can't) meet you at the airport.

We must use it when we mean 'will know how to':
> I can't write very well in English yet, but I'**ll be able to** when I finish this book.

## D  Prepositional phrases

A number of common phrases in English are made up of a preposition and a noun. Here is a list of the common ones for reference:
**in**, (go) **to** bed; **at**, **in** (= inside), (go) **to** church; **in**, (go) **to** court; **at** home; **in**, (go) **to** hospital; **at**, (go) **to** market; **on** paper (= written down, not spoken); **in**, (go) **to** prison; **at**, (go) **to** school; **at**, (go) **to** sea; **at**, (go) **to** university; **at**, (go) **to** work.
The definite article is only used when we clearly refer to a particular school, hospital etc.
> My mother's **in hospital**.
> I'm going **to the hospital** today to take her some flowers.

Modes of travel and transport take *by* + noun, without *the*:
> You can travel **by car/bus/coach/train/plane** etc.
> You can travel **by road/rail/air/sea** etc.

* Note that we do not use a preposition with *home* when we use a verb of movement:
> Is she **at home**? but I'm **going home** now.

* Note that the exception to the use of *by* is to travel *on foot* (not walking).

## E  Revision for Unit 7

In addition to the notes above, you will find it helpful in completing the writing tasks in this unit to revise 1A, 1D, 1E, 2D, 6A, 6B, 6C, 6E.

# Unit 8

## A  Tenses: past perfect tenses

When the main verb is in the past simple or past continuous tense, as in almost all narratives, we use the past perfect tenses to describe actions that took place before it.
> It **was** a wet afternoon. It **had started** raining about midday and it **had been raining** since then.
> When the last wagon **had gone by**, Jack **opened** the gate.

* Note that the past perfect tenses are the furthest back in past time we can go, so that two previous actions, one after the other, will both be past perfect in this sort of sequence.
> Before he **worked** on the railways, Jack **had worked** in a factory, and before that he **had been** a sailor.

## B  *Could* and *was able to*

*Could* is used as the past form of *can* when we refer to things that we had the ability to do or knew how to do in the past (see *can*, 6C1):
> I **could ride** a bicycle when I was five years old.
> I **could speak** Spanish soon after I arrived in Spain.

It is therefore used in narrative to describe such ability or knowledge:
> Jack **could see** a man sitting in the car.

When we want to indicate the difficulty involved and the achievement required in order to do something in the past, we use *was able to*:
> Tom **couldn't run** as fast as his rivals at first, but he knew the course better and so he **was able to** win the race.

* Sentences where *was able to* is used instead of *could* can be written with *managed to* or *succeeded in* without changing the meaning. Note the constructions used in these examples:
> Because he knew the course better, he **was able to** win the race/he **managed to** win the race/he **succeeded in** winning the race.

## C Negative forms

### 1 Negative subjects and complements

A subject in negative form, like *no one* or *nothing* takes an affirmative verb:
> **No one** (*not* anyone) *had rung to say the train was late.*
> **Nothing** (*not* anything) *happened on the flight across the Atlantic.*
> **None** *of the people in the queue* (*not* anyone) *spoke English.*

As a complement we can use either of the following:
> *There **was no one**/There **wasn't anyone** at the station.*
> *There **was no sign**/There **wasn't any sign** of the driver.*

### 2 either... or, neither... nor

Study the use of negative forms in these sentences:
> *He didn't look at his father or his girl friend (, **either**).*
> *He looked **neither** at his father **nor** at this girl friend* (much more formal).
> *Before the race, everyone thought that **either** Mayne **or** Cummings would win.*
> *Nobody thought that **either** Tom **or** anyone else from the village would win.*
> *They thought **neither** Tom **nor** anyone else from the village would win* (much more formal).
> *Tom did not think he would win, and his girlfriend didn't think he would win, **either**.*
> *Tom did not think he would win, and **neither/nor** did his girlfriend.*
> ***Neither** Tom **nor** his girlfriend expected that he would win* (formal).

## D Defining Relative Clauses

Study the table and then look at the examples and notes that follow:

| Type | Subject pronoun | Object pronoun |
|---|---|---|
| person | who(that) | —(that)(whom) |
| thing | that(which) | —(that)(which) |
| possessive | whose | whose |
| prepositional | | —+preposition* <br> preposition + whom/which |

Defining relative clauses identify the person or thing we are talking about. Without them, the sentence would not be clear.
> *The man **who** had won the race twenty years ago was his father.*

When these clauses refer to the object of the sentence, the relative pronoun is usually left out (contact clause):
> *The man **Tom beat** was called Cummings.*

\* It is normal to avoid pronouns in prepositional clauses either by putting the preposition at the end of a contact clause:
> *That's **the man I was talking to**.*

or by using *where* or *when* as relative adverbs in references to place and time:
> *That's the house **where** I was born.* (The house **I was born in**.)
> *Do you know the time **when** the race starts?*

## E because, because of

*Because* is followed by a clause with a verb form in the correct tense after it; *because of* is followed by a noun or a gerund.
Compare the following sentences:
> *Jack could not see the car clearly **because** it was misty.*
> *Jack could not see the car clearly **because of** the mist.*

## F Unless

*Unless* is usually convertible to *if... not*:
> *I could see that we would stand in the queue for hours **unless** someone did something/if someone did not do something.*

In some sentences, the real opposite of *unless* is *provided* (or *providing, so long as, as long as*). These words and phrases mean 'if, but only if':
> *I agreed to meet him for dinner **unless** the plane arrived late/**provided** the plane arrived on time.*

## G Word order: all and both

Note the position of *all* and *both* in these sentences:
> ***All** (of) the leading runners came from the city.*
> *The leading runners **all** came from the city.*
> ***Both** Cummings and Mayne expected to beat Tom.*
> *Cummings and Mayne **both** expected to beat Tom.*

## H Remember and Remind

1 *Remember* has two main meanings. The first is 'have the memory of'. In this case the verb form that follows will be a gerund:
> *I can **remember** winning the race twenty years ago, but I don't **remember** the names of the other runners.*

The second meaning is 'not forget'. Here it is followed by a clause with *that* or an infinitive:
> ***Remember that** the others don't know the course very well.*
> ***Remember to save** your effort until you come to the hill.*

2 *Remind* means 'make someone remember' or 'make someone not forget'. In each case it has a personal object. Note the construction in each case:
> *The medal on the wall **reminded** Tom of his father's victory.*
> ***Remind** me to write to Aunt Barbara.*

**Reference Section**

## I Vocabulary

In attempting the written tasks for further practice in this unit, you may need some of the words below. Look up their meanings in a dictionary if you do not know them already:

1 *rob a person of something, rob a bank; steal something from a person, steal money; duplicate key; pick a lock; smash a window; open a safe; threaten someone with violence, with a gun; 'Hands up!'; escape.*
2 *haunt a house; wear a white sheet; appear, disappear; become invisible.*
3 *blackmail; keep something secret; threaten to tell the police; be guilty of a crime.*

## J Revision for Unit 8

In addition to the notes above, you will find it helpful in completing the writing tasks in this unit to revise 2A, 2B, 2C, 2D, 2E, 3A, 3B, 3C, 6E.

## Unit 9

## A There is/are and have

Compare these sentences:
**There are** three drawers in the desk.
It (the desk) **has** three drawers.
**There was** a three-speed gear on the cross-bar.
It (the bicycle) **had** a three-speed gear on the cross-bar.

## B Have to/don't have to/ don't need to/needn't

*Have to* is used like *must* to express obligation (see 6D2); there is a small difference between them in that *have to* expresses obligation imposed on us from outside by other people or circumstances:
My room at home **has to serve** two purposes.
Lack of obligation is expressed by *don't have to, don't need to* or *needn't*.
I **do not have to/need to use** the table lamp during the day.
I **needn't use** the table lamp during the day.
Use the following table for reference for the future and past forms of these modals:

* The form *didn't need to* is used when the person had no obligation to do something and consequently did not do it:
I **didn't need to go** to work yesterday because it was a holiday.
If the person did something although it was not necessary, we use the form *needn't have* + past participle:
I **needn't have taken** the bicycle to the repair shop. There was nothing wrong with it (but I did not know this, and took it to the shop).

## C Passive forms

1 The passive is formed by the verb *be* in the appropriate tense and the past participle of the main verb. Look at these examples:
The bicycle **was made of** steel.*
The furniture (always singular) **is made of** wood.
The frame **was painted** black (*not* in black).
The furniture **was made by** experts in a factory with great care.
*When the original material is no longer recognisable, we use *made from*:
Wine **is made from** grapes. (We cannot see the grapes, but we can still see the steel the bicycle is made of, or the wood the furniture is made of).
2 The participle can be used in apposition in certain sentences without the repetition of the passive form:
The bicycle had a dynamo (that was) **driven** by the back wheel.
They were wondering if the bus **would arrive** on time.

## D Progressive comparison

Apart from the main comparative forms already listed (5A), we can show that two actions develop in a related manner by using two comparative forms in parallel:
**The faster** I rode, **the brighter** the light was.
**The more** he eats, **the fatter** he gets.

## E Revision for Unit 9

In addition to the notes above, you will find it helpful in completing the writing tasks in this unit to revise 2A, 2D, 2E, 3A, 3F, 5A, 5B, 8A, 8B.

| Purpose | Present form | Future form | Past form |
| --- | --- | --- | --- |
| orders | must | must | had to |
|  | have to | will have to | had to |
| obligation | must | must | had to |
|  | have to | will have to | had to |
| no obligation | don't have to | won't have to | didn't have to |
|  | don't need to | won't need to | didn't need to* |
|  | needn't | won't need to | didn't need to* |

# Unit 10

## A Tenses: present perfect tenses

The present perfect continuous tense is almost always found in the affirmative, because it suggests continuing action up to and including the present, but for repeated actions up to now we use the present perfect simple. Compare the following:

*I **have been working** as a secretary for the past eighteen months.*
*I **have never used** a word processor.*
*I **have applied for** several jobs recently.*

We associate *for* and *since* with the present perfect tenses, *ago* with the past tenses (see 1C). Compare the first example above with:

*I started working as a secretary eighteen months **ago**.*

## B Connectors and modifiers

### 1 Explaining causes and results

Note the following:
**because of this/that, for this reason, therefore, as a result, consequently.**
The first is the least likely to be used in formal correspondence. Note the word order of the following sentences:

*I am very interested in the job and am **therefore/consequently** enclosing my curriculum vitae.*
*I am very interested in the job and **as a result/for this reason** am enclosing my curriculum vitae.*

On the whole, the shorter forms – *therefore, consequently* – are preferred in business correspondence.

## C Register

Register, the use of socially appropriate language, is very important in formal letters. It is above all necessary to be natural but respectful. Consequently, we do not use short forms (*I'll*, *you'd* etc.) or colloquial expressions, but long rhetorical phrases, which usually employ words of Latin origin, are not desirable, either.

### 1 Self-confidence

Revise 1D to see the difference between *hope*, *expect* and *look forward to*. It is polite to say:
*I hope you will take my application into consideration.*
A more self-confident candidate would write:
*I trust my application will be of interest to you.*
However, in expressing interest in a job, you should not say 'I hope I will like it' or 'I am quite interested' but
*I believe I have the appropriate qualifications.*
*I am very interested in the job.*

In the same way, a confident candidate will not say: 'I think I can do the job quite well', but
*I am confident (sure) that I have the ability to do the job.*

### 2 Politeness

Revise 1B3 and 4A4 for the use of conditional forms.

## D Useful words and phrases

Revise 4B and also note the following:
*Qualifications* (academic, technical, on paper) *and experience* (learnt in one's working life); *curriculum vitae* (list of qualifications and experience); *make an application*, *apply for a job* (post, more formal, but *not work*, which is uncountable); *advertise a job in the newspaper*, *advertisement*; *interview*, *attend an interview*; *enclose*, *attach information* (for example, curriculum vitae); *track record* (previous experience, but used mainly for success in sales); *good prospects* (opportunities for success in a job); *undertake responsibility*.

## E Revision for Unit 10

In addition to the notes above, you will find it helpful in completing the writing tasks in this unit to revise 1B1, 1B3, 1C, 4A, 4B, 7A, 8E.

Reference Section

# Unit 11

## A *may/might*

*May* and *might* express possibility in the present and future. We use *might* when we do not think that something is very probable. The negative forms are *may not* and *might not*.

    Scooters **may seem** a sign of progress, compared to bicycles, but I don't think so.
    The results of space research **may be useful** to us in the future.
    They **might be**, but I don't believe it.

* *Can* is only used for possibilities that are always possible:
    Anyone **can** make a mistake.
* Do not develop the habit of avoiding *may* and *might* by saying 'It is possible that...' because this is very rarely used.

## B *should*

We use *should* or *ought to* for advice in general terms and to express our opinions on subjects where we have no power to change the course of events. The negative forms are *shouldn't* and *ought not to*:

    You **should be** more careful when you ride your scooter.
    The Government **should provide** cycle lanes in cities.

These forms do not have the force of *must/mustn't* because the speaker cannot oblige the other person to do as he/she says.

## C *must* (logical)

Apart from its meaning of obligation (see 6D), *must* can express a logical deduction, suggesting: 'I am sure that...', 'it is obvious that...' With this meaning, the negative form is 'can't':

    It **must cost** far more to send a rocket to the moon than to feed a million people for a year.
    It **can't cost** that much! I don't believe rockets are so expensive.

## D Impersonal constructions

### 1 *It* + adjective

Two constructions are possible where an adjective follows *it* + a form of *be* at the beginning of a sentence or clause. Compare these sentences:

    **It is** easy (for people) to see why young people prefer scooters.
    **It is** clear that scooters are dangerous.

Common adjectives followed by *for* and the infinitive are:

*boring, dangerous, difficult, easy, expensive, healthy, necessary.*

Common adjectives followed by *that* are:
*certain, clear, curious, likely, lucky, probable, strange, surprising, true.*

* The alternative construction to *it* + adjective + infinitive is to begin the sentence with a gerund form; we rarely use the infinitive at the beginning of a sentence:

    **It is** not **difficult to ride** a scooter.
    **Riding** a scooter is not difficult.

### 2 *It* + passive verb form

Compare these sentences:

    **It is thought** that the landing on the Moon did not advance human knowledge very much.
    **People think** that the landing on the Moon did not advance human knowledge very much.

We prefer the impersonal form, *It is thought, It is believed*, when we do not want to associate the idea with specific groups of people.
The sentence above could be rewritten with a different construction and word order:

    The landing on the Moon **is not thought** to have advanced human knowledge very much.

## E Concession clauses

### 1 Although

*Although* is often used as an alternative to *but*; it is preferable in written argument. Because the main clause usually comes second, it has more strength than *but*, and therefore sounds more persuasive. *Even though* is a stronger form of *although*.

    The landing on the Moon was spectacular **but** did not advance human knowledge.
    **Although** the landing on the Moon was spectacular, it did not advance human knowledge.

* *Though* can be used instead of *although* in these examples. The difference between them is that *though* can appear at the end of a sentence or phrase, where it means 'however':

    It may be useful in the future. It doesn't do us much good, **though**.

### 2 While

*While* is used for balanced sentences, where the two halves of the statement, although contradictory, are equally important. Compare these two ways of saying the same thing:

    For some people space research is a proof of man's adventurous spirit; **on the other hand**, for others it is a waste of money.
    **While** for some people space research is a proof of man's adventurous spirit, for others it is a waste of money.

### 3 In spite of (Despite)

**Although** is followed by a clause, *in spite of* by a noun or gerund. Compare these three ways of saying the same thing:

*Although zoos have improved, many animals are still kept in cages.*
*In spite of zoos having improved, many animals are still kept in cages.*
*In spite of the improvement in zoos, many animals are still kept in cages.*

## F  *The* – use and omission

### 1 Omission

We do not use *the* with the following:
1 **Games and sports**
   *I play football every week.*
2 **Subjects of study**
   *She studies physics and chemistry.*
3 **Languages**
   *A lot of Welsh people speak Welsh but most Scots speak English.*
4 **Meals**
   *What time did you have breakfast?*
5 **Clock times**
   *At eight clock.*
6 **Gerunds**
   *He likes skiing.*
7 **Collocations** (preposition + noun)
   *What time did you go to bed?*
(For a list of these, see 7D.)

### 2 Use of *the*

We use the definite article with:
1 **Weights and measures**
   *Petrol is sold by the litre.*
2 **Groups or classes of people**
   *The young often get impatient with their parents.*
   * We can also say 'Young people'. The verb that follows in this case is plural.
3 **Rivers, seas, mountain ranges**
   *The Amazon is in South America.*
   * We do not use *the* for the name of a single mountain:
   *Everest is the highest mountain in the Himalayas.*
4 **Unique objects, points of the compass**
   *The sun, the moon, the earth, the world.*
   *The north, the south, the east, the west.*
5 **Time expressions**
   *The past, the present, the future.*
   * But note the time expressions *in future* (from now on) and *in the future* (not from now on, but at some future time):
   *In the future men may live on other planets.*

### 3 Use and omission of *the*

We use *the* when we are talking about something specific, not when we are speaking in a more general sense. We usually indicate the specific reference either by referring to something already mentioned or by a modifying phrase or clause:

*She has just started going to school. The school (she goes to) is quite near home.*

Abstract nouns in general terms do not take *the*:
*Progress is inevitable.*
Compare:
*The progress resulting from scientific research is inevitable.*

* If you are in doubt about the rules, consider this sequence, which shows that we use *the* only when the noun is modified by a relative clause or by a phrase including *of*:

*Life is worth living.*
*Modern life is often tiring.*
*My grandparents' life was very peaceful.*
*The life they led was very different from ours.*
*Life in the nineteenth century was quieter.*
*The life of people in the nineteenth century was quieter.*

** A further problem concerns species of animals. In general, we refer to them in the plural, without *the*:
*Elephants live longer than most animals.*

When we refer to a particular species we can use the plural:
*Indian elephants are smaller than African elephants.*

but it is common to use *the* with a singular noun:
*The Indian elephant is smaller than the African elephant.*

## G  Noun clauses – *what*

*What* means the thing(s) that and can appear as subject, object or complement:

*What matters most to animals is freedom.*
*Young people overestimate what a scooter can do.*
*In choosing between a scooter and a bicycle, safety is what matters most.*

## H  *Too* and *enough*

Compare these sentences and note the word order:
*Those who are too (not too much) young to have a scooter may find bicycles slow.*
*Those who are not old enough to have a scooter may find bicycles slow.*

* Note that *enough* comes after an adjective or adverb but before a noun:
*They usually haven't got enough money to buy a scooter.*

## I Connectors and modifiers

### 1 Indicating or agreeing with facts
**in fact**, **actually** (= in fact, *not* 'now'), **as a matter of fact** (= in fact, though it may sound surprising), **the fact (of the matter) is that**..., **really** (= in fact); **in effect**, **in practice** (in contrast to *in theory*); **of course** (= as you probably already know), **naturally** (= of course).

### 2 Building up an argument
See 5D1, but also note:
**first of all**, **to begin/start with** (beginning an argument, = in the first place);
**at first sight** (= apparently, but contrasts with in fact); **in addition**, **what is more**, **on top of that**, **besides** (= and another thing), **in the same way** (used to make a further point of the same kind);
**on the one hand ... on the other hand** (balanced argument).
\* *on the contrary* contradicts the previous statement so we never use it for our own arguments, only when we are quoting other people's arguments or replying to them.
\*\* *in contrast*, clearly indicating an opposite opinion or fact.

### 3 Expressing a personal opinion
**In my opinion**, **in my view**, **from my point of view**, **personally**; **as I see it**, **as far as I am concerned**, **if you ask me** (conversational).

### 4 Giving examples
**For example**, **for instance**.

### 5 Reaching conclusions
**anyway**, **in any case** (whatever the reasons, situation may be;
**after all** (having taken everything into account);
**as it is** (since things are the way they are).

## J Revision for Unit 11
In addition to the notes above, you will find it helpful in completing the writing tasks in this unit to revise 5A, 5B, 5C, 5D, 6D, 7A, 9C, 10B.

# Unit 12

## A Verb + gerund/infinitive

### 1 Gerund only
Some common verbs followed by a gerund are:
**avoid**, **dislike**, **enjoy**, **finish**, **not mind**, **practise**, **can't help**, **can't stand**.
A gerund also follows a verb + preposition:
 *My father has **given up smoking**.*
Note in particular the following, using the preposition *to*:
**amount to**, **be (get) accustomed to**, **be (get) used to**, **look forward to**, **object to**:
 *She **is looking forward to going** on holiday.*

### 2 Infinitive without *to*
*Let* and *make* take the infinitive without *to*:
 ***Let** her **go**.*
Most auxiliary verbs: **can**, **may**, **must**, **had better**, **would rather** etc., take the infinitive without *to*:
Exceptions are **have to**, **ought to**, **used to**. But compare *be/get used to* (part 1).
\* *Help* can be used with or without *to*:
 ***Help** him **(to) do** it.*

### 3 Verbs taking gerund and infinitive
A small number of verbs can take either gerund or infinitive. Note the following:
**Hate, like, love.**
The gerund is the usual form with hate, but the infinitive occurs:
 *I **hate to interrupt** you while you're working.* (I'm sorry to interrupt you on this particular occasion.)
 *I **would hate to live** there.* (Conditional form – see would like).
The gerund is used for *like* and *love* in general terms, meaning 'enjoy', 'find agreeable'. The infinitive is used when *like* means 'prefer':
 *Ian **likes doing** adventurous things.*
 *I **like to get away** from the crowd and not go where everyone else goes.*
The conditional form, would like, is always followed by the infinitive:
 *I **would like to go** to a Mediterranean island for my holiday this year.*
For remember, see 8H.

## B Preference
*Would rather* is the form normally used on specific occasions and in hypothetical situations:
 *I**'d rather** go to a quiet place in Yugoslavia **than** lie on the beach in a crowd.*
Note the repetion of the same verb form after *than* – 'go ... lie ...'

# Reference Section

*Prefer* is used for general preferences. Note the constructions used:
> Maureen **prefers** news programmes **to** sports programmes.
> Maureen **prefers watching** news programmes **to watching** sports programmes.

In a particular case, however, when choosing the programme she wants to watch on a certain evening, she would say:
> I'**d rather** watch the news programme **than** the sports programme.

## C Useful words and phrases

*go on holiday; lie on the beach; enjoy sailing, swimming, skiing, sledging, windsurfing* etc. but *playing tennis* and other games; *book a flight, seat on coach, train, room in a hotel; spend time lying on the beach, sightseeing; package tour, adventure holiday, excursion, trip.*
*watch TV, listen to the radio, viewer, listener; programme, series, episode* (one of a series), *documentary; choose a programme, switch to a different programme, channel.*

## D Revision for Unit 12

In addition to the notes above, you will find it helpful in completing the writing tasks in this unit to revise 3A, 5A, 6E, 10B, 11I3.

# Unit 13

## A Exclamations

In exclamations *how* is used with adjectives and adverbs (like *much*), *what* with nouns. Study the following examples:
> **How enjoyable** it was!
> **What lovely weather** we had!
> **What a lovely weekend!**
> **How much** I enjoyed last weekend!

The use of the adjective before the noun does not alter the rule that *what* should be used.
In indirect speech we use the same forms and word order:
> I had to write to you to say **how enjoyable** my stay was.
> I wanted to tell you **how much** I enjoyed last weekend.

## B *So/such*

### 1 In exclamations

*So* relates to *how* and is used with adjectives and adverbs, *such* relates to *what* and is used with nouns. Study the following examples and compare them with those for exclamations in section A:

> It was **so enjoyable**!
> We had **such lovely weather**!
> We had **such a good time**!
> We enjoyed ourselves **so much**!

### 2 Degree clauses

These expressions can be continued in clauses:
> I felt **so foolish** that I wanted to apologise.
> I felt **such a fool** that I wanted to apologise.
> We enjoyed ourselves **so much** that we are looking forward to going there again.

## C Indirect questions

### 1 Introductory words

Questions formed without a question word are introduced in indirect form by *if/whether*. Questions formed with a question word retain the same word.

| Direct | Indirect |
| --- | --- |
| '**Did I** offend Kate?' Mary thinks. | Mary wonders **if/whether** she **offended** Kate. |
| 'How **did I** get lost?' Mary thinks. | Mary can't imagine how she **got lost**. |

### 2 Form and word order

In an indirect question there is no question mark at the end of the sentence, the affirmative (*not* question form) is used, and the subject comes before the verb, as in the examples above.

## D Register

In writing to thank people or apologise, it is important to use the right adverb to qualify what one says. Note the meanings and usage of the following, as well as the word order in a sentence:
**actually** = in fact (*not* now);
**certainly** = without a doubt, undoubtedly, but
**surely** = almost certainly, very probably.
Note the question mark:
> She **certainly** knows the way. She lives next door.
> **Surely** she hasn't got lost? She's been here before.

**frankly** and **honestly** are similar, but a person who says 'frankly' may use it in order to tell an unpleasant truth.
**Sincerely** is not usually used alone but appears as a standard form at the end of letters (see 1A5);
**extremely** = very;
**naturally** = of course, but note the word order:
> She **naturally** didn't mean to hurt you.
> **Of course**, she didn't mean to hurt you.

**properly** = in the right way, appropriately;
**on purpose** = deliberately, intentionally;
**really** can mean in fact, but we also use it for emphasis:

**Reference Section**

*I **really** enjoyed myself* = I enjoyed myself very much.
**seriously** is used to show that the speaker is sincere, and not joking.
Adverbs commenting on whether events were good or bad are: **luckily, unluckily, fortunately, unfortunately**.

## B Revision for Unit 13

In addition to the notes above, you will find it helpful in completing the writing tasks in this unit to revise 1A, 1B3, 1E, 2A, 2B, 6F, 8A, 11I3.

# Unit 14

## A Reported speech

Study 2A3 (tense changes), 2B (say and tell), 13C (indirect questions) and look at the table of time and place changes that occur in reported speech:

| Direct | Reported |
| --- | --- |
| here | there |
| this | that |
| now | then |
| yesterday | the day before, the previous day |
| tomorrow | the day after, the next day, the following day |
| last week | the week before, the previous week |
| next week | the week after, the next week, the following week |
| ago | before |
| come | go (went) (if relationship to the place has changed) |

The best way to see how the different rules function together is to see how a dialogue is reproduced in reported speech. Compare the following with the dialogue on p.34, lines 19–29. Note that expressions like 'Well, you see, ...' are normally omitted.

Trevor **asked** the girl **if she would mind** answering a few questions.
Fiona **asked** him what he **was** talking about and **why Bill was taking** pictures.
Trevor **said they were** interested to see **her there**, mixing with the crowd.
He **thought it was** very democratic.
Fiona **said she supposed that was** some sort of joke, but **she didn't** think it **was** funny. **She had** only got twenty minutes to do **her** shopping, and then **she had to** get back...
Trevor **thought she was going** to the Palace. **He asked her if** the Prince **was** looking after the children.
Fiona **said she hadn't** got any children. **She said he must be** mad, and **told him that if he didn't** go away and leave her alone, **she would** call the police.

## B Introducing verbs in reported speech

A large number of introducing verbs may be used in reported speech to specify the way things were said. Use this table for reference not only as a reminder of the appropriate verb for a given purpose but also to study the constructions that are used with it.

| Verb | Direct | Indirect/reported |
| --- | --- | --- |
| accuse | You did it, didn't you? | She **accused him of doing** it. |
| admit | Yes, I did it. | He **admitted that** he **had done** it. |
| advise | You should go home. | He **advised her to go** home. |
| agree | You're quite right. | She **agreed with** me. |
| | All right! I'll do it. | He **agreed to do** it. |
| apologise | I'm very sorry. | He **apologised** (**for** what he **had done**). |
| complain | This is a waste of time! | He **complained that** it **was** a waste of time. |
| demand | Apologise! | He **demanded that** I should apologise. |
| deny | No, I didn't do it. | He **denied having done** it/**that** he **had done** it. |
| describe | It's quite big. | She **described** it **to** me. |
| explain | It happened like this. | He **explained how** it had happened/**what had happened**. |
| greet | Hello! How are you? | He **greeted me**. |
| invite | Would you like to come to tea? | She **invited me** to (come to) tea. |
| offer | I'll help you, if you like. | She **offered to help** me/**open** the window. |
| | Shall I open the window? | |
| refuse | I won't do it. | She **refused to do** it. |
| suggest | Why don't you/You should take the day off. | He **suggested that** I should take the day off. |
| threaten | I'll hit you if you do that again! | He **threatened to hit** me (if I did that again). |
| warn | It's dangerous to put your head out of the window in a train. | I **warned him against/about putting** his head out of the window in a train. |
| | | I **warned him not to put** ... |
| | Where am I? | I **wondered** where I was. |

**Reference Section**

## C *as/like*

### 1 *as/like* (+ noun/pronoun)
*As* refers to a person's profession or a part he plays as an actor; *like* is used for comparison.
> Fiona works **as** a secretary.
> She is **like** the princess (but she isn't the princess).

### 2 *as/like* (+ verb/noun or pronoun)
We can only use *as* for comparison if it is followed by a verb form. Compare the following:
> He works hard, **like** me.
> He works hard, **as** I do.

*Like* cannot be followed by a verb form in a clause:
> **As** I was saying when you came in, we had a good journey.

## D *on one's own, by oneself*
These forms are both used to mean, 'alone, without anyone else accompanying one'. Compare the use of the forms in these sentences:
> Trevor was surprised that the princess had gone shopping **on her own**/**by herself**.

## E *have/get something done*
These constructions are used for things we do not do for ourselves. We cannot cut our own hair very easily, for example, so we go to the barber's or the hairdresser's. The form is *have/get* + object + past participle of the verb. Compare:
> **The hairdresser does** Fiona's hair like the princess's.
> **Fiona has** her hair **done** like the princess's.

There is not much difference between *get* and *have*. *Get* suggests making more effort, while *have* is more passive. Compare:
> I'm going to the hairdresser's to **get** my hair **done**.
> I **had** my hair **done** yesterday.

The first sentence suggests making the journey to the hairdresser's, the second sitting quietly in the chair while the hairdresser did her hair.

## F Revision for Unit 14
In addition to the notes above, you will find it helpful in completing the writing tasks in this unit to revise 2A, 2B, 2E, 6E, 8A, 8B, 8H, 13C.

# Unit 15

## A Passive forms
In all cases the passive is formed by the verb *be* in the appropriate tense and the past participle of the main verb. Use the table below for reference if you want to convert active to passive forms.
The only continuous forms normally found are the present and the past.
The passive sometimes occurs with an agent (*by*...) when our main interest is in a thing – a building, a book, a picture etc.
> The Clifton Suspension Bridge **was designed by** Isambard Brunel.

It is better to use active forms in general terms, but the passive is necessary in such sentences when the agent is not mentioned:
> The church **was built** on the site of an abbey.

## B Non-defining relative clauses
Before studying this section, revise 8D (defining relative clauses). All the clauses in that section were necessary to complete the sentence. Non-defining relative clauses, however, do not identify the people or things we are talking about, but give us additional information about them. They are essentially a written form. In normal spoken English we tend to convey two separate pieces of information in two sentences:
> **Bath is thirteen miles away.** It still preserves the atmosphere of the eighteenth century.

In written English the separate ideas of the distance from Bristol and the atmosphere of Bath can be joined together in one sentence with a non-defining relative clause:
> Bath, **which is thirteen miles away**, still preserves the atmosphere of the eighteenth century.

Clauses like this usually appear between commas, but if the person or thing referred to is the object of the main clause, the relative clause can appear at the end:

| Tense | Active | Passive |
| --- | --- | --- |
| Present simple | They **make** bread here. | Bread **is made** here. |
| Present continuous | They **are building** a house. | A house **is being built**. |
| Future simple | They'**ll open** it next week. | It **will be opened** next week. |
| Past simple | Someone **broke** the window. | The window **was broken**. |
| Past continuous | They **were growing** rice. | Rice **was being grown**. |
| Present perfect | They **have finished** the job. | The job **has been finished**. |
| Modals | They **may sell** their house. | Their house **may be sold**. |
| Infinitive | He was pleased **to help** her. | She was pleased **to be helped**. |

# Reference Section

*Tomorrow we are going to Bath, **which is thirteen miles away**.*

In all cases a relative pronoun is required. Study the table below and learn the correct forms. It is not possible to use contact clauses, doing without the relative pronoun (see 8D).

| Type | Subject pronoun | Object pronoun |
|---|---|---|
| person | who | whom |
| thing | which | which |
| possessive | whose | whose |
| prepositional | — | preposition + whom/which |

As in the case of defining relative clauses using a passive form (see 9C2), the participle can be used in apposition without repeating the relative pronoun or part of the verb *be*:

*The university, (which is) **built** on a hill in Clifton, was founded in 1876.*

\* Remember that a clause of this kind is always preceded by a comma. It is also useful to remember that the use of a name indicates that the clause is non-defining except in cases where the speaker may know two people or places with the same name:

*He said that London, **which is the capital of England**, has a population of 100,000.*
*No. **The London he was talking about** is in Canada.*

## C *Where*: relative adverb

Note the use of *where* in defining relative clauses (8D*). *Where* can also be used in non-defining relative clauses. The best way of recognising the difference is to see that in this case it follows a name. Compare:

*We visited **the house where Shakespeare was born**.* (defining)
*We visited **Shottery, where his wife was born**.* (non-defining)

\* Note the use of the comma in the second sentence and its position.

## D Vocabulary

In attempting the written tasks for further practice in this unit, you may need some of the words below. Look up their meanings in a dictionary if you do not know them already:
1. *sightseeing*; public buildings: *cathedral, mosque, museum, art gallery*; monuments: *(equestrian) statue (commemorating) ..., column, pillar, fountain*; *shopping centre, traffic-free zone, boutique, souvenir shop*.
3. *population; founded in ..., built by ..., conquered by ..., castle, fortress, tower, relics of antiquity, Roman, Greek, Moorish etc. remains; market, trade, industry; town planning, reconstruction.*

## E Revision for Unit 15

~ddition to the notes above, you will find it helpful in the writing tasks in this unit to revise 1C, 2D, 7A, 7B, 8D, 9C, 10B, 11E, 11F.

# Unit 16

## A *Should/shouldn't have*

Before studying this section, revise 11B (should). We use the past forms *should/shouldn't have*... with the past participle to indicate mistakes that people have made in the past. These forms are therefore often used when we are admitting our own errors or complaining about something that has gone wrong.

*Your representative **should have come** to the airport to meet us.*
*He **shouldn't have left** the tourists to find their own way to the hotel.*
*We **should have given** our clients more information about the holiday.*

## B Connectors and modifiers

In addition to those already studied (5D, 10B, 11H), note the following:

### 1 Modifying what you are saying

**to some (a certain) extent, up to a point, more or less, partly, mostly, at least** (limiting a general statement to a particular case)
*The travel agency are very inefficient, **at least** in Mocosa.*
**under the circumstances, as far as I know** (but I don't claim to be an expert).
All these limit the effect of what is being said.
**not to mention, to say nothing of, obviously, needless to say** (it isn't necessary to say this because it is obvious)
*All the tourists had to carry their own luggage; **needless to say**, they complained about it.*
**let alone** (without needing to mention)
*He couldn't book a ticket satisfactorily, **let alone** run a travel agency.*
All these increase the importance of what is said, either by concentrating our attention on it or suggesting it is additional to something that is obvious.

### 2 Others

**according to** (= in the opinion of, ... says that...)
***According to** the weather forecast, we'll have rain tomorrow.*
**to make matters worse**, indicating something bad happening after another bad event had already happened:
*It started raining and, **to make matters worse**, I hadn't brought an umbrella.*
**in short, in brief** (summarising what has already been said in greater detail).

# Reference Section

## C Register

Both in complaining and in answering complaints, it is necessary to be firm and polite, not insulting or over-apologetic.
In complaining, it is useful to remember these phrases: *complain* (to someone) (about something); *make a complaint*; *cause for complaint*; *misleading information* (claims what is not true); *inaccurate information* (not correct); *bad* (*poor*) *service*; *inefficiency*; *rudeness*; *lack of consideration for customers* (who buy things) *or clients* (who pay for services); *I must protest...*; *the company owes us an apology*; *... draw your attention to ...*; *raise a point*.
In answering complaints, note 1E3, 8E and 10B, but also: *your complaint has been passed to me for attention*; *inquire into the circumstances*; *accept responsibility for ...*; *very much regret any inconvenience ...*; *due to a shortage of staff, unforeseen circumstances*.

## D Revision for Unit 16

In addition to the notes above, you will find it helpful in completing the writing tasks in this unit to revise 1C, 1E3, 2A, 2B, 2D, 2E, 4A, 4B, 5D, 6E, 8E, 10B, 11B, 11I, 13D, 14A.

# Unit 17

## A Conditional sentences (Types 1 and 2)

Conditional sentences are of three main types. **Type 1** refers to a specific situation in real time. **Type 2** refers to a hypothetical situation. **Type 3** refers to a situation in past time, which cannot now be changed. The clause containing *if* can appear before or after the main clause. Study the examples of the first two types below:

### 1 Type 1

*If I **see** him tomorrow, I **will tell** him about the party.*
A common alternative structure here is to use the imperative instead of a future tense in the main clause (see 6B):
*If you **see** him tomorrow, **tell** him about the party.*
Modals can also be used in the main clause:
*If he is **coming** by car, you **can come** with him.*

### 2 Type 2

*If I **knew** the answer, I **would tell** you.*
It is clear that I do not know the answer, so this is a hypothesis.
*The past simple or continuous in the *if* clause is, in fact, a subjunctive, unnoticeable except with the verb *be* in the first person:

*If I **were** you, I **would listen** to what she says.*
In the third person, *were* and *was* are both commonly found.
** Note the equivalent here to the sentence in Group 1 with *can*:
*If he **came** by car, you **could come** with him.*
*** This type of conditional sentence relates naturally to *should* (see 11B) in sequences like this:
*The Government **should** only tax the rich. If they only **taxed** the rich, there **would not be** so many poor people.*

## B Co-ordinating relative clauses

Before studying this section, revise non-defining relative clauses (15B). Co-ordinating relative clauses are different because they refer to the whole of the main clause and the only pronoun ever used in them is *which*. Compare:
*Governments tax people in order to obtain money, **which is spent on services like schools and hospitals**.*
*My father says the Government takes all the money he earns in taxes, **which is not fair**.*
In the first sentence, *which* refers to money – 'the money is spent on services' (non-defining); in the second sentence is refers to the fact that the Government takes all the money in taxes – 'this (action) is unfair'.

## C Vocabulary

In attempting the written tasks for further practice in this unit, you may need some of the words and phrases below. Look up their meanings in a dictionary if you do not know them already.

1. *enter for/pass/fail an examination*; *continuous assessment*; *test people's real abilities*; *learn by heart*.
2. *automation*; *create unemployment*; *put people out of work*; *make them redundant*; *efficiency*; *calculation*; *provide accurate data*.
3. *juvenile delinquent, delinquency*; *crime*; *robbery, theft*; *be arrested, be taken to court*; *punishment, be on probation, be sent to prison*.
4. *violence, vandalism*; *generation gap*; *lack of respect for authority*; *bring up children*; *set standards*; *instil values*.
5. *Government*; *authority*; *power*; *international co-operation*; *Security Council*; *World Health Organisation*; *UNESCO*; *Secretary-General*.

## D Revision for Unit 17

In addition to the notes above, you will find it helpful in completing the writing tasks in this unit to revise 5D, 6B, 8C1, 8F, 8G, 10B, 11B, 11D, 11E, 11F, 11I, 15A, 15B.

Reference Section

# Unit 18

## A Revision for Unit 18

You will find it helpful in completing the writing tasks in this unit to revise 2A, 2B, 2D, 2E, 6E, 8D, 11F, 13B2, 14A, 14B, 15B, 15C.

# Unit 19

## A *By the time that...*

Look at the note on *by* (2D*) and then study these sequences:
  **By the time** we arrive, the film **will have started**. (future)
  **By the time** we arrived, the film **had started**. (past)
*By* means 'at some time before...' in these sentences. Note that the main verb will be in the future perfect tense (*will have* + past participle) if we are referring to future time, and in the past perfect tense in past time.

## B Vocabulary

In attempting the written tasks for further practice in this unit, you may need some of the words and phrases below. Look up their meanings in a dictionary if you do not know them already.
1 *junction; pavement; shop window; route; street trader; monument; fountain.*
2 *stall; wares; delivery van.*
5 *hamper; picnic basket; tent; shelter; ants; wasps.*

## C Revision for Unit 19

In addition to the notes above, you will find it helpful in completing writing tasks in this unit to revise 2A, 2D, 2E, 3B, 3C, 3D, 3E, 3F, 6E, 8A, 9A, 11F, 15B, 15C.

# Unit 20

## A *in case*

*In case* means 'because... may/might'. It is usually followed by the present tense in present and future time and the past tense or past perfect tense in past time. Look at these examples:
  We **have (will have)** a break between lectures **in case** you **get** tired (because you may/might get tired).
  He **took** an umbrella **in case it rained** (because he thought it might rain).
  Julie **explained** everything in detail **in case** the participants **hadn't read** the programme (because they might not have read the programme).

* It is used in certain phrases like *in case of accident, in case of emergency* to mean 'if there is an accident, emergency...' But it cannot be used in a clause instead of *if*:
  Come to see me **if** you haven't understood the timetable completely. (If you have understood it, you don't need to come and see me.)
  Come and see me **in case** you haven't understood the timetable completely. (Come and see me to make sure you have understood it, because you may have missed something.)

## B *meet, get to know, know*

Getting to know a person or country is an intermediate stage between meeting the person or visiting the country for the first time and knowing them.
  I **met** her on a course in England (first time you saw her).
  I **got to know** her on the course (talked to her, understood what she was like).
  Now I **know** her very well. We are good friends.
* *Meet* and *know* have other meanings, of course. Note in particular:
  I'**ll meet** you at the station (go there to welcome you).
In this case, it is not necessarily the first time you have seen the person.

## C Useful words and phrases

In making an informal speech, a number of expressions are useful. Note the following:
  *We may (might) as well start now* (I think it would be all right if we started now); *I'd like to draw your attention to..., remind you of...; if you have (there are) any questions,...; if you look at... you will see...; would you mind paying attention, please?*

## D Revision for Unit 20

In addition to the notes above, you will find it helpful in completing writing tasks in this unit to revise 1D, 2D, 5D, 6E, 9C, 15A.

# Unit 21

## A Noun clauses – *whether, whatever, however*

In written argument there are a number of techniques of style that make the argument clearer and more fluent. One is the use of noun clauses to join ideas together. Compare these sentences:

Reference Section

*People often use the word 'freedom' as an excuse to do what they want to do. It doesn't matter whether this upsets someone else.*
*People often use the word 'freedom' as an excuse to do what they want to do, **whether (or not)** this upsets someone else **(or not)**.*
*He'll do what he likes. It doesn't matter what you think about it.*
*He'll do what he likes, **whatever** you think about it.*
*The problem must be solved. It doesn't matter how much it costs.*
*The problem must be solved, **however** much it costs.*

## B *Most, the majority of*

Note the correct forms:
   **Most** people agree with me (*not* The most of the people).
   **The majority** of people agree with me.

## C Vocabulary

In attempting the written tasks for further practice in this unit, you may need some of the words and phrases below. Look up their meanings in a dictionary if you do not know them already.
1  *murder, rape, robbery with violence, terrorism, hijacking; hanging, execution; life imprisonment; murderer, robber, terrorist, victim; innocent, guilty, not guilty; arrest, try convict, sentence; judge, jury.*
2  *housewife, career woman, professional qualifications; go out to work, stay at home; equal pay for equal work; feminist.*
3  *armed forces, army, navy, air force; general, officer, conscript, volunteer; patriotism, nationalism, pacifism; attack, defence; camp, barracks.*

## D Revision for Unit 21

In addition to the notes above, you will find it helpful in completing writing tasks in this unit to revise 7A, 9B, 10B, 11B, 11D, 11E, 11F, 11G, 11I, 15A, 16B, 17A.

# Unit 22

## A Connectors and modifiers

In addition to the connectors and modifiers you have already studied, not the following, which all mean 'apart from that' – *in addition, furthermore, moreover*. The last two are more formal and more literary and should only be used in appropriate contexts.

## B Revision for Unit 22

Revision of the following will be helpful in completing the summary: 3F, 5D, 10B, 11F, 11I2.

# Unit 23

## A Conditional sentences (Type 3)

Before studying this section, revise conditional sentences (types 1 and 2) (17A) and *should/shouldn't have...* (16A).
   *If I **had stepped out** into the road, the motor-cycle **would have hit** me.*
   *But I **did not step out** into the road, so the motor-cycle **did not hit** me.*
\* The main variation here is that the result of a past action may still be noticeable. In that case, the main clause will have the conditional form (*would*), not the conditional perfect (*would have*):
   *If the motor-cycle **had hit** you, you **would be** in hospital now.*
\*\* Note the connection between *should/shouldn't have...* and this type of conditional:
   *You **shouldn't have opened** the car door. If you **hadn't opened** the car door, the accident **wouldn't have occurred**.*

## B *Quite/rather*

Both these words can mean 'comparatively'. In such cases, *quite* is used when the speaker is in favour of the person or thing, *rather* when he/she is not.
   *Vanessa's manner was **quite** pleasant.*
   *Vanessa had **quite** a pleasant manner.*
   *Carol's manner was **rather** aggressive.*
   *Carol had a **rather** aggressive (rather **an aggressive**) manner.*
\* The use of *quite* or *rather* depends on the speaker's point of view, not on the adjective itself:
   *Vanessa is **quite** young so she has plenty of time to reach the top in her career.*
   *I think Elena is **rather** young for this job. She has no previous experience.*
With comparative forms, *rather* is always used, whether the adjective is good or bad in meaning:
   *I thought the second candidate was **rather** more intelligent than the first.*
\*\* Native English speakers frequently use *quite* to mean 'completely, absolutely' and *rather* to mean 'better than expected', but it is wiser at this stage in writing compositions to concentrate on the main distinction made here.

## C Revision for Unit 23

In addition to the notes above, you will find it helpful in completing writing tasks in this unit to revise 2A3, 2B, 2C, 3A, 5D, 11I5, 14A, 14B, 16A, 17A.

**Reference Section**

# Unit 24

## A Vocabulary

In order to interpret the graphs, you need to understand the words and phrases below. Look up the meanings of any unfamiliar words not fully explained here in a dictionary.
1. *league, FA (Football Association) cup, (Football) league cup; champions, promoted, promotion, relegated, relegation; success, failure; attendance; spectators; rise, increase in attendance; decline, fall in attendance; attendance rose, increased, fell, declined, fluctuated (rose, fell, rose etc.); slight, consistent (steady), noticeable, sharp rise/fall.*
2. *Parliament, the Government, the Opposition, political party; general election; constituency (voting area); MP (Member of Parliament); trend (general tendency); accentuate the trend (make pattern of rise/fall more noticeable).*

## B Revision for Unit 24

In addition to the notes above, you will find it helpful in completing the writing tasks in this unit to revise 1C, 5A.

# Unit 25

## A Revision for Unit 25

In completing the exercises and writing tasks for this unit, you will need to pay particular attention to the revision of 2D and 2E (prepositions of time and time expressions); 8D (defining relative clauses); 15B (non-defining relative clauses); 23A (conditional sentences, Type 3). It will also help you to look again at 3A, 8B and 15C.

# Unit 26

## A Register

In making a formal speech, certain phrases are frequently used in order to be polite. Note the following:
*Ladies and Gentlemen; I have great pleasure in welcoming you... (It is a great pleasure for me to welcome you...); we are honoured (pleased) to have with us...; our distinguished guests; on behalf of the Committee (Jury), I...; last but not least (the last person/fact mentioned but not the least important); we are very grateful to..., we would like to express our thanks to... we would like to thank... for...*

## B Revision for Unit 26

the writing tasks for this unit, you will find it
se 1D, 5D, 10C, 11I.

# Unit 27

## A Noun clauses – *how, what*

As a rhetorical device in argument, we can substitute clauses with *what* or *how* for phrases involving nouns. The use of *what* with nouns and *how* with adjectives is the same as in exclamations (13A). Compare the following:
   *The degree of seriousness of this problem depends on one's perspective.*
   ***How** serious this problem is depends on one's perspective.*
   *The extent to which this problem is serious is demonstrated by public concern.*
   ***What** a serious problem this is is demonstrated by public concern.*
In both cases, the second alternative is neater and more convincing.
\* However, where we can use the adjectives listed in 11D1 in an impersonal construction, this is preferable. Compare:
   ***What** a serious problem this is is easy to see.*
   *It is easy to see that this is a serious problem.*
   ***How** serious a problem this is is quite clear to everyone.*
   *It is quite clear to everyone that this is a serious problem.*
The second alternative sounds much more natural in modern English.

## B *as if*

Look again at the use of *as if* in 3B. In an example in present time we use the present perfect tense after *as if* to indicate what we imagine people's experience or feelings are:
   *He looks **as if** he has enjoyed the party.* (His expression, behaviour suggest that he has enjoyed it.)
We use the past perfect tense after *as if* in such sentences when this imaginary expression is obviously not true:
   *Motorists treat me **as if** I did not exist.* (Clearly, I exist, but they ignore me or pretend I am not there.)

## C Revision for Unit 27

In addition to the notes above, you will find it helpful in completing the summary in this unit to revise 9B, 11B, 11F.

# Unit 28

## A Vocabulary

In attempting the written tasks for further practice in this unit, you may need some of the words and phrases below. Look up their meanings in a dictionary if you do not know them already.
1. The necessary vocabulary here is contained in 17C3.
2. *ban, prohibit smoking; introduce non-smoking areas; fine smokers; effects – lung cancer, heart disease, chronic bronchitis, catarrh; breathe impure air, cough, choke.*

3 Much of the vocabulary is contained in the passage on p. 59, but the following are additional: *be involved in an accident, crash*; *crash* (verb); *crash helmet*; *accelerate, overtake cars* (*on the inside*); *lose balance, control*; *take risks*; *show off*.

## B  Revision for Unit 28

In completing the writing tasks in this unit, you will find it helpful to revise, in particular, 5D, 11B, 11F, 11I, 17A.

# Unit 29

## A  Tenses; writing about a book, play or film

Because a work of art is permanent, we use the present simple tense as the main narrative tense, not the past simple, as in a normal narrative – compare 2A, 8A. Consequently, we write:

*The first scene of Hamlet **takes place** in the castle of Elsinore, in Denmark. It **is** night, and a sentry, Bernardo, **comes** to take the place of the sentry on guard.*

Where we would use the past perfect tense in narrative in referring to previous actions and the conditional to future actions, here we use the present perfect or past tenses for the past, and future tenses for the future:

*When Hamlet's friends **tell** him that they **have seen** the ghost, they also **say** that they **think** it **will speak** to him, although it **did not speak** to them.*

Compare the narrative form:

*When Hamlet's friends **told** him that they **had seen** the ghost, they also **said** that they **thought** it **would speak** to him, although it **had not spoken** to them.*

The only time when we need the past perfect tenses is when we wish to mention something that occurred in the book, play or film before an action we are already referring to in the past:

*The ghost of Hamlet's father **tells** him that his uncle Claudius **killed** him because he **had been having** an affair with Hamlet's mother and **had decided** to seize the crown.*

## B  Vocabulary

*author* (of books), *writer, novelist* (of novels)
*scriptwriter* (film dialogue), *dramatist*
*playwright* (plays), (films) *director* (films)
People in books, plays and films are called *characters*. The *main characters* are the *hero* (e.g. Hamlet), the *heroine* (e.g. Ophelia), and the *villain* (e.g. Iago). The others are *minor characters*.
Novels are divided into *chapters*, and occasionally, *books* or *parts*; plays into *acts* and *scenes*; films into *scenes* and *shots* (one particular camera picture); television serials into *episodes*.

Scenes in plays are divided into *dialogue* and *speeches* (one character speaking for a long time); actors speak *lines*.
Novels are *read* by *readers*.
Plays are *acted* on the *stage* in front of *audiences* in *theatres*.
Films are *made* in *studios* on the *set* (specially built background using natural scenery)
A film is *shown* on the *screen* to a *cinema audience*.
Television programmes are *watched* by *viewers*.

## C  Revision for Unit 29

In addition to the notes above, you will find it helpful in completing the written tasks in this unit to revise all sections of unit 2, 3D, 3E, 8D.

# Unit 30

## A  Revision for Unit 30

In completing the writing task in this unit, you will find it helpful to revise 4A, 4B, 6E, 6F, 11A, and all sections of unit 16.

# Unit 31

## A  *used to/would*

*Used to* is a past form contrasting with the present. Note that it has no present form – we use the present simple:

*I **used to get up** early when I **was** at school.* (Now I have left school, I don't get up early.)
*He **gets up** early to go to school every day.*

In narratives in the past tense, we find *used to* in contrast to the present, for example, to indicate changes that have taken place:

*When I **was** a child I **used to spend** my holidays at my grandparents' house.*

In such contexts, *would* is preferred for a repeated action in the past; it often appears in the main clause of a sentence when the subordinate clause begins with *whenever* or *every time*. It is not necessarily a contrast to the present:

*In those days, children **used to arrive** at school at six o'clock in the morning. The teacher **would place** the first to arrive at the top of the class, but **whenever** anyone **made a mistake** during the day, he **would move** them to the bottom.*

## B  *may, might, must* (logical) – past forms

Revise 11A and 11C and then look at this section. In considering explanations for past actions, we usually begin by thinking of a number of possibilities. Imagine that you

# Reference Section

saw someone in the street who looked very like a friend of yours but was many years older. At first, you thought that there was probably no connection:

*It **may have been** a coincidence. I **may have made a mistake**. He/she **may not have looked** very much like my friend* (perhaps he/she didn't really look like him/her).

But you are likely to think that it is just possible that he/she was a relative:

*He/she **might have been** a cousin or an uncle.*

In some cases, the explanation that may occur to you is obviously not correct:

*It **couldn't/can't have been** his/her father/mother because he/she is dead.*

When you see your friend again, you mention what you saw, and he/she says:

*Oh, my elder brother/sister has been abroad for many years, but now he/she is staying with us. You **must have seen** him/her.*

Now you are sure for a logical reason that you saw the brother or sister, you can conclude: *Yes, it **must have been** him/her.*

\* Do not confuse the form of *must* used here with its past form in sentences where it indicates obligation, *had to* (see 9B).

\*\* The difference between *can't have* and *couldn't have* + past participle is not always clear in normal speech but in general *can't have* suggests 'I'm sure I haven't...' and *couldn't have* suggests 'I'm sure I didn't...'

The table that follows summarises the different forms available:

| Use | Present | Past |
| --- | --- | --- |
| possibility | She **may (not) know** | She **may (not) have known** |
| not likely | She **might (not) know** | She **might (not) have known** |
| deduction | She **must know** | She **must have known** |
| deduction (impossible) | She **can't know** | She **can't/couldn't have known** |

## C Revision for Unit 31

The exercises in this unit give you the opportunity of revising all narrative tenses thoroughly. You should pay special attention to 1B1, 2A, 8A, 15A, 17A and 23A, as well as to the notes above. You should also revise 2E2 thoroughly for the time expressions it contains. The same revision will be helpful to you in completing the writing tasks in the unit.

## Unit 32

### A Revision for Unit 32

In order to complete the exercises and writing tasks in this unit, you will find it helpful to revise 2A3, 5D, 10B, 11I, 14A, 14B.

## Unit 33

### A Revision for Unit 33

In order to complete the exercises and writing tasks in this unit, you will find it helpful to revise 3D, 3E, the whole of section 5, 10B, 11D, 11E, 11I, 15B, 16B, 17B.

## Unit 34

### A Revision for Unit 34

plete the exercises and writing tasks in this
nd it helpful to revise 5A, 5B, 8E, 11B, 14A,

## Unit 35

### A Vocabulary

In attempting the written tasks for further practice in this unit, you may need some of the words and phrases below. Look up their meanings in a dictionary if you do not know them already.

1. *youth club, sports grounds* (*football pitches, tennis courts* etc.); *library, museum, concert hall; study grant; reduced fares, admission fees.*
2. *scenery, landscape; period of architecture, arch, column; ecology, preservation of historic buildings.*
3. *discrimination; machismo.* See also the list for 21C2.
5. *fatal accident; seriously injured, serious injuries; bend, junction; swerve, skid.* See also text on p. 23.3.

### B Revision for Unit 35

In order to complete the exercises and writing tasks in this unit, you will find it helpful to revise 5D, 10B, 11B, 11D, 11E, 11G, 14C, 17A, 17B, 21A, 27A.

## Unit 36

### A Revision for Unit 36

In order to complete the writing tasks for this unit, you will find it helpful to revise 31B.

# Index to Reference Section

## How to use this index

Note that each reference number indicates the unit in which the structure is first required in order to complete a writing task so the information found in the Reference Section will be helpful when you are completing the tasks. From Unit 7 onwards, there are also revision notes, indicating that structures already used in previous tasks may be required again.

To help you find the correct entry in the Reference Section, here are some examples:

*ago* 1C = Unit 1, section C
**Conditional sentences** 17A, 23A = Unit 17, section A and Unit 23, section A
**Degree clauses** 13B2 = Unit 13, section B, part 2

---

**Adjectives** comparison 5A; position/word order 3A
**Adverbs** comparison 5B; of frequency, word order 3F
*ago* 1C
*all* word order 8G
*already* 7B
*although* 11E1
**Apology** 1E3
**Appearance** verbs describing 3B
**Article** definite 11F
*as* 5A3, 14C
*as if* 27B
*at* 6E1

*because/because of* 8E
*both* word order 8G
*by oneself* 14D
*by the time that* 19A

*can* 6C
**Clauses** concession 11E; co-ordinating relative 17B; defining relative 8D; degree 13B2; future time 6B; non-defining relative 15B; purpose 7A
**Clothes** verbs describing 3C
**Comparison** adjectives 5A; adverbs 5B
**Concession clauses** 11E
**Conditional sentences** 17A, 23A
**Congratulation** 1E4
**Connectors and modifiers** 5D, 10B, 11I, 16B, 22A
**Co-ordinating relative clauses** 17B
*could* 8B

**Defining relative clauses** 8D
**Definite article,** *the* use and omission 11F
**Degree clauses** 13B2
*despite* 11E3
*different from* 5C
*don't have to/don't need to* 9B
*during* 1C

*either* 8C2
*enough* 11H
*even though* 11E1
**Exclamations** 13A, 13B1
*expect* 1D

*for* 1C
**Future** plans and intentions 1B2; reference in past time 1B4, 2A2; time clauses 6B

**Gerund** and infinitive 12A1, 12A3
*get...done* 14E
*get to know* 20B

*have* 9A
*have...done* 14E
*have to* 9B
*hope* 1D
*how* exclamation 13A; noun clauses 27A
*however* noun clauses 21A

*if* in conditional sentences 17A, 23A
**imperative forms** 6A
**Impersonal constructions** 11D
*in* 6E1, 6E2
*in case* 20A
*in order to* 7A2; *in order not to* 7A5
*in spite of* 11E3
**Indirect questions** 13C
**Infinitive** and gerund 12A1, 12A3; and present participle 2C; in purpose clauses 7A1, 7A3; without *to* 12A2
*into* 6E2
**Introducing verbs** in reported speech 14B
*it* and adjective 11D1; and passive verb form 11D2

*know* 20B

**Letters** official 4A; personal 1A
*like* 14C
*look forward to* 1D

# Index

*the majority of* 21B
*may* 11A; *may have...* 31B
*meet* 20B
*might* 11A; *might have...* 31B
**Modifiers** 5D, 10B, 11I, 16B, 22A
*most* 21B
*must* logical 11C; obligation 6D2; orders 6D1; prohibition (*mustn't*) 6D3
*must have* logical 31B

**Narrative, past tenses in** 2A1
*needn't* 9B
**Negative forms, subjects and complements** 8C1
*neither* 8C2
*no longer* 7B
**Non-defining relative clauses** 15B
*nor* 8C2
**Noun clauses** 11G, 21A, 27A

*off* 6E2
**Official letters** 4A
*on* 6E2
*on one's own* 14D
*onto* 6E2
*or* 8C2
*out of* 6E2

**Passive forms** 9C, 15A
**Past continuous tense** 2A1
**Past perfect tenses** 8A
**Past simple tense** 2A1
**Past tenses, and present perfect** 1B1
**Personal letters** 1A
**Polite forms** 1B3, 1E; requests 6F; 10C2
**Preference** 12B
**Prepositions** giving directions 6E3; of place 6E; of time 2D
**Prepositional phrases** 7D
**Present continuous tense** 3D
**Present participle** 2C
**Present perfect tenses** 1B1, 10A
**Present simple tense** 3D
**Progressive comparison** 9D
**Purpose clauses** 7A

**Relative clauses** co-ordinating 17B; defining 8D; non-defining 15B
*remember* 8H
*remind* 8H
**Reported speech** 14A; introducing verbs 14B; tense changes 2A3

*same as, the* 5C
*say* 2B
*should* 11B; *should have...* 16A
*since* 1C
*so* and *as* 5A3; and *such* 13B
*so as to* 7A2; *so as not to* 7A5
*so that* 7A4
*still* 7B
*such* 13B

*tell* 2B
**Tenses** future plans and intentions 1B2; future reference in past time 1B4, 2A2; Past 1B1; 2A1; Past perfect 8A; Present 3D; Present perfect 1B1, 10A; in reported speech 2A3; *would* 1B3, 31A; writing about a book, play or film 29A
**Thanks** 1E4
*the* use and omission 11F
*there is/are* 9A
**Time expressions** 2E
*too* 11H

*unless* 8F
*used to* 31A
**Useful words and phrases** 1E, 4B, 10D, 12C, 20C

**Verb** + gerund/infinitive 12A; + infinitive/present particle 2C
**Verbs** describing people's appearance 3B; describing people's clothes 3C; introducing in reported speech 14B; introductory in indirect questions 13C; not usually found in continuous forms 3E
**Vocabulary** 2F, 8I, 15D, 17C, 19B, 21C, 24A, 28A, 35A.

*wait (for)* 1D
*was able to* 8B
*what* exclamation 13A; in noun clauses 11G, 27A
*whatever* 21A
*where* relative adverb 15C
*whether* 21A
*while* 11E2
*will be able to* 7C
**Word order** adjectives 3A; adverbs of frequency 3F; *all* and *both* 8G; indirect questions 13C2
*would* 1B3, 31A
*would rather* 12B

*yet* 7B